A Question of Balance

A Question of Balance

A Study of Legal Equality and State Neutrality in the United States, France, and the Netherlands

Brenda J. Norton

LEXINGTON BOOKS
Lanham • Boulder • New York • London

Published by Lexington Books
An imprint of The Rowman & Littlefield Publishing Group, Inc.
4501 Forbes Boulevard, Suite 200, Lanham, Maryland 20706
www.rowman.com

Unit A, Whitacre Mews, 26-34 Stannary Street, London SE11 4AB

British Library Cataloguing in Publication Information Available

Library of Congress Cataloging-in-Publication Data

Names: Norton, Brenda J., 1969-
Title: A question of balance : a study of legal equality and state neutrality in the United states, France, and the Netherlands / Brenda J. Norton.
Description: Lanham : Lexington Books, an imprint of The Rowman & Littlefield Publishing Group, Inc., 2016. | Based on author's thesis (doctoral) - Baylor University, 2013. | Includes bibliographical references and index.
Identifiers: LCCN 2015040208 (print) | LCCN 2015047880 (ebook) | ISBN 9781498523967 (cloth : alk. paper) | ISBN 9781498523974 (electronic)
Subjects: LCSH: Freedom of religion--France. | Freedom of religion--United States. | Freedom of religion--Netherlands. | Religious minorities--Legal status, laws, etc.--France. | Religious minorities--Legal status, laws, etc.--United States. | Religious minorities--Legal status, laws, etc.--Netherlands. | Muslim women--Legal status, laws, etc.--France. | Muslim women--Legal status, laws, etc.--United States. | Muslim women--Legal status, laws, etc.--Netherlands.
Classification: LCC K3258 .N67 2016 (print) | LCC K3258 (ebook) | DDC 342.08/52--dc23 LC record available at http://lccn.loc.gov/2015040208

∞™ The paper used in this publication meets the minimum requirements of American National Standard for Information Sciences Permanence of Paper for Printed Library Materials, ANSI/NISO Z39.48-1992.

Printed in the United States of America

Contents

Acknowledgments

I thank my husband, Ken Coffman. Not many men would have said "Go for it" when their wife, a practicing attorney of many years, announced that she was switching careers to academics. At Baylor University, I must thank my friend and mentor, Jerold Waltman. You have certainly heard more about legal theory than you ever imagined you would. To the students I have already had the privilege of teaching, you continue to challenge my mind and show me new ways of thinking about how to achieve a better democracy.

Chapter One

Introduction

In the lobby of the United Nations General Assembly building in Manhattan there hangs a gift from the Netherlands, a perpetual pendulum.[1] A perpetual pendulum slowly sways in time with the rhythm of the Earth, never straying from a fixed boundary circle. The Earth, while it may feel motionless and stable to us, is in continuous motion on its own axis and around the sun. Its core must remain liquid and moving or all life will die. These movements must not stray beyond the boundaries set by nature or all life will die. Even when we feel an earthquake the Earth's axial spin and movement around the sun remain constant. Like the earth, democracy is also in constant motion. It is messy and constantly changing and no one can clearly define it. We see evidence of its movement through the actions of individuals and groups, ever changing in time and place, but which must remain within boundaries of its own if it is to retain its essence.

Scientists can calculate precisely the amount of movement, or lack thereof, necessary to sustain life on Earth. We cannot, however, precisely calculate the boundaries of democracy. But by observing events in different geographical areas with similar democratic structures we can attempt to sketch an amoeba-like edge beyond which democracy cannot breathe. The West is experiencing events which are pushing the pendulum of democracy to the edge, and some argue over it, due to an increase in religious pluralism.

The West has been and is a Christian majority area. Its societal structure largely emanates from the implementation of Christian values. In the West the concepts of dignity of the person, free will, and a transcendent justice all reflect Christian values morphed into universal human rights. Western societal characteristics consequently include a constitutional structure and the recognition of individual rights.[2] When this structure was being shaped, the majority of people identified themselves as Christian, and the theories influencing the development of society claimed Christianity as their foundation. Thus, arguments about political equality and religion revolved around the same foundational axis.

Western liberal democracy has a dual foundation of limited government implementing the will of the majority and protecting individual autonomy within a sphere of fundamental rights. This foundation is implemented through a constitutional framework with some schema for the recognition of separate powers to legislate, administer, and interpret rules by which those governed consent to abide. All government institutions are supposed to implement the foundational principles of liberal democracy and balance the will of the majority with the protection of individual rights.

When adopting a constitutional structure the polity seeks to provide administrable legal standards which are drawn from moral and political principles. The structure shapes the relationship between religion and government and restricts legislative choice with regard to religion and other basic rights. Within this broad framework, legislatures may freely adopt laws which reflect their political values. Constitutional courts are to strive for something more. They are to interpret constitutional standards using specific legal interpretive techniques which may generate an outcome that may run counter to the view of the political branches.

The area of religious belief and practice is often considered the first of these individual spheres of private choice.[3] Thus, there is a continual balancing required between the enactment of the will of the majority through political (legislative and executive) institutions and the protection of the individual from the tyranny of the majority. In carrying out this balancing act, Western liberal democracies usually try to maximize tolerance of religious ideas and practices while treating all persons equally. For most of modern history judicial decisions and political action were based on similar philosophical mores regarding religious practices. Since the mid-1950s these mores have increasingly stressed individual rights and equal treatment. Some scholars argue that these countries have become so secularized that the ideas of tolerance and equality have been distanced, if not detached, from their Christian roots and transformed into secular universal human rights.[4] Religion has become differentiated and privatized to such an extent those Western societies take for granted that they tolerate all religions and treat all persons equally.

Nonetheless, this toleration and equality has been chiefly applied to differing Christian religious practices. Through globalization and immigration Western societies are increasingly finding non-Christian people in their midst. When confronted with non-Christian practices, the populace often reacts negatively, even to practices accepted from Christians. For example, a nun can wear full habit with wimple, and her garb is generally accepted. However, a Muslim woman wears a *hijab* or *burqa,* and she is suspected of having subjected herself to an unhealthy degree of male dominance, of not being capable of making an individual choice to practice her religion by dressing in a certain manner, or even worse being associated with terrorists.[5]

Secularism, of course, remains a powerful force in the West, but religious disputes are once again becoming political issues. This repoliticization is causing each polity to rethink fundamental notions of the boundaries of religious freedom, equality, and state neutrality. Three countries whose systems are based on the Western liberal democratic philosophy and which are religiously pluralist, the United States (US), France, and the Netherlands, are reacting in different ways. In this book we will examine how these countries are coping with these new religious adherents. In comparing the countries, are there any common factors driving their actions, or are the actions traceable to each state's historical-institutional structure? If there are common factors, can they be used to formulate a theory of why the action has taken place and predict where it may occur next?

A comparison of these three countries' judicial and political actions is enlightening because they all share certain basic similarities. All three countries identify themselves as institutionally secular democracies, have a system of separation of powers, and have constitutions establishing similarly functioning democratic republican structures. They all have enacted protections equivalent to the US Bill of Rights, including proclamations respecting equality, individual freedom, and the endorsement of state neutrality toward religion. These countries have similar economies and all were founded by and remain majority Christian populations. Though the role of the courts differs in each, the separation of powers in these democracies sets up an inherent tension between politically driven legislative and executive action that presumably expresses the will of the majority and the judicial protection of individual rights.

Moreover, from the demographic perspective, all three countries have experienced similar patterns of Muslim immigration. According to United Nations population surveys of the three countries, the United States has the largest percentage of overall immigrant population and France the fifth. The Netherlands is not far behind.[6] The percentage of Muslims in each of the populations exhibits a different pattern. Approximately 1 to 3 percent of the US population, 8 percent of the French, and approximately 6 percent of the Dutch self-identify as Muslim.[7] None of the countries has foundational populations which are Muslim, and the majority of Muslims in each is immigrants rather than native born or native-born converts. The population density of the countries differs greatly. The Netherlands is one of the most densely populated countries with 497 inhabitants per square kilometer, much denser than France (117) and the United States (32).[8] UN rankings place the Netherlands as sixty-first largest in population and thirty-fifth in land mass while France is twenty-first in population and twentieth in area, and the United States is third in both categories. In area the Netherlands' land mass is about twice the size of New Jersey. France is approximately the same size as Texas.

Even with a politically and legally prominent emphasis on religious freedom and equality in the United States, France, and the Netherlands, Muslim women have suffered discrimination for wearing Islamic dress. The politics of the *hijab* and *burqa* lie at the intersection of the political (executive and legislative) and legal (judicial) spheres. The political sphere emphasizes majority rule and societal unity, while the legal tends to protect the individual right of expression. Consequently, the political and legal spheres have each attempted to enforce differing versions of the concepts of equality and neutrality toward religion. Global movement of individuals into the United States, France and the Netherlands has rendered it essential for groups coming from different cultural and religious traditions to find common ground if a reasonable degree of order and social cohesion are to be attained. The path to such cohesion may be taken through assimilation, syncretization, or multiculturalism. Any of these, though, begins with tolerance.

Tolerance is seen in the ideas of equality and neutrality. The notion of equality has two distinct aspects. First, it is an individual liberty from external, particularly governmental, control. This is embodied in the concept of rights, i.e., the individual is free to make autonomous decisions about her life. One foundational form of equality is the belief that religious belief and expression are matters of personal choice. Second, any obligation to society is that of a contract between equal, consenting individuals requiring that all people are to be treated the same. Any outward manifestation of disparate treatment is viewed as an inequality and must be justified. The law must not favor or disfavor any group without sufficient reason.[9]

Each individual agrees to compromise those aspects of individual choice perceived as a threat to underlying equality. Thus, there is an inherent tension between individual expression and community equality. All polities embracing Western liberal theory must balance community and individual interests. A particular polity may give greater deference to one or the other, but the institutional structure is not supposed to act in a manner which *unnecessarily* suppresses considerations of one for the other.

The concept of neutrality is both unity and rights oriented. It emanates from the political sphere and is part of the social contract theory that the state is limited to action on those matters which impact society while all other matters are left to the sphere of personal autonomy. There is a need to feel valued not only individually but also as a member of the group. "[N]eutrality is Janus-faced: it may be a device of inclusion for minorities, who understand neutrality as the equal right to pursue their way of life as they see fit; but it may also be a device for exclusion, via strengthening the necessarily particular boundaries and sense of collective self of the group that so excludes."[10]

The purpose of this work is to study judicial and political reaction to the increased presence of Islam in these three countries through an analysis of judicial decisions and political action debating Muslim women's dress. Is there a divergence between how each is applying the concepts of individual rights of conscience and practice and equal treatment? Why are different liberal democratic polities, all of which value tolerance, reacting differently to Islamic women's dress?

A prominent rationale for restricting the wearing of Islamic dress by women is that the practice runs contrary to the social norms of the country. Social norms are enforced informally by the population or formally by the enactment of laws. In liberal democracies enforcement by law is only for those things considered fundamental to democracy. Democracy entails both a unity of persons and individual freedom. When must the freedom of religious practice give way to the promotion of social unity? Is the social norm of an uncovered face or head so fundamental to these societies that it trumps the fundamental right of free exercise of religion?

This study is a cross-cultural and cross-national survey of judicial decisions and legislative action in each country since its first decision on Islamic rights after the inception of the 1970s migration. Through this survey we examine whether there is a tendency to apply the same philosophical principles to Islamic and Christian issues on analogous facts. Have the courts been expanding rights or merely holding to principles already accepted in the country? If they are expanding rights, an argument can be made that they are at risk for implementing a juristocracy. If they are restricting Islamic rights unequally, they are violating democratic principles.

We will then survey the political sphere through legislative action, political rhetoric, and public outcry to determine if there is an increase in the limitation of rights for non-Christians based on their religion as opposed to neutral democratic factors. Did any change in rhetoric and legislative action occur as a result of perceived judicial overreaching and, if so, was it primarily a correction to the balance of powers with only a secondary religious impact?

Chapter 2 will give a brief summary of the rise of the issues in each of the countries and throughout the West. The third chapter will survey the literature of the development of liberal democratic theory with an emphasis on the two foundations of rule by majority and the sphere of autonomy with regard to religious practices. This will include a discussion of the development of the principles of equality, neutrality, and individual rights, including their philosophical and theological roots. The next chapter will show how these have been implemented in the supranational context and how this binds the states surveyed.

The next three chapters will survey each of the three countries separately through their historical and philosophical lenses. Chapter 5 will explore the unique French *laïcité* and its roots. France originally had a strong partnership between the monarch and the Roman Catholic Church, and then after the Revolution France experienced a dramatic shift to a strong anti-religion government. This strong secularity in the unique French form of *laïcité* softened with the passage of time. Religion was still strongly privatized chiefly by social mores rather than government action. The rise in immigrants from Muslim countries has reinstituted a strong *laïcité* and forced privatization of Muslim religious practices.

Chapter 6 will discuss the unique relationship of church-state in Dutch pillared society. The Netherlands' historical pillared society was largely dismantled by the time of the Muslim immigrant wave. Dutch society was considered the most tolerant of the European nations. However, events in the Netherlands and other countries led to a swift and strong reversal of toleration for religious activities which do not fall within the traditional pillars. The Dutch have enacted the strongest anti-immigrant laws of the nations studied and have done so expressly to keep out "undesirable" cultural and religious "others." There has been a recent moderating of political winds which may harken a return to Dutch tolerance by the general population. Or is it merely a result of extremist political parties losing ground due to other failures? And where has the Dutch judicial system stood during these political changes?

Chapter 7 will focus on the United States and its foundation as a Christian plurality embodying Enlightenment political philosophy. The United States has never had an institutionalized national religion and has always had a large immigrant population. The development of US law, while *de jure* secular, has historically been *de facto* mainline Protestantism with recent trends toward Christian ceremonial deism. Further, of the three countries studied, the United States has experienced the most active judicial involvement in the expansion of individual rights.

After looking at each of the countries separately, chapter 8 will investigate whether there are common factors at play or if the reactions are mere reflections of local conditions. Regardless of whether common factors are found, it is important to continually review the balance Western societies strike, or should strike, between the principles of equality and neutrality. In a liberal democracy freedom of conscience/religion and speech are supposed to be given wide expression and only limited when absolutely necessary to protect order and other fundamental rights. However, are the ideas of toleration, equality, and freedom as much a result of the social and institutional structures in place as the ideal of liberal democratic theory? Is the practice of the ideal of tolerance merely the reinforcement of an already existing boundary of what is tolerable in the dominant culture? When the ideal of toleration is put into practice, is it just a reinforcement of the local culture's definition of what is tolerable or is there a universal boundary which can be identified through the balance between the principles of equality and neutrality?

NOTES

1. A perpetual pendulum is also called a Foucault pendulum and was first created in 1851 to prove the movement of the Earth. In order to counteract the friction of air, which would eventually stop the pendulum, the pendulum in the UN building has a small electromagnet underneath it.

2. It can be argued whether concepts of dualism existed in Judaism or Greek and Roman polities, but without question the presence of Christianity shaped Western social and political thought for centuries. See Said Amir Arjomand, "Religion and Constitutionalism in Western History and in Modern Iran and Pakistan," in *The Political Dimension of Religion*, ed. Said Amir Arjomand (Albany: State University of New York Press, 1993); Carl Friedrich, *Transcendent Justice* (Durham, NC: Duke University Press, 1964); Brian Tierney, *Religion, Law, and the Growth of Constitutional Thought, 1150–1650* (New York: Cambridge University Press, 1982).

3. Rex Ahdar and Ian Leigh, *Religious Freedom in the Liberal State* (New York: Oxford University Press, 2005), 1.

4. Ahdar and Leigh, 38–64.

5. *Hijab* and *burka* or *burqa* are terms which have different meanings in different places. In this study I define the terms in the manner most commonly used in the countries surveyed. A *hijab* covers the hair, ears, and neck, leaving the face exposed. It is also often referred to as a head scarf. A *burqa* is a full-body covering which usually includes a face veil (*niqab*) so that only the eyes and hands are exposed. In all three countries, *hijab*, *burqa*, and *niqab* are frequently lumped together under the heading "veiling." The items are only worn by women of the Islamic faith. Just as there is no one uniform name there is no one uniform style or color. Nor is there a single theological justification for wearing or not wearing them. This lack of uniformity in theology and use is a factor in the controversies that have been generated. For a fuller discussion about the different styles and arguments for and against use see Anne Roald, *Women in Islam* (New York: Routledge, 2001); John Bowen, *Why the French Don't Like Headscarves* (Princeton: Princeton University Press, 2006). Also, I will not attempt to define religion in general but will use the term generically as a self-identifier. If an actor, institutional or individual, claims that it/(s)he is serving a religious purpose, I will accept this and not attempt to determine whether it constitutes religious action in general. If the state acts as if the matter is a religious one, I accept that categorization.

6. UN Population Facts, http://www.un.org/esa/population/publication/popfacts/popfacts2009.pdf (accessed June 16, 2012).

7. Various surveys give different figures for the number of Muslims in each of the countries, but all are close to these figures. I used US Department of State figures from the 2010 religious freedom report for each country, http://www.state.gov/g/drl/rls/irf/2010 (accessed June 16, 2012). The figures vary because (1) none of the countries' official censuses record religious affiliation, and (2) "Muslim" may reflect country of origin, ethnicity, or religious self-identification. Identification as a Muslim does not correlate to Muslim religiosity. Land mass figures may vary because some statistics include inland and coastal water areas as part of land mass (dry land v. territorial claim).

8. UN Economic Commission for Europe, http://www.unece.org/stats/social-demographics; http://www.unece.org/pxweb/quickstatistics/readtableasp?qs_id=22 (accessed June 14, 2012).

9. See John Rawls, *A Theory of Justice* (Cambridge, MA: Harvard University Press, 1998), and *Political Liberalism* (New York: Columbia University Press, 1996).

10. Christian Joppke, "State Neutrality and Islamic Headscarf Laws in France and Germany," *Theory and Society* 36 (2007): 314, http://www.springer.com/social+sciences/journal/11/86.

Chapter Two

Forces of History

In physics there are four forces acting on all matter. These forces do not work in equal measure in all places at all times, but at no time are any completely absent. In human society there are certain forces which exist in some form at any time and place. Two of these forces are religion and nation-state.[1] Even if religiosity of the population is currently low, the cultural and political formation of any Western nation-state can be traced to historical religious concepts. The forces of religion and state may act in concert or in conflict but are always in some level of tension as the state, in whatever institutional form, is concerned with the everyday order of human activity while religion is concerned with the enactment of the Ultimate Truth. The historical process of religion-state relations is referred to as the "domestication of religion . . . [i]t is the process by which nation-states make religions fit for their national projects."[2]

In ancient Rome, emperors presided over a pantheon of official religions. In the Roman Empire religious groups were able to act because the government allowed them to exist. Illicit or illegal religious believers had to feel so strongly about their religion that they risked death or else altered their beliefs to coincide with an accepted religion.[3] On the one hand, the state may find religion a useful good for imbuing citizens with a moral compass which aids state policies. At the same time religious practitioners may alter their beliefs or practices to accommodate state interests in order to survive. On the other hand, when religious actors do not meet the state's criteria for moral behavior or do not acquiesce to the state's pressure, the state implements means of suppression. Religious groups who do not think the state is paying proper deference to or respect for their higher calling challenge, or may even overthrow, state institutions. Thus, the needle of religion-state relations vacillates between one extreme of complete autonomy and control by religion of state and the other of complete autonomy and control by state of religion.

Throughout the Middle Ages in Europe the Christian religion, in the form of Roman Catholicism, exerted the greatest force on the position of the pendulum.[4] The local ruler may have come to his position by heredity or force, but he needed the pope's approval to validate his authority to rule. Failing to garner this approval the ruler literally had a target on his back and no one owed him fealty.[5] Secular rulers chafed under waxing and waning church power and wealth and sought ways around it. In some instances, different kingdoms utilized separate popes, while others refused the protection of their sword to clergy who did not support their policies.[6] While much of the theology of the Protestant Reformation focused on otherworldly matters, the groups became more dependent on the sword of the secular ruler due to the religious wars. The state was able to control religious groups with threats of banishment, and the secular ruler became the one to declare the proper religion for his people, *cuius regio eius religio*.[7]

Religious pluralism did exist during this time, albeit a heavily controlled pluralism. A small minority of Jews and Muslims were allowed to live in segregated communities by the grace of the church and ruler. The oppressed minorities subjected to periodic banishment or death were ever mindful of their place and careful not to request equal rights. There was no uniform belief in the mind of the majority that the minority believer had any inherent right to exist within the kingdom or Christendom.[8] With the Protestant Reformation pluralism turned to issues of Christian diversity and whether it was a cultural good or a contagion to be regionally controlled. Even in areas where multiple Christianities were allowed to exist they did so within an institutionally enforced limitation on social, political, and economic rights.[9]

Recognition of human dignity has been a staple throughout the development of Western Christian-state relations.[10] The creation of mankind in the image of God imbues humanity with some aspect of sacredness. Theologians interpreted this sacredness in a wide variety of ways, including total depravity due to the original sin of the Fall. The inherent element of sacredness was never totally extinguished, which meant that redemption was possible given a proper worldly experience and focus of the heart.[11] Thus, the concept of human dignity and need for a right, ordered world are deeply ingrained into the Western psyche.

With the Protestant Reformation and later Enlightenment philosophy these concepts became more centralized to Western culture.[12] Theological focus on individual salvation and the need to follow God's speaking to one's heart fostered both human dignity and the development of an idea of an individual's right to choose her religion.[13] One was free to follow one's heart but the state could still declare "just not here" in the interest of the community. The believer could emigrate to a state where she could join others who shared her beliefs or to a new land where like-minded people could establish a colony in their own image of God's order.[14] State toleration of religious diversity often was manifested by merely allowing a neighboring state with a different state religion to exist. Even in states that allowed a variety of denominations to exist within their borders, there was still a cap on diversity by state sanction and support.[15]

Throughout this time the small seeds of the idea of democracy and rule of law had been growing. Both also depend for part of their formation on the sacredness of human dignity. In democracy the individual is the unit of social origin. While the individual may consent to restricting her ability of unlimited action for the good of the community and grant to the state the authority to enforce this consent, the individual remains the locus of original power due solely to her humanness.[16]

Democracy, just as human dignity, did not begin with the Protestant Reformation or Christianity. What occurred as a result of the Reformation, Enlightenment, and Industrial Revolution was a spread of the idea that democracy was the proper, even God-decreed, order for the West.[17] Democracy is dependent on at least two principles—the will of the majority balanced by the freedom of the individual, and the rule of law. Both center the locus of action in human society in the individual human. However, this individual is limited by living as a member of the society. The society is the determiner of individual rights. This determination can be enforced through social ostracization or be institutionalized as law.[18]

The rule of law focuses on the concept of human dignity; all are equal and entitled to the same consideration in the agreed-to government structure and also in wider society. Human dignity became the central legal concept post World War II and is the driving force behind conceptions of liberal democratic systems and human rights.[19] It is human dignity which requires the rule of law and equality under the law. Legal systems depend on the conceptualization of dignity as justification for their stated human rights, as a criterion for resolving conflict between competing rights and establishing legal precedent, the foundation for resolving future conflicts. However, it is also human dignity which undergirds the continuing problem of who decides what is dignity or equality.[20] Is it all just a matter of perspective, and thus relative, or is there a border beyond which we can declare that something violates human dignity and inequitably treats the individual, the locus of worth in human society?

Early Christians saw law as part of God the lawgiver's plan for order; thus, "natural law" was acting in accordance with God's plan.[21] But who determined what this plan was and who is subject to it? The Pope or theologian granted themselves the authority to declare God's plan and direct how that plan should be put into practice in the organization of human society. The natural law established a hierarchical system with the ruling elite holding a God-given right to their place. They enacted laws to regulate the conduct of lesser humans, yet as God-chosen law givers they were above their enacted human law.[22] With the expansion of democracy the individual became the enactor of law *and* subject to it. The power of the individual acting in a group was placed in the government. The individual remained the locus of authority as he chose his government, but the individual who remained within the territory subjected himself to its authority via the rule of law. Rule of law thus became the normative regulator of society, not the declarations of religious leaders.[23]

Alongside all of this is modernization. Modernization includes the above theological and philosophical turns and adds the economic dimension caused by the Industrial Revolution. One of these turns is a new economic order of independent labor for wage with the worker choosing when, where, and for what wage he works. The worker is free to leave a job and the employer is free to deny the worker employment. This economic alteration led to increased movement of peoples. Workers since the beginning of the Industrial Revolution have increasingly emigrated in search of economic opportunities to a now taken-for-granted view that moving within a nation-state or to a new nation-state is acceptable. The movement of people and mass media development has created a global world. With this globalization, particularly with immigration of peoples, Western society increasingly encounters persons who rest their philosophy of religion-state relations on a different foundational axis. One of these groups is Muslims.

Approximately one in ten people in advanced industrial democracies, including the three studied countries, is of foreign birth. Most European Muslims immigrated in two waves: first, in the 1960s and 1970s as guest workers at the invitation of European governments, and second, in the 1980s.[24] Few native-born European people convert to Islam. The majority of French citizens identify themselves as Roman Catholic. The majority of Dutch identify themselves as Protestant. Christian religiosity is, however, low in both countries, though it varies by region. Religiosity among Muslims is correlated to religiosity among Christians in the same areas.[25]

In the US, Muslim immigration also occurred primarily in two waves: post–World War I with the fall of the Ottoman Empire and from the 1970s through the present. They have come from a wide variety of countries and are generally geographically dispersed, unlike in European countries in which the immigrant groups traditionally cluster together by country of origin.[26] Additionally, the US has a home-grown form of Islam rooted in Black Muslim organizations. This purely African American–created style of Islam remains small.[27] Religiosity, Christian or Muslim, varies widely by geographic and rural/urban areas in the US.[28]

Coexistence with immigrant groups has occurred in the West, as they are allowed to live and work here. However, societal equality and political and judicial neutrality have varied in time and place. For example, few Americans currently hold the view that a fellow American of Irish Roman Catholic descent should not be accorded an equal place in society or should suffer discriminatory treatment by government. It was but a mere one hundred years ago, though, that they were seen as lower class and were not welcome here.[29] Historically, European countries did not have large immigrant populations, and until the 1960s American immigrants were, for the most part, from other Christian societies; thus, religious rights issues centered on Christian denominational differences that were not vastly different theological perspectives.[30] The immigration of non-Christians into these three countries has forced the polity and people to rethink what they mean by tolerance, equality, and state neutrality to religion.

In a liberal democracy freedom of conscience/religion and speech are supposedly entitled to wide ranges of expression and only limited when absolutely necessary to protect order and other fundamental rights. However, the ideas of toleration, equality, and freedom are as much a product of the social and institutional structures in place as the ideal of liberal democratic theory. Is the practice of the ideal of tolerance merely a reinforcement of an already existing boundary of what is tolerable in the dominant culture?

NOTES

1. I will not define religion but will use the term generically as a self-identifier. If an actor, institutional or individual, claims it/(s)he is serving a religious purpose. I will accept this and not attempt to determine what constitutes religion or religious action. Additionally, I acknowledge that the term "state" is a modern concept but it is a nice shorthand way of referring to nonreligious institutions which exert a claim to legitimate authority over a territory and its population to the exclusion of or superior to all other claims of authority and which, after World War II, holds a specific status in international law.

2. Thijl Sunier, "The National 'Domestication' of Religion in Europe," in *Religious Newcomers and the Nation State*, ed. Erik Sengers and Thijl Sunier (Delft: Eburon Academic Publishers, 2010), 2.

3. Simeon Guterman, *Religious Toleration and Persecution in Ancient Rome* (Westport, CT: Greenwood Press, 1971).

4. Brian Tierney, *The Middle Ages* (New York: Knopf, 1970).

5. Uta-Renate Blumenthal, *The Investiture Controversy: Church and Monarchy from the 9th to the 12th Century* (Philadelphia: University of Pennsylvania Press, 1988).

6. "Whose realm, his religion"; Brian Tierney, *The Crisis of Church-State, 1050–1300* (Toronto: University of Toronto Press, 1988).

7. Diarmaid MacCulloch, *The Reformation: A History* (New York: Penguin, 2003); Peace of Augsburg (1588), pertinent sections can be found at http://www.pages.uoregon.edu/sshoemak/323/texts/augsburg.htm; Peace of Westphalia (1648), http://www.avaon.law.yale.edu/17th_century/westphal.asp (accessed June 15, 2012).

8. Robert Chazan, ed., *Church, State and Jew in the Middle Ages* (New York: Behrman House, 1980); Theodore Steinberg, *Jews and Judaism in the Middle Ages* (Westport, CT: Praeger Publishers, 2008).

9. Brad Gregory, *The Unintended Reformation: How a Religious Revolution Secularized Society* (Cambridge, MA: Harvard University Press, 2012); Steven Ozment, *The Age of Reform, 1250–1530: An Intellectual and Religious History of Late Medieval and Reformation*

Europe (New Haven, CT: Yale University Press, 1986); Benjamin Kaplan, *Divided by Faith: Religious Conflict and the Practice of Toleration in Early Modern Europe* (Cambridge, MA: Harvard University Press, 2007).

10. Arjomand, 70 et seq.; Friedrich, 4 et seq.; Colin Morris, *The Discovery of the Individual, 1050–1200* (Toronto: University of Toronto Press, 1987); Giovanni Bognetti, "The Concept of Human Dignity in European and US Constitutionalism," in *European and US Constitutionalism,* ed. George Nolte (New York: Cambridge University Press, 2005), 85–107.

11. Friedrich, 11 et seq.; Tony Burns, "Aquinas's Two Doctrines of Natural Law," *Political Studies* 48 (2000): 929–46.

12. Ozment; Kaplan.

13. Gregory, 96–98.

14. Gregory, 129–80.

15. Ahdar and Leigh, 38 et seq.; Alex Sweet, *Governing with Judges* (New York: Oxford University Press, 2000).

16. Burns, 929–46.

17. Gregory, 129–80; Harold Berman, *Law and Revolution, II: The Impact of the Protestant Reformation on the Western Legal Tradition* (Cambridge, MA: Harvard University Press, 2003).

18. Harold Berman, *Law and Revolution: The Formation of the Western Legal Tradition* (New York: Cambridge University Press, 1983); Brian Tamahara, *On the Rule of Law* (New York: Cambridge University Press, 2004).

19. Doron Shultziner and Itai Rabinovici, "Human Dignity, Self-Worth, and Humiliation: A Comparative Legal-Psychological Approach," *Psychology, Public Policy, and Law* 18, no. 1: 105–43 (2012), http://dx.doi.org/10.1037/a0024585.

20. Christopher McCrudden, "Human Dignity and Judicial Interpretation of Human Rights," *The European Journal of International Law* 19, no. 4: 655–724 (2008), http://dx.doi.org/10.1093/ejil/chn043.

21. Brian Tierney, *The Idea of Natural Rights: Studies in Natural Rights, Natural Law, and Church Law, 1150–1625* (Atlanta: Scholars Press, 1997).

22. Burns, 929–46.

23. Brian Tierney, *Religion, Law and the Growth of Constitutional Thought, 1150–1650* (New York: Cambridge University Press, 1982).

24. Jörgen Nielsen, *Muslims in Western Europe,* 2nd ed. (Edinburg: Edinburg University Press, 1975).

25. UN World Population Facts, http://www.un.org/esa/population/publication/popfacts/popfacts2009.pdf (accessed June 16, 2012); US International Religious Freedom Report, http://www.state.gov/g/drl/rls/irf/ 2010 (accessed June 16, 2012).

26. Edward Curtis IV, *Muslims in America: A Short History* (New York: Oxford University Press, 2009); Kambiz Ghamaea Bassiri, *A Short History of Islam in America: From the New World to the New World Order* (New York: Cambridge University Press, 2010).

27. C. Eric Lincoln, *The Black Muslims in America* (Boston: Beacon Press, 1961).

28. US International Religious Freedom Report, http://www.state.gov/g/drl/rls/irf/2010 (accessed June 16, 2012).

29. For a historical example see *Pierce v. Society of Sisters of Mary and Jesus*, 268 U.S. 510 (1925) adjudicating an Oregon law, enacted at the direct urging of the KKK, banning all private school education for grades K–12 in an effort to close all Roman Catholic parochial schools in Oregon. In fact, the KKK's efforts unseated a governor who refused to support their law and put in office legislators and a governor who supported their anti-Catholic efforts. Philip Jenkins argues that Roman Catholics are still subject to greater prejudice than other religious groups. Philip Jenkins, *The New Anti-Catholicism: The Last Acceptable Prejudice* (New York: Oxford University Press, 2003).

30. I am not discounting the differences between Roman Catholicism and Protestantism and between Protestant denominations. These differences have led to wars and oppression. They have had a profound impact on state and society formation, particularly in Europe, as they were a direct cause of territorial religion, which may be an important factor in why the countries in

this study are reacting differently to Islam. However, all Christianity has a common theological foundation which is not shared by Islam.

Chapter Three

Theoretical Context

The modern world is inherently pluralist. In fact, this is one of the markers of modernity. Persons band together in units other than family, clan, or tribe. This new unit must find some means of staying unified despite cultural differences.[1] In the modern world diversity is the reality. Globalization has the effect of "powerfully dislocating national cultural identities."[2] Even if one has never ventured out of her small village in the Alps or Alaska, communications, goods, and visitors from the outside world expose one to non-traditional ideas, which at a minimum causes one to accept their plausibility *ipso facto*.

Multiculturalism can be just a description of fact; there is cultural diversity in modern societies because people are not limited to family, clan, or tribe. It can also be normative: an ideology or policy that promotes, even institutionalizes, diversity. It preserves and even promotes the individual expression of identity. Nicholls's definition of the varieties of pluralism also defines the varieties of multiculturalism—"all share a common concern with the degree of unity and the type of unity which actually exists in a particular state, or which ought to exist."[3] Multicultural policies vary widely in Western states. They may be expressed as equal respect of cultures to an active institutional promotion of diversity. All focus on the interaction of different cultures and the amount of cultural cohesion which is necessary to the state. Is the majority national culture so important that minority cultural practices must be curtailed or abandoned for the good of the many, or can the minority cultural practice be added to form a mosaic national culture?

The evolution of religion into a human right rather than theological or elitist assertions of supremacy places diversity at the center of thought. It recognizes that a search for meaning and drive for moral earnestness is a positive thing which can aid all of humankind. It also recognizes that there are a variety of roads to meaning and views on moral righteousness. It theologically and socially sets aside the question of one ultimate Truth in favor of social cohesion through recognition that no matter how fervent your faith that of another may be correct. Doubt is an axial given. In religion as human right it is the acceptance of tolerance which holds primacy of place.

Equal treatment, among believers and nonbelievers, is the goal. In order to achieve equality the believer must consent to certain restrictions on theology and practice, and nonbelievers must acquiesce in the believer's individual right of conscience and the opportunity to practice her beliefs. It requires a continual balancing of individual and community needs to maintain a peaceful coexistence. It requires respect for others. "[R]espect is a keyword for any understanding of human rights in general and freedom of religion or belief in particular. It does not primarily refer to this or that concrete religion which we may still consider wrong or unreasonable. Rather, respect is due for the *underlying ability of human beings to have and develop deep convictions in the first place*."[4] It is the "manifestation of the human ability of responsible agency"[5] which commands respect. It is this insight which forms the basis for all human rights. It is not a new insight but it has taken on greater importance in the modern era with the increasing diversity of society. The more humans move about and communicate across the Earth the more often they are exposed to different ideas, thereby expanding our plausibility structure. Some react to this by adding to their list of tolerances while others become more rigid and seek to force a return to familiar constructs. By constantly expanding what is tolerated we open our society to the possibility of tolerating the next new idea to which we are exposed.

Tolerance has both behavioral and attitudinal aspects.[6] It entails a respect toward ideas or behaviors with which one may disagree. In this way tolerance is inclusive. Lee Bollinger defines tolerance as a "self-restraint toward what we believe to be without societal value."[7] It is not acceptance to the point of "approval or endorsement. . . . [T]he connotation is that [the other's idea] is untrue or undesirable but that an individual, or the community 'puts up with' it nonetheless."[8] However, this minimal behavioral tolerance fails to contain the attitudinal aspect required of true tolerance. Tolerance must also manifest a sympathetic or respectful attitude. "A tolerant person is one who tries to see what is good or true in the ideas and practices of others, and who assumes whenever possible that others are acting in good faith."[9]

Tolerance also has limits; it is not licentiousness. "There are times when tolerance constitutes moral weakness and is itself to be properly condemned, just as there are times when responding 'intolerantly' is a sign of admirable moral strength."[10] Charles Taylor describes tolerance in terms of a rebuttable presumption. One begins with a presumption that there is value in another's idea or practice, as it "takes supreme arrogance to discount this possibility *a priori*," and this arrogance violates liberal democratic principles of equality.[11]

As Bollinger and Taylor point out, however, this does not mean that no evaluation takes place. This evaluation is a measurement against liberal democratic principles forming the basis of the social contract only. Does the idea or practice implement an inequality, does it fail to limit government, and does it maximize individual freedom of conscience? If a religious practice does not violate democratic norms it is to be permitted or accommodated. "To 'accommodate' suggests . . . treating a different religion with respect, and trying to find ways to avoid suppressing or infringing upon that religion, without actually adopting it."[12]

Another outgrowth of the acceptance of human responsible agency is an altered view of the origin of human dignity. The Universal Declaration of Human Rights of 1948 begins by proclaiming that "recognition of the inherent human dignity and of the equal and inalienable rights of all members of the human family is the foundation of freedom, justice and peace in the world." This acknowledgment of the concept of inherent human dignity was not new, as it has long been exalted in the works of Confucius, Stoic philosophy, the Hebrew and Christian Bible, and the Q'uran. The change demonstrated in the 1948 Declaration separates the concept from denominational theology or philosophy and declares it universal. Human dignity now belongs to the entirety of the human race "*just because they are human beings.*"[13] As Bielefeldt points out, the declaration "links the 'inherent dignity' of all human beings to their 'equal and inalienable rights,' which means that respect for human dignity receives an institutional backing in internationally binding rights of everyone."[14] But the right is not limited to positivist legal reasoning; it encompasses a moral motivation to which all are called. The human by virtue of being human holds dignity and is thus entitled to rights of freedom and equality, including the inalienable right to freedom of religion.

> First, freedom of religion or belief is a *universal right* which all human beings have a claim to just because of their inherent dignity as "members of the human family." Secondly, given its liberating thrust as a *right to freedom*, it aims at empowering people to realize their potential of responsible agency and thus freely find their ways in the field of religion or belief, as individuals and together with others. Finally, in keeping with its universalistic nature, freedom of religion or belief must be respected and implemented in a *non-discriminatory manner*, since equality in human dignity necessarily implies equality of all in their basic rights.[15]

Every Western constitution contains a freedom of conscience or religion clause. This freedom is not uncontrolled. The state may give preference to recognized religions or monitor and restrict religious practices; religious pluralism is state controlled to some extent in every country. If one accepts the starting point of normative universalism set forth above, all restrictions on the self-understanding of humanness through religion are improper. But how do we form a social group and protect other human rights if there is no restriction on religious rights? We cannot. What the normative universalism through religious rights calls for is the application of the right without impinging on other rights and which is not so broad as to lose its significance. Not every opinion or practice ascends to the point of being a protected religious belief or ritual. The question is where do we draw the line? In the case of the *burqa* and *hijab,* do we define them as relating to a "deep and existential conviction and concomitant individual and communitarian ethical or ritualistic practice," or are they remnants of a former political system which must be shed when seeking to become a member of a new political system?[16] Michael Weiner opines that this is evident in the UN Special Rapporteur on Freedom of Religion, characterizing the proper scope of state regulation of religion as being guided by the principle of *in dubio pro libertae*—any doubt should benefit liberty.[17]

In considering how to grant the widest freedom of religion one must consider both positive and negative freedom. In law this means one is as free to do something as she is not to do it. With religion one is free to believe and practice in the same margin that one is free not to believe or practice. Promotion of one or the other is to violate the general essence of a freedom. Thus, the state which fully implements freedom of religion is the one which neither advantages nor disadvantages either religion or nonreligion. This does not mean anything goes, as any exercise of the human right of religion must be balanced against the practice of other human rights that include the rights to safety and order. If there is a *direct* conflict of interests, religious rights may be restricted. But what is a *direct* conflict? Is the directness determined solely by local feelings, or is there a boundary past which we can say that the universal right of freedom of religion is violated? What is that boundary?

Since we are dealing with inalienable rights, the onus is always on the one who would impose restrictions to prove that the exercise is in direct conflict with other fundamental interests, that the proposed restriction is the least restrictive, and that it is reasonably related to resolve the conflict. In Western states these restrictions usually involve the protection of a negative right (the right for a nonbeliever not to have to participate in the believer's ritual), the protection of other fundamental rights (speech, voting, etc.), and issues of public safety, order, health, and morals. In pursuing resolution of these latter issues the state serves as determiner of what it deems necessary for safety, order, and health. The majority of society imposes additional moral restrictions through social practices and mores. Thus, minority religions have frequently found themselves restricted in practices and rituals which are different from those practiced by the majority of society. This leads to the second issue of how to implement freedom of religion—how to achieve equal treatment.

Freedom and equality are inextricably intertwined. Without freedom to choose for oneself there would only be an equality of sameness. Thus, freedom is not uniformity; it is an implementation of an *a priori* principle that each is entitled, as a human being, to develop and pursue their own beliefs. Thus, equality is diversity and diversity is equality.

In ensuring equality toward religion the state begins by seeking nondiscrimination—the neutral state. In attempting to achieve neutrality the state regulates its own conduct and that of society. Thus, the state must promote a climate of openness and tolerance to counter prejudices and discriminatory practices by private actors. For the state to be the arbiter of neutrality it must be careful to not be perceived as granting special status to a religion, religions, or nonreligion. In implementing reasonable restrictions the state must prove that it is acting both *de jure* and *de facto* without discrimination.

> The principle of neutrality represents the high normative aspiration of the State to consistently act in a *fair, inclusive and nondiscriminatory manner* vis-a-vis the existing or emerging religious and philosophical diversity in society. This is a very demanding task and one may rightly object that such an aspiration is finally utopian.[18]

The pendulum will never stop moving on the grid of neutrality and equality. As society is constantly encountering new religious ideas, the liberal democratic state must constantly consider how to act in a nondiscriminatory manner while maintaining a cohesive societal order. In a state which guarantees freedom of religion, religious minorities have the right to demand adjustment of legal restrictions when they impact religious convictions. Conversely, the state has the right to demand, in seeking order, safety, morals, and insurance of other freedoms, that certain practices be forfeited. Thus, the state and religion seek an accommodation for each other's interests.

For the state to be neutral it must at some level be secular in the sense that it is not solely implementing a single religious doctrine. Nondiscrimination by the state means the state must not be overly identified with any religion or belief other than that of nondiscrimination. Government neither advantages nor disadvantages any specific religion; any fostering of national cohesion through religion must give equal weight to all religions and nonreligion. It is respectful of all beliefs so long as those beliefs do not impinge on others or the government's conception of democracy. Bielefeldt calls this a "respectful non-identification" and Rawls a "veil of ignorance."

Actors in the political sphere place fullness of democracy, consensus pluralism, as the fixed point of perfection around which other ideas, including religious, may be allowed to exist but which must not become the center point. State secularism and neutrality are the operative means by which the state implements the inalienable right of freedom of religion. Conversely, the believer alters her theological claims of Ultimate Truth to accept the existence of other views of Ultimate Truth and their right of existence. In accepting this right of existence the Ultimate Truth is expanded to include a tolerance of another view and a restriction in practice to allow the other to exist. Further, the believer agrees to submit to the state's regulation to protect the freedom of others and foster social cohesion. To reach a consensus for coexistence each group must give up some aspect of exclusivity and accept equal existence of other viewpoints. This allows the formation of a pluralist society around points of common agreement, with the first one being tolerance of differences unless they threaten the continuation of the consensus. The issues are how to balance these interests and what are the boundaries of tolerance.

The history of a people creates the psychological, sociological, political, and religious order in a territory which forms a state. In the modern world this state begins with a boundary wider than family, clan, or tribe, so there is some level of inherent plurality. Globalization "dislocate[s] the centered and 'closed' identities of a national culture. It does have a pluralizing impact on identities producing a variety of possibilities and new positions of identification and making identities more positional, more political, more plural and diverse."[19] Identity is a choice and to be fully democratic, treating all equally, the state is to allow individualization of identity. At the same time, the state needs to find some means of binding people together to maintain itself; thus, it must promote a common identity for its citizens.

The question is, given this inherent plurality which is increasing with globalization, whether anyone can ever reach the goal of true equality and neutrality. If one can never reach the goal, why measure action against perfection? Isn't the ideal or perfect really an imperfect because it fails to account for the *a priori* pluralism? I assert that the answer is no because the ideal, while unattainable, marks the singularity for the constantly moving society. By knowing the singularity of ideal balance, we can observe how far from ideal the movement of society is at any point in time. By establishing the ideal and the outer boundary, we can now observe events and determine whether they move us closer toward the ideal or toward breaking the outer boundary of democracy.

The state and society can each work together to check the other and move toward the ideal. But there is also a danger of them using each other to work together for individual purposes to create abuses and move to the outer boundary. Appeals to national identity by state and social accords are frequently used to foment public resentment of minority immigrant groups and to implement discriminatory regulation that characterizes new cultural practices as dangerous to national unity. The immigrant minority is seen as a contagion which must be eradicated to save the nation. The social actor, motivated by fear and contempt, moves aggressively against the minority out of both a feeling of vulnerability and a "pretense of moral superiority."[20]

The neutral state is not one which turns a blind eye to the question of religion, and it does not purge public space of all religious symbols. Purging is not a neutral action because it actually advantages the view that religion is inappropriate. It is exclusive of religion disadvantaging all religion. Neutrality is "a political fairness principle" to foster freedom of religion. The secular state is not a secularist state. It is a state in which there is "political secularism" not "doctrinal secularism." Doctrinal secularism promotes a secular ideology over any other religion. Political secularism operates in service of nondiscrimination in religion; the state remains "open, fair and inclusive."[21] Because we are dealing in pure theory and the practicalities of human thought and conduct never fit into the neat boxes of theory, there are overlaps, gray areas, and constant tension in action and inaction. If the actor, state, or individual or social group stops to ask itself these questions before restricting religious practice, we may move closer to the utopian.

Will Kymlicka opines that liberalism originates in the liberal state's separation of itself from religion. But it cannot be completely neutral when it comes to religion.

> However hard it tries to be neutral, even the liberal state will always favor a certain language, its decisions about public holidays, the contents of public education, and its myths and ceremonies will always reflect or favor the "societal culture" of the majority group at the cost of those of minorities. Accordingly, "benign neglect" (that is neutrality) is not a solution. If equality and justice are to prevail, the state must proactively "recognize and endorse or support" the cultures of minority groups.[22]

There is a need to feel valued not only individually but also as a member of the group. Thus, Kymlicka argues the state must recognize and make room for religious and cultural expression.

Brian Barry, however, sees multiculturalism as a divider of society via an institutional perpetuation of differences which undermines equal distribution of economic and political resources. Further, it hinders formation and implementation of universal policies of inclusion and equality. In different ways, both Barry and Rawls posit the merit of a universal liberal egalitarianism which restricts free exercise of religion in favor of a system of neutral law, arguing that equal treatment without regard to cultural or religious identity better achieves liberal democratic ideals, a "separate is never equal" argument. Equal treatment achieves political inclusiveness while allowing private preservation of the essentials of cultural or religious identity.[23]

But who is responsible for ensuring this equality? It may rest in the political as implementer of the will of the majority because they are in control of the terms of the social contract. However, in liberal democracies this power does not rest solely in the political because there are foundational principles to check the possible tyranny of the majority. This check usually occurs through the judicial branch, whose task it is to ensure that foundational principles of equality, freedom, and state neutrality to religion are maintained. But who checks the judiciary?

Ran Hirschl declares that the judicial branch has in recent years exceeded its function in many polities, and a juristocracy has arisen.[24] A juristocracy is an elevation of the judicial role to policymaker by judicial fiat, serving as a *policy* check on legislative action. This elevates the power of the judiciary to that of an unelected legislator and not merely a check on improper legislative action. Hirschl asserts the judicial branch through this juristocracy has expanded its role and "elected" itself the final authority. In turn, the legislator and public form public policy debates in legal terms and capitulate to this new judicial role, thus judicializing politics. The public policy debate on hotly contested issues no longer ends in the political sphere; rather they end when the judicial makes the final ruling a policy decision. These have resulted in either a backlash by the political arm to overturn by legislative action judicial decisions deemed excessive by the majority or by capitulating and drafting legislation which will satisfy the policies of the judiciary, not majority will, thereby increasing the tension between the legislative and judicial spheres.

Equality is a controversial subject in law. In all Western law, there is agreement to the "concept" of equality, the right to equality, but there is disagreement about what it is in practice and how to achieve it.[25] There are two main streams of thought: one is that equality means the elimination of all difference while the other asserts that, while differences beyond one's control (such as race) should be eliminated, differences of fundamental choice should be preserved. A major component of both is the question of what to do about cultural differences, particularly religious ones. Should we preserve cultural differences (multiculturalism) or should they be lessened or eliminated in order to form a cohesive, equal society? All questions of equality involve the just distribution of resources, physical and symbolic. Thus, all theories of equality focus on how to achieve a just distribution of resources.

Dworkin, working from the point of view of the individual, advocates an "envy free" distribution of resources. He begins with the question of whether anyone is envious of another's available resources and argues that equality means a distribution, enforced by law, which leaves no one envious of another and only compensates for differences beyond one's control. Thus, he would support a law prohibiting discrimination based on race in employment but objects to a law which requires employers to give employees time off for religious activities.[26]

Walzer approaches the issue from the perspective of the nature of the good distributed.[27] Each good is inherently different and must be measured by its place in the sphere of a person's life (work, education, religion). He argues for application of different criteria for different spheres, a position which requires that we consider the fundamental importance of the sphere to the individual. Walzer's theory protects cultural differences which are deemed "important enough." The issue then is who determines what cultural practice is "important enough." Whether enacted by law or social acceptance, the majority decides what is an acceptable cultural practice. Thus, critics claim Walzer's theory contains an inherent inequality in favor of majority opinion.

Kymlicka argues for group-specific rights to mitigate disadvantages of minority positions in society.[28] Iris Young and Anne Phillips push further, saying the state should take steps to ensure an active political voice for minority members, according them an equal opportunity to have their points of view implemented.[29] While Cecile Laborde argues that a tempered French republicanism incorporates liberal democracy's equality and neutrality better than Kymlicka's preferentialism. Do any of these work, in the practical sense, for the veiling debates? Are all of these attempts to justify or criticize actions viewed as either falling within or over the amorphous edge of democratic equality?

Working alongside equality is neutrality. Modern liberal democracies assert they are "neutral" toward religion as part of their recognition of individual rights of conscience and culture. However, neutrality is as slippery as equality. Neutrality can be divided into two broad stances: particularistic and universalistic, also known as unity and rights-oriented.[30] It has been common for the political sphere to emphasize the first and legal the second. Each sees the other as an opponent and claims that its view is democratically superior.

All versions of democracy include some consideration of neutrality, as the state is an institution made up of individuals with theoretically equal say in governance. The state must not favor or disadvantage any one group—it must be equal as well as neutral. Traditional liberal democratic theory holds that religion is one of the fundamental areas in which the state must be neutral. John Locke thought that the state should only concern itself with "every man's possession of things of this life" while leaving "the care of each man's soul . . . entirely to every man's self."[31] Locke considered this neutrality purely from a Protestant view, limiting the state's neutrality to a Protestant vision of neutrality, not a religiously pluralist one. As the West has become more pluralist and accepting of different religions, the neutral state has come to be defined as "one that deals impartially with its citizens and which remains neutral on the issue of what sort of lives they should lead."[32] Thus, the neutral state is to separate itself as far as possible from religion. No seriously considered theorist argues that the separation can be complete. The argument comes over what level of separation is sufficient to maintain order and social cohesion on the one hand and individual liberty on the other. The introduction of large numbers of Muslims in the United States, France, and the Netherlands is challenging stability in this balance. Recent action on Islamic women's religious dress in each of the countries demonstrates that reaction is not just a result of public fear of the other but also a political backlash against legal rights-oriented neutrality and equality.

NOTES

1. R. D. Grillo, *Pluralism and the Politics of Difference: State, Culture, and Ethnicity in Comparative Perspective* (New York: Clarendon Press, 1998), 5–11.
2. S. Hall, "The Question of Cultural Identity," in *Modernity and Its Future,* ed. S. Hall, D. Held, and T. McGrew (Cambridge: Polity Press, 1992), 299–302.
3. Grillo, 5, quoting D. Nicholls, *Three Varieties of Pluralism* (London: Macmillan, 1974). See also James Beckford, *Social Theory and Religion* (New York: Cambridge University Press, 2003).
4. Heiner Bielefeldt, "Freedom of Religion or Belief—a Human Right under Pressure," *Oxford Journal of Law and Religion* 1, no. 1 (2012): 17.
5. Ibid.
6. Stephen Smith, *Getting Over Equality* (New York: New York University Press, 2001), 96.
7. Lee Bollinger, *The Tolerant Society: Freedom of Speech and Extreme Speech in America* (New York: Oxford University Press, 1988), 182.
8. Smith, 96.
9. Smith, 97.
10. Bollinger, 11.
11. Charles Taylor, "The Politics of Recognition," in *Multiculturalism: Examining the Politics of Recognition*, ed. Amy Gutman (Princeton: Princeton University Press, 1994), 66–73.
12. Smith, 98.
13. Bielefeldt, 18.
14. Bielefeldt, 19.
15. Bielefeldt, 20.
16. Bielefeldt, 21.
17. Michael Wiener, "The Mandate of the Special Rapporteur on Freedom of Religion or Belief—Institutional, Procedural and Substantive Legal Issues," *Religion and Human Rights* 2 (2007): 2, http://dx.doi.org/10.1163/187103107X218911.
18. Bielefeldt, 24.
19. T. H. Ericksen, *Ethnicity and Nationalism: Anthropological Perspective* (London: Pluto Press, 1993), 145–49.
20. Bielefeldt, 28.
21. Bielefeldt, 34.
22. Will Kymlicka, *Multicultural Citizenship* (New York: Clarendon Press, 1995), 111.
23. Brian Barry, *Culture and Equality: An Egalitarian Critique of Multiculturalism* (Cambridge, MA: Harvard University Press, 2001); John Rawls, *A Theory of Justice*, (Cambridge, MA: Harvard University Press, 1998) and *Political Liberalism* (New York: Columbia University Press, 1996).
24. Ran Hirschl, *Towards Juristocracy* (Cambridge, MA: Harvard University Press, 2004), 1.
25. See Rawls, *A Theory of Justice*; H. L. A. Hart, *The Concept of Law* (New York: Oxford University Press, 1961).
26. Ronald Dworkin, *Taking Rights Seriously* (Cambridge, MA: Harvard University Press, 1977).
27. Michael Walzer, *Spheres of Justice: A Defense of Pluralism and Equality* (New York: Basic Books, 1983).

28. Kymlicka, 111.

29. Iris Young, *Justice and the Politics of Difference* (Princeton: Princeton University Press, 1990).

30. Chistian Joppke, "State Neutrality and Islamic Headscarf Laws in France and Germany," *Theory and Society* 36 (2007): 313–42, http://www.springer.com/social+sciences/journal/11/86. As we shall see, the approach from either side lies in whether you begin from individualism or communitarianism. Are you more concerned with restriction by government and seek to retain a broad individual sphere or are you more concerned with creation of a community order such that individualism must make concession to integrate to the satisfaction of the institutional structure or it can be excluded?

31. John Locke, Letter Concerning Toleration (1689), http://www.etextlib.virginia.edu.

32. Peter Jones, "The Ideal of the Neutral State," in *Liberal Neutrality*, ed. Robert Goodin and Andrew Reeve (New York: Routledge, 1989), 9.

Chapter Four

Supranational Forces

The theories discussed in the preceding chapter are not merely academic exercises because democratic states attempt to implement them internally and agree to be bound by their force when they consent to international norms. Most often these international norms take the form of international aspirational agreements such as UN declarations. The United States, France, and the Netherlands have all signed and agreed to abide by several UN declarations on human rights, including religious freedom and minority and women's rights.[1] While these documents are not legally binding they declare an ideal force to which each state agrees to be bound. In addition to these aspirational agreements, France and the Netherlands have agreed to legally bind themselves to two bodies: the Council of Europe (COE) and the European Union (EU). Thus, when discussing the intersection of law, politics, and religion, particularly in the European context, we must consider not only the sovereign state's institutions; we also must consider the impact of forces exerted by international and pan-European institutions.

INTERNATIONAL DECLARATIONS

UN declarations are not binding international law. They are a form of peer pressure and a point of pride for signatories to assert their leadership. The UN employs special rapporteurs to publish yearly reports on any country's failure to comply with the declarations, and the General Assembly can pass condemnations against any noncompliant country to pressure it to conform. Countries will often consider this pressure in taking local action. A state may elect to be viewed as acting out of the mainstream or as a leader of certain ideologies. The US, France, and the Netherlands have all served on the UN Human Rights Council, successor to the UN Commission on Human Rights, and submit periodic national reports on adherence to human rights norms.[2] In these reports and other pronouncements the US, France, and the Netherlands have sought to be portrayed internationally as leaders of human rights norms and assert that these norms apply internationally to all political states and cultures.[3]

The first document to which all three countries agreed is the UN Declaration of Human Rights adopted in 1948. It is a global recognition of inherent rights perceived as fundamental to human dignity, and its signatories agree to conduct themselves according to certain norms that include freedom of religion in thought and practice and equal treatment of all persons. The 1948 Declaration on Human Rights has been combined with other UN declarations, including the International Covenant on Economic, Cultural, Social, and Political Rights and the International Covenant on Civil and Political Rights, to form the International Bill of Rights (1976). All three countries also joined with the UN General Assembly in adopting the Declaration on the Elimination of all Forms of Religious Intolerance and Discrimination (1981). The US, France, and the Netherlands are also signatories to the Organization for the Security and Co-operation in Europe's (OSCE) Helsinki Final Act (1975), which requires signatories to "respect human rights and fundamental freedoms," including religious freedom, and incorporates the UN Declaration on Human Rights into its terms.

The terms of the International Covenant on Civil and Political Rights (ICCPR) of 1996 are substantially similar to those of other UN declarations and covenants.[4] The ICCPR provides for implementation of its norms through national constitutional structures and recognizes that a variety of sociopolitical structures are capable of guaranteeing agreed upon universal human rights norms, including the place of religion and equal treatment. In three articles the ICCPR provides for religious freedom, equal treatment, and protection of minorities:

> Article 18
>
> 1. Everyone shall have the right to freedom of thought, conscience and religion. This right shall include freedom to have or to adopt a religion or belief of his choice, and freedom, either individually or in community with others and in public or private, to manifest his religion or belief in worship, observance, practice and teaching.
>
> 2. No one shall be subject to coercion which would impair his freedom to have or to adopt a religion or belief of his choice.
>
> 3. Freedom to manifest one's religion or beliefs may be subject only to such limitations as are prescribed by law and are necessary to protect public safety, order, health, or morals or the fundamental rights and freedoms of others.
>
> 4. The States Parties to the present Covenant undertake to have respect for the liberty of parents and, when applicable, legal guardians to ensure the

> religious and moral education of their children in conformity with their own convictions.
>
> Article 26
>
> All persons are equal before the law and are entitled without any discrimination to the equal protection of the law. In this respect, the law shall prohibit any discrimination and guarantee to all persons equal and effective protection against discrimination on any ground such as race, colour, sex, language, religion, political or other opinion, national or social origin, property, birth or other status.
>
> Article 27
>
> In those States in which ethnic, religious or linguistic minorities exist, persons belonging to such minorities shall not be denied the right, in community with the other members of their group, to enjoy their own culture, to profess and practise their own religion, or to use their own language.[5]

These articles make clear that freedom of religion has a communal dimension but that it remains fundamentally an individual right and that this right may be manifested in public or private. The Human Rights Committee, overseer of the implementation of the ICCPR, has opined that this means the following: "The observance and practice of religion or belief may include not only ceremonial acts but also such customs as the observance of dietary regulations, the wearing of distinctive clothing or head coverings."[6]

The limitations contained in sections 2 and 3 of article 18 are the elements which cause the most controversy in state implementation. The state must show that the limitation is prescribed by law, and the law must be "necessary to protect public safety, order, health, or morals or the fundamental rights and freedoms of others." This necessity clause exception is the one used by states to justify restrictions on the wearing of religious dress.

Through these declarations each of these countries commits to fashion its national law and policy to comply with liberal democratic ideals promoting religious freedom, equality, and state neutrality expressed in the international declarations. In addition, in the European context there are two supranational agreements which are binding on France and the Netherlands.

COUNCIL OF EUROPE AND EUROPEAN UNION

In 1946, seeking ways to rebuild Europe and prevent another world war on European soil, Winston Churchill called for something akin to a "United States of Europe."[7] States were not willing to concede national sovereignty *in toto* so a compromise organization was formed, the Council of Europe, of which France and the Netherlands are founding members.[8] The council tag line is "human rights—democracy—rule of law." The COE is completely separate from the EU. Even though the council cannot make binding laws, it has become an important political body chiefly due to the work of its Court of Human Rights. The members of the council have signed the European Convention on Human Rights (ECHR), setting forth human rights standards by which the sovereign-state members agree to be bound, and created a European Court of Human Rights to enforce those standards.[9] The ECHR provides that contracting parties "shall secure to everyone within their jurisdiction the rights and freedoms defined in section 1 of this Convention" and that each party is obligated to ensure that its institutions and officials make no law or take no action infringing on the ECHR. Thus, the signatories must take the provisions of the ECHR into consideration when carrying out state functions.

Section 1 of the ECHR is a "bill of rights" that recognizes rights of privacy, expression, assembly, and religion. One article of the bill of rights states:

> 1. Everyone has the right to freedom of thought, conscience and religion; this right includes freedom; to change his religion or belief and freedom, either or alone or in community with others and in public or private, to manifest his religion or belief, in worship, teaching, practice and observance.
>
> 2. Freedom to manifest one's religion or beliefs shall be subject only to such limitations as are prescribed by law and are necessary in a democratic society in the interests of public safety, for the protection of public order, health or morals, or for the protection of the rights and freedoms of others.

In 2002 a nondiscrimination provision was added to the ECHR, which provides that:

> 1. The enjoyment of any right set forth by law shall be secured without discrimination on any ground such as sex, race, colour, language, religion, political or other opinion, national or social origin, association with a national minority, property, birth or other status.
>
> 2. No one shall be discriminated against by any public authority on any ground such as those mentioned in paragraph 1.[10]

Under each right granted in the ECHR there is a necessity clause restriction which restricts the right granted "only to such limitations as are prescribed by law and are necessary in a democratic society in the interests of public safety, for the protection of public order, health or morals, or for the protection of the rights and freedoms of others."

The Human Rights Court has jurisdiction over member states' national laws and judicial decisions for review in accordance with the standards set forth in the ECHR, creating binding international law. The court must balance the individual freedom protection with the state interest protected by the necessity clause.

Protocol 11, enacted in 1998, expanded jurisdiction of the court to claims by individuals. This grant of jurisdiction is unusual in that not only are member states subject to claims brought by other member states and court decisions on them, but they are also bound by court decisions filed by any individual, after exhaustion of all state remedies.[11] "Protocol 11 remade the regime into an efficient mechanism for monitoring domestic politics in regimes that could pose a serious threat to peace and stability on the continent. The cost to Western states was stronger supervision of their own system of rights protection."[12] The protocol put the court into a position of structural supremacy to state institutions—"a kind of 'super agent' empowered to enforce the law against the states themselves."[13] This creates a judicialization of the council through the court's jurisdiction and interpretation of state laws. This causes the judicial body to have a significant effect on state policy and lawmaking in the member states. While theoretically the council could override a court decision, it would be difficult and to date the council has not done so. This allows the court to "operate in an unusually permissive zone of discretion." The zone of discretion exists where a court "exercises compulsory jurisdiction over questions concerning state noncompliance; states are under a legal obligation to comply with their rulings; and the decision rule governing override—unanimity—reduces the probability of reversal virtually to nil."[14] Because the council is a composite of sovereign states, the ability to override by unanimous vote is greatly weakened. Thus, the court dominates the evolution of the state regime so long as the member states accept the concept of judicial precedent. Further, the court "possesses the de facto power to determine the scope of its own competences and therefore to expand or contract the zone of discretion."[15] In areas where the regime's legislative process is likely to reach an impasse, the judicial process substitutes itself and becomes the instrument through which revision through interpretation is achieved.[16]

The court views the ECHR as a "living instrument" which is to be interpreted dynamically as society evolves, granting to itself wide discretion to act as policymaker for issues under the ECHR.[17] According to the court, any state limitation on the enumerated rights must fall within the necessity clause to be valid. The court decides what state action qualifies under the necessity clause, so it decides what state action is legitimate according to the court's own standards of necessity. The national constitutions of the Netherlands and France also contain their own "necessity" clauses limiting the freedom of religion and other civil rights within their borders. Thus, the states must consider not only their own constitutional balancing but also that imposed by the ECHR when crafting law or policy on religious issues.

The court utilizes a proportional analysis to decide issues of individual versus state's rights. In applying necessity analysis the court applies

> a "least restrictive means" test (a "narrow tailoring" requirement in American terms) in the context of balancing regime values against the interest being pleaded by the defendant state. A state measure that fails to meet the necessity requirements is, under the regime's law, a "disproportionate" exercise of discretion under the treaty, and the defendant state loses.[18]

The court uses this strategy to move state policy to conform with its interpretation of the ECHR by finding a violation until the state alters its law.

Sweet and Brunell assert that this animates a "majoritarian activism" between states and the court in that the court alters its interpretation in response to evolving norms expressed by a sufficient number of states. The court's decisions both restrict state action deemed inconsistent with the ECHR and supports activist states via majoritarian activism by adopting new standards embraced by a majority of states and imposing them on states lagging behind. Until the French *burqa* ban, this movement was only to the expansion of individual rights. Further, no state that has lost its national regulatory autonomy in an area has ever regained it, as no court opinion has ever been overridden by the council or any member state.[19] Accordingly, the decisions of the court on issues of religious dress are extremely important in assessing state action with regard to Islamic women's religious dress in the Netherlands and France.

The court ruled that the wearing of religious symbols in public is not a per se threat to public safety, order, or the rights of others.[20] In applying the necessity test the court uses a proportionality analysis in ruling on restrictions of rights. It defines necessity as "a pressing social need; thus the notion necessary does not have the flexibility of such expressions as useful or desirable."[21] The court has consistently held that "necessity" is not synonymous with "indispensable," "admissible," "ordinary," "reasonable," or "useful and desirable." It defines democratic society as one which is pluralist, tolerant, and broadminded. The court has held that the state is in a better position to determine the local issues of society and, therefore, a broad margin of discretion should be granted to it. Thus the court seeks to balance the margin of appreciation granted to the state to determine local issues and consensus on European values to be imposed on the state. This balancing takes place in two ways: first, a balancing of individual and society, and, second, state and European consensus. T. Jeremy Gunn has distilled this balancing to a tripartite test:

1. "[T]he measure must [first] be appropriate . . . for attaining its objective, [it has] the theoretical capacity to accomplish its aim."
2. "The measure is necessary . . . to achieve its intended purposes," which means that no less restrictive alternative is available.

3. "[T]he measure must be proportional to the objective," meaning that the restriction is narrowly tailored.[22]

The court repeatedly recognized the delicate balancing that must take place with regard to religion-state relations, given the ECHR's supranational position and the member sovereign state's authority to regulate the place of religion within its borders.[23] In the case of *Dahlab v. Switzerland*, wherein a public primary school teacher was prohibited from wearing the *hijab* by an administrative rule, the court explained its approach thus:

> The Court refers, in the first place, to its case law to the effect that freedom of thought, conscience and religion, as enshrined by Article 9 of the Convention represents, one of the foundations of a "democratic society" within the meaning of the Convention. In its religious dimension, it is one of the most vital elements that go to make up the identity of the believers and their conception of life, but it is also a precious asset for atheists, agnostics, skeptics and the unconcerned. The pluralism is indissociable from a democratic society which has been dearly won over the centuries, depends on it. While religious freedom is primarily a matter of individual conscience, it also implies a freedom to manifest one's religion. Bearing witness in words and deeds is bound up with the existence of religious convictions. . . . The Court further observes that in democratic societies, in which several religions coexist within one and the same population, it may be necessary to place restrictions on this freedom in order to reconcile the interests of the various groups and ensure that everyone's beliefs are respected.[24]

However, with regard to the *hijab*, the court held that it

> appears to be imposed on women by a precept which is laid down in the Koran and which . . . is hard to square with the principle of gender equality. It therefore appears difficult to reconcile the wearing of an Islamic headscarf with the message of tolerance, respect for others and, above all, equality and non-discrimination that all teachers in a democratic society must convey to their pupils.[25]

In the case of *Sahin v. Turkey*, ruling on a Turkish law prohibiting any student from wearing a *hijab* at a public university, the court held:

> Where questions concerning the relationship between State and religion are at stake, on which opinion in a democratic society may reasonably differ widely, the role of the national decision-making body must be given special importance. . . . In such cases, it is necessary to have regard to the fair balance that must be struck between the various interests at stake; the rights and freedoms of others, avoiding civil unrest, the demands of public order and pluralism.[26]

On appeal to the higher Grand Chamber, it stated:

> Pluralism and broadmindedness are hallmarks of a "democratic society." Although individual interests must on occasion be subordinated to those of a group, democracy does not simply mean that the views of a majority must always prevail: a balance must be achieved which ensures the fair and proper treatment of people from minorities and avoids any abuse of a dominant position.[27]

This balancing can be seen in two recent cases from the UK involving employees who are required to wear uniforms adding personal necklaces with cross pendants.[28] The court held that

> given the importance in a democratic society of freedom of religion, the Court considers that, where an individual complains of a restriction on freedom of religion in the workplace, rather than holding that the possibility of changing job would negate any interference with the right, the better approach would be to weigh that possibility in the overall balance when considering whether or not the restriction was proportionate.[29]

The court held the wearing of the religious garb need not be a requirement for all practitioners of the religion, just that the some, including the wearer, believes it to be an act of piety for it to fall within the protection of religious freedom laws. However, the court balanced the freedom of the individual against employers concerns for the workplace. In the case of Chaplin, a state nurse, a necklace with a cross pendant with a work uniform could be prohibited by the employer due to safety concerns. The employee should have been allowed to wear the cross if it was kept tucked away so a reasonable accommodation must be made by the employer. In the second case, the court held a British Airways employee should have been permitted to wear the cross because uniform accommodations had been made for other religious garb and it did not cause a significant distraction from the desired corporate look.[30] Thus, whether student or employee, the court utilized a balancing test of state interest against individual right to wear religious garb until the French *burqa* ban came before the court.

Prior to the French *burqa* ban, the council issued resolution 1743, recognizing that there is a difference between the forced wearing of the *burqa* or *niqab* and a woman choosing to wear the garments.[31] The resolution recognized that a general ban on wearing the garments may infringe on the rights of women who freely choose to wear the garments, thereby violating their personal rights. The only legitimate restrictions are on the forced wearing of the garments, state security, or work requiring religious neutrality or a visible face.[32] According to the resolution, the state should view any woman forced to wear religious dress as a domestic violence victim and provide the needed support and rehabilitation to her.[33] Finally, the resolution pointed out that the true consequence of the ban might be to force women in difficult domestic or economic situations to choose between their cultural and religious traditions and their desire or need to work outside the home, thus actually forcing the women to remain isolated and hindering their ability to fully integrate into society.[34] The assembly calls on member states to

> develop targeted policies intended to raise Muslim women's awareness of their rights, help them to take part in public life and offer them equal opportunities to pursue a professional life and gain social and economic independence. In this respect, the education of young Muslim women as well as of their parents and families is crucial. It is especially necessary to remove all forms of discrimination against girls and to develop education on gender equality, without stereotypes and at all levels of the education system.[35]

In a position paper, human rights commissioner Thomas Hammarberg asserted that a general ban would be improper under the ECHR.[36] He reasoned that such bans are incompatible with the privacy and religion articles of the ECHR and that states had not shown the exception required by the necessity clause. He asserts the states have not shown how the wearing of the *burqa* or *niqab* significantly undermines public safety, order or the rights of others. Further, the commissioner argues that there are other less restrictive measures to satisfy state claims for bare faces and heads for identification purposes and that states have not shown these alternatives are inadequate or even that there are serious or persistent identification problems. In line with the resolution, he expressed disapproval of the bans' failure to distinguish between women who freely choose to veil and those who are forced. He found that the bans failed to meet their asserted goal of assisting in women's equality and integration into society by isolating them. Rather, the bans increased intolerance against Muslim women.[37] He concluded that the only reasonable restrictions on women would be those on women who are in state representative capacities, such as police, judges, civil servants, who commonly interact with the public.

After the French ban, member states of the COE began to resist a perceived push by France to impose its views on the place of religion in the public sphere at the European level. They adopted resolution 1928, calling on member states to enact reasonable accommodations to religion and religious practices in the public space, including rendition of government services and education.[38] Additionally, a group of scholars from around Europe sent an open letter to the chair of the Committee on Legal Affairs and Human Rights objecting to the manner in which a report on the "Protection of Minors against Sectarian Influence" was being drafted by French representative Rudy Salles. The group stated Mr. Salles admitted that "the purpose of the report is to convince other European countries to adhere to the French model of fighting against so-called 'sects' or 'sectarian movements,'" which model, the group asserts, has been strongly criticized by the UN and is in violation of the Human Rights Court's ruling in the case of *Jehovah Witnesses of Moscow v. Russia.*[39] The political arm of the commission remains at a position of state neutrality and legal equality while judicial retreated solely when deciding the French *burqa* ban. Both the political and judicial influence state action by France and the Netherlands.

The US, France, and the Netherlands are not free to enact national laws and determine religious freedom and women's rights in any way they desire. The norms of equal treatment and broad individual rights are not mere academic opinion; they have been embraced by each of these states as the norms not only for themselves but also for other states. Thus, an analysis of the degree to which each of these countries is implementing these ideals and norms in national policy and law is appropriate.

NOTES

1. Universal Declaration of Human Rights 1948; UN Declaration on all Forms of Intolerance and Discrimination Based on Religion or Belief 1981; Convention on all Forms of Discrimination against Women. The US signed the Convention on women but the Senate did not ratify it. All UN documents can be found at http://www.un.org.
2. The Human Rights Council consists of forty-seven elected UN members from defined regions. Currently France is actively lobbying for election to the council in 2014. The US is on the counci,l and the Netherlands just completed a term and is not eligible for reelection for one election cycle.
3. See UN periodic reports, http://www.un.org/depts/dhl/unbisref_manual/humanrights/Humanrights/periodicreport.html.
4. The US has opted out of protocol 1 on the issues of capital punishment and juveniles. In ratification the Senate provided that the treaty is not self-executing in that it creates no cause of action in state courts and the US does not subject itself to the jurisdiction of the commission for claims brought by individuals.
5. France has not accepted article 27.
6. General Comments Adopted by the Human Rights Committee, 1993. UN Doc CCPR/C21/Rev/1/Add.4 adopted 29 July 1993, http://www.unchr.ch.
7. Winston Churchill, "Speech to the Academy of Youth," Zurich, Switzerland, September 1946. Interestingly, Churchill did not include the UK in his call for a United States of Europe. http://www.assembly.coe.int/Main.asp?link=/AboutUs/zurich_e.htm (accessed June 14, 2012).
8. The other founding members are the UK, Belgium, Denmark, Ireland, Italy, Luxembourg, Norway, and Sweden. Ian Bache, Stephen George, and Simon Bulmer, *Politics in the European Union* (New York: Oxford University Press, 2011). See also http://www.conventions.coe.int. In addition to the binding law of the ECHR, both France and the Netherlands must consider EU directives in implementing local law. In 2000 the European Parliament adopted a Charter of Fundamental Rights of the European Union and issued Directives on Equal Treatment regarding employment, women, and religious and ethnic minorities within the union. The European Court of Justice (ECJ) recognizes the right to religious freedom as a principle of EU community law, which is binding on member states. While the ECJ has the authority to enforce the Charter on Rights, most human rights cases brought in the European context are filed with the Human Rights Court under the ECHR, so the ECJ only rarely addresses human rights issues. Further, the ECJ generally follows the court holdings in deciding rights cases brought to the ECJ.
9. See http://www.coe.int/60years (accessed June 16, 2012). Martyn Bond, *The Council of Europe: Structure, History, and Issues in European Politics* (New York: Routledge, 2011). The court structure was substantially changed by protocol 11 in 1998.

10. France has not ratified this protocol.

11. To date there are only three international courts whose members have consented to jurisdiction over individual claimants, the European Court of Human Rights, the World Trade Organization, and the European Union's ECJ. Both the WTO and ECJ deal mainly with economic issues.

12. Alex Sweet and Thomas Brunell, "Trustee Courts and the Judicialization of International Regimes," *Journal of Law and Courts* 1, no. 1 (Spring 2013): 62. Protocol 11 was prompted by the inclusion of former Soviet states into the COE.

13. Sweet and Brunell, 62.

14. Sweet and Brunell, 65–66.

15. Sweet and Brunell, 66.

16. Sweet and Brunell, 66.

17. *Loizidiou v. Turkey*, application no. 15318/89, judgment 18, December 1996, http://www.hudoc.echr.coe.

18. Sweet and Brunell, 69.

19. Sweet and Brunell, 77–81.

20. *Arslan and Others v. Turkey*, application no. 23462/94, judgment of 8 July 1999; *Arslan and Others v. Turkey*, application no. 41135/98, judgment of 23 February 2010.

21. *The Moscow Branch of the Salvation Army v. Russia*, application no. 72881/01, judgment of 5 October 2006.

22. T. Jeremy Gunn, "Deconstructing Proportionality in Limitations Analysis," *Emory International Law Review* 19 (2005): 467.

23. Y. Arai-Takahashi, *The Margin of Appreciation and the Principle of Proportionality in the Jurisprudence of the ECHR* (Antwerp: Intersentia, 2002); J. A. Sweeney "Margins of Appreciation: Cultural Relativity and the ECHR," *International and Comparative Law Quarterly* 54 (2005): 459–74.

24. *Dahlab v. Switzerland*, application no. 42393/98, ECHR 2001-V, para. 83.

25. Ibid.

26. *Leyla Sahin v. Turkey*, fourth section, application no. 44774/98, and judgment of 29 June 2004, para. 100.

27. *Leyla Sahin v. Turkey*, application no. 44774/98, Grand Chamber judgment of 10 November 2005, para. 108.

28. *Case of Eweida and Others v. UK*, applications no. 48420/10, 59842/10, 51671/10, 36516/10, judgment of 15 January 2013. The Grand Chamber refused hearing May 29, 2013.

29. Case from fn 27—Eweida.

30. *Case of Eweida and Others v. UK*, applications no. 48420/10, 59842/10, 51671/10, 36516/10, judgment of 15 January 2013.

31. Council of Europe, Parliamentary Assembly (2011) Resolution 1743 on Islam, Islamism, and Islamophobia in Europe, http://www.assembly.coe.int/Main.asp?link=Documents/AdoptedText /ta10/RES1743.htm. Pertinent sections are 14–17. Hereafter PACE 1743, [article number].

32. PACE 1743, article 16.

33. PACE 1743, articles 16 and 19.

34. PACE 1743, article 17.

35. PACE 1743, article 17.

36. Thomas Hammarberg, "Ruling Anywhere That Women Must Wear the Burqa Should Be Condemned but Banning Such Dresses Here Would Be Wrong," http://www.coe.int/t/commissioner/Viewpoints/100308_en.asp (accessed June 14, 2012).

37. See also the commissioner's official blog on the subject, Thomas Hammarberg, "Penalising Women Who Wear the Burqa Does Not Liberate Them" (2011), at http://www.commissioner.cws.coe.int/tiki-view_blog_post.php?postId=1557 (accessed June 15, 2012).

38. PACE Resolution 1928, adopted 24 April 2013, http://www.assembly.coe.int.

39. "Professors and Religious Leaders Write to Parliamentary Assembly," http://www.eifrf-articles.org/Professors-and-religious-leaders-write-to-Parliamentary-assembly.html (accessed June 14, 2012). The Jehovah's Witnesses received a ruling from the European Court of Human

Rights permitting their registration. *Jehovah's Witnesses of Moscow v. Russia*, 302/02, 10 June 2010.

Chapter Five

France

Liberté, Egalité, Fraternité

France considers itself one of the most egalitarian societies in the world and a leader in the implementation of democratic ideals; however, when it comes to religious freedom that assertion is debatable.[1] While the United States is sometimes referred to as a melting pot due its long history of immigration, modern scholars have noted it is more analogous to a salad or ethnic stew in which each ingredient adds flavor to the overall final product without losing some of its own unique characteristics.[2] France is the true melting pot of cultures; each is expected to so meld with the French culture that there is no discernible sign of the original, and if the newcomer does not meld voluntarily, the state will ensure she does so.[3] It is assimilation, not an integration or multiculturalism. This assimilation is visible in the French style of religion-state relations.

The French style of church-state relations revolves around the concept of *laïcité*. As will be described in more detail below, *laïcité* is not merely separation of church and state. *Laïcité* creates a French face of neutrality which emphasizes state-enforced unity over individual rights. In the early French republics the legal and political systems sought to create a new republican identity by stressing national uniformity. As the republic became more established the legal sector began granting more deference to individual choice, slightly relaxing the stress on uniformity. The recent increase in Muslim immigrants, however, has raised suspicions of anything different and caused a return to forced uniformity. The French government has focused on Muslim women's religious dress as the public point to demonstrate its authority to enforce French uniformity. One wonders why this small group is perceived as a major threat to French democracy and why the state is becoming more illiberal due to this threat. To understand, one must understand the history of church-state relations in France and French republicanism.

HISTORY

From the middle ages to the French Revolution the Roman Catholic Church was closely tied to the French monarchy.[4] After Clovis I became the first European monarch to pledge allegiance to the Roman doctrine over Arianism in 498, the Roman Catholic Church considered France *fille annee de l'Eglise* (elder daughter of the church).[5] The Roman Church's attainment of pledges from European monarchs enabled it to become the sole theological power on the Continent. From the time of Clovis to the revolution, the church and monarchy worked hand in hand to control all aspects of French society. There was tension in the relationship which centered on the amount of control over the church exercised by the French monarchy (*Gallicanism*) and submission to the Roman pope (*ultramontainisme*). The close relationship with the French monarchy grew to the point that French kings decided they had the authority to determine who should be pope and moved the papacy to Avignon, resulting in a period of multiple popes.[6]

The French monarchy remained staunchly Roman Catholic during the Protestant Reformation and many of the religious civil wars occurred on French soil. The monarchy and Roman Catholic Church effectively eliminated Protestantism in France. When the people rejected monarchy, they rejected the church, so dissent and nonbelief became the way out of the status quo. The church and monarchy were so closely intertwined that in throwing off the monarchy, the people sought to reject the power of the Roman Catholic Church over society.

The French Revolution, while dated at July 14, 1789, was not a smooth trajectory to the present state like that which occurred in the US. A part of this tortured history can be attributed to the fact that America revolted against an external colonial power, whereas the French Revolution was a civil war with all its attendant emotional turmoil. After the American Revolution many loyalists left America, but in France the opponents continued to live side-by-side with the revolutionaries. In 1790, the republic dissolved all monastic vows, severed relations with all religious organizations, dismissed bishops and appointed new ones without consultation with the pope, and all clergy were required to pledge primary allegiance to the republic and became employees of the state. The church became divided between those who pledged loyalty to the republic and those who remained aligned with Rome.

Historians generally view this time as the destructive beginning of a civil war on religion in France which revealed an "instinct for intolerance."[7] Any perceived group or class difference was strongly suppressed as a rejection of the strict class distinction which had prevailed under the *Ancien Regime*. After the revolution, the rejection of Catholicism was so strong that there was an attempt to replace it with a new French Republican religion in which the altar of Notre Dame de Paris, the Mother Church of the nation, was renamed by scratching into its surface that it was now to be the altar of reason. The state issued a new calendar with months renamed and religious holidays removed. In addition, property belonging to the Catholic Church was seized and redistributed.

The Declaration of Rights of Man and Citizens of 1789 set the post-revolution tone for the relationship between religion and society. The preamble states that "the ignorance, neglect or contempt of the rights of man are the sole cause of public calamities and of the corruption of governments, [thus we declare] the natural, unalienable, and sacred rights of man." These include that "[m]en are born free and remain free and equal. Social distinctions may be founded only upon the public good." The declaration defines liberty as that which "injures no one else" and is limited when it impinges on the enjoyment of others of those same rights. The law may prohibit such actions as are deemed "hurtful to society," and no one should be "disquieted" because of his religious opinions "provided their manifestation does not disturb the public order established by law."[8] Gerard Noiriel argues that the "context of anti-aristocratic and anti-clerical mobilization explains, far beyond the philosophy of the Enlightenment, the essential aspects of the Declaration of the Rights of Man and Citizens. Behind the haunting theme of equality is found a violent rejection of all privileges (and all stigmatisations) based on origin."[9]

After the revolution the relationship between church and state seesawed, depending upon which regime was in control. After the Napoleonic Wars, the republic was rejected in favor of the return of monarchy. Monarchy was overthrown again in 1848 after which a brief Second Republic gave way to Napoleon III's empire. The democratic state was able to achieve lasting control in 1871 with the advent of the Third Republic. Throughout this time the Roman Catholic Church sought to remain relevant to society. The active involvement of the church on behalf of the monarchy and Napoleon in the political struggles ensured it would remain a target of suspicion, if not hatred, with the return of the republic. The current French government is the Fifth Republic, founded in 1958. The constitution of 1958 incorporates the Declaration of Rights of Man and Citizen of 1789 and the preamble to the 1946 constitution and continues in effect the 1905 law on the separation of church and state.

The 1946 preamble incorporated into the current constitution provides that "the people of France proclaim anew that each human being, without distinction of race, religion, or creed, possesses sacred and inalienable rights." It further proclaims "political, economic, and social principles," including equal rights of women "in all spheres"; no discrimination in employment "by virtue of [one's] origin, opinion or beliefs"; that "[t]he Nation shall provide the individual and family with the conditions necessary to their development"; and secular education for all.[10]

Article 1 of the constitution of 1958 declares "France shall be an indivisible, secular [*laique*], democratic and social republic. It shall ensure the equality of all citizens before the law, without distinction of origin, race, or religion. It shall respect all beliefs."[11] The constitution establishes a republican form of government with strong central powers divided between three branches.

The executive is headed by a popularly elected president in a two-round election. The president appoints the head of government, the prime minister. The president can dissolve the National Assembly and call early elections. Thus, the president and National Assembly must work together or the government will fall.

The legislative branch is bicameral—the Senate and National Assembly. The Senate is chosen by an electoral college and has limited power. The main legislative body, the National Assembly, is popularly elected by regional district.

The third branch is the judicial with separate branches for civil and criminal cases and administrative law. There is no *stare decisis*, as France is a civil law system; however, it does follow *jurisprudence constant*, which in practice acts in virtually the same manner as *stare decisis*. The Council of State (*Conseil d'État*) and the Constitutional Council (*Conseil Constitutionnel*) are the two highest bodies acting as courts and deciding whether or not the administrative branch has complied with the Constitution. The Council of State is the supreme administrative court and an advisory body to the executive branch.[12] Its members are selected from various government departments and agencies. Important cases from administrative law courts, a very important division in France, can be brought up to the council and, while it is not technically a court, it serves as court of last resort for decisions involving national regulations. It can evaluate whether a regulation comports with the procedural jurisdiction of the administrative body and with higher law, in other words, constitution, national legal principles, treaties, and so on. It also serves in an advisory role to the executive branch with the authority to determine, prior to introduction in Parliament, whether a law proposed by someone other than a member of Parliament is constitutional and whether any executive order is properly issued or if the matter should be handled by Parliament. Because the council rules on all executive actions, its pronouncements shape legal interpretation and policy of state.

The Constitutional Council is the highest constitutional authority in France.[13] The council is composed of former presidents who choose to sit; nine other members are appointed for one nine-year term evenly by the president of France, the president of the National Assembly, and the president of the Senate. It determines whether proposed statutes that have passed both houses of Parliament comply with the constitution, the Declaration of Rights of Man and Citizen, and the principles underlying them. It also determines whether the proposed laws are in keeping with treaties such as the European Convention on Human Rights (ECHR). Some laws must be submitted to the council before enactment, while others are submitted upon request by certain government officials or majority of either the National Assembly or Senate. The only way to override decisions of the councils is by amendment of the constitution (not an easy task), so their rulings are very important to French law and political development.

1905 LAW

The 1905 law was not the first law of separation of church and state, but it has become iconic to the French and is the axis of all later church-state relations and views on the place of religion in France. During the Third Republic (1870–1940), unification was paramount, suppressing all identities other than national. The Third Republic focused on the creation of a national unity which suppressed regional differences in the interest of creating a fused French identity. This fusion into one identity continues to mark the French psyche to the point that other identities, regional, religious, or immigrant, are considered un-French and are a type of deviancy which must be kept private.[14] French liberty is expressed through equality and fraternity. The commitment to individual autonomous liberty is "realized in a distinctive autonomous, political 'community of citizens'" that is most visible in religion-state relations.[15]

The 1905 law did not spring out of nothingness and was preceded by a series of laws between 1880 and 1905 which sought to suppress religious influence, particularly Catholic.[16]

> [D]uring these formative periods, (1789 and 1879–1905) *laïcité* did not embody the high principles of tolerance, neutrality, and equality; rather it, emerged from periods of conflict and hostility, most of which targeted the Roman Catholic Church. . . . Between 1880 and 1905, more than two dozen laws were promulgated that promoted *laïcité* in ways ranging from placing civil disabilities on those who had received a religious education to preventing religious manifestations in streets during funeral processions. The spirit of *laïcité* could act with the same intolerance that it accused others of exemplifying.[17]

In 1901 the Law on Associations greatly restricted the ability of religious organizations to form, and any without the proper legal approval were subject to confiscation of their property.[18] The Catholic churches refused to register and remained illegal until after World War I (WWI). The republic still continues to license all religious organizations, and property of unlicensed ones is subject to confiscation. Thus, in France the central government decides what is religion and what religions are legal. The initial desire to restrict the Catholic Church's intrusion in all aspects of society has resulted in a continuing will of the state to define and restrict religion in general.

The 1905 law provides: "The Republic ensures the freedom of conscience. It guarantees the freedom of worship, subject only to restrictions imposed in the interest of public order." Article 2 states that the republic "does not recognize, finance or subsidize any religious group." However in practice the republic does recognize religions because all must obtain state approval to exist, and it does subsidize them by subsidizing religious schools. Further, the 1901 law for formation of religious associations as cult or sect continues with cults being religious organizations recognized under the 1905 law while sects are not. The 1905 law declared all religious buildings then in existence property of the state, but the religious bodies using them were allowed to continue to do so for free.

Under article 19, the republic became responsible for the maintenance of all religious buildings in use at the time, which includes most of the country's famous cathedrals. The state has the right to close any religious building at any time. The law ended all direct state subsidies for religious bodies. It also prohibited any religious display at government sites. However, in 1921 the Parliament authorized the expenditure of state funds to build the Grand Mosque in Paris in commemoration of Muslims serving with the French military in WWI. In addition, many religious schools, mostly Catholic, are subsidized by the government.

In 1921 the government reinstated portions of the Napoleonic Concordat of 1801, which dictates that it consult with the Vatican about the appointment of all clergy serving in France. Additionally, the Ministry of the Interior includes a Bureau of Religious Affairs responsible for licensure of all religious organizations and having the right to tax, fine, or close any religious organization which is not licensed. The law of 1905 affirmed "liberty of conscience" and guaranteed the free exercise of religion "except as necessary for the public interest."[19] The elimination of religious symbols from public display is seen as paramount because religion is divisive and a threat to the public interest of order.

Jean Baubérot cites the passage of the 1905 law as a "Copernican revolution" setting the relationship between politics and religion in France.[20] The period just before the passage was a time when the republic was perceived to be threatened by "clerical fanaticism" of the Roman Catholic Church, which could only be defeated by the "comprehensive secularism," in the style of a

Rawlsian comprehensive doctrine. Freedom of religion was interpreted as freeing the citizen from the corrupting effects of established religious institutions, as was the sacred republic which would save the people. The revolution contained in the 1905 law "never seems to have been really internalized by the dominant French mentality" as they remained privately Roman Catholic.[21]

LAÏCITÉ

Laïcité is a term which eludes exact translation but is essential to understanding French society.[22] The term, its variety of interpretations, and its importance to France are the subject of hundreds of books and articles. Controversies surrounding it are as numerous as those surrounding the US Constitution's First Amendment religion clauses. *Laïcité* is commonly translated as secularism; however, this definition is inadequate and misleading. "There is no firm definition of *laïcité*: neither officially established nor generally accepted."[23] A popular French dictionary defines it as "a political notion involving the separation of civil society and religious society, the State exercising no religious power and the churches exercising no political power."[24]

The implementation of *laïcité* is not so neutral. In use it "conveys . . . a profound suspicion" expressed in "a somewhat tense attitude where religion is concerned."[25] Jeremy Gunn says, "[I]t describes a particular attitude about the proper relationship between church and state . . . [t]he connotation of the state protecting itself from the excesses of religion . . . [while in the US 'religious freedom'] would be more likely to have the connotation of religion being protected from the excesses of the state."[26] The French freedom of religion emanates from the philosophy of Rousseau in contrast to the American Lockean version. Blandine Krieger explains the difference as being a Lockean individual holding concrete rights while the Rousseauian version abstracts the individual from personal traditions to transfer rights to the law (state). Rights are through the political power of the state, which must guarantee a public space devoid of individualism, particularly religion. It is the contrast of "freedom through the state against freedom from the state, society as a 'coming together' and 'living together' against a society as isolated rights-bearing individuals or (worse) as isolated communities defined by religion, race, or ethnicity."[27]

A speech of President Jacques Chirac in 2003 wherein he proposed a law banning the wearing of religious clothing in schools demonstrates the mythical quality of *laïcité*. In his speech President Chirac asserted,

> *Laïcité* is inscribed in our traditions. It is at the heart of our republican identity. . . . The cornerstone of the Republic, the bundle of our common values of respect, tolerance, and dialogue, to which I call all of the French to rally. . . .

> Its values are at the core of our uniqueness as a Nation. These values spread our voice far and wide in the world. These are the values that create France. . . . *Laïcité* guarantees freedom of conscience. It protects the freedom to believe or not to believe. It assures everyone of the possibility to express and practice their faith peaceably, freely, though without threatening others with one's own convictions or beliefs. France is the land of diversity in which *laïcité* promotes tolerance. [*Laïcité* is] one of the great accomplishments of the republic. It is a crucial element of social peace and national cohesion. We can never permit it to weaken.[28]

Laïcité was added to the constitution in the 1946 preamble, but it appeared during the Third Republic (1870–1940) in laws and policies defining the proper relationship of religion and the state. At the time the form was strongly anticlerical and is known now as *laïcité du combat.* Gunn argues that "[f]rom the late eighteenth to the early twentieth century, [*laïcité*] came to refer to policies designed to restrict (or even eliminate) clerical and religious influence over the state."[29] As Poulat observes *laïcité* was not a unifying concept and to view it as such "is to forget and ignore the initial violence that was imposed in the process of separating church and state."[30]

France has come to have three forms of *laïcité: laïcité du combat* (strongly assertive); *laïcité plurielle* (also known as *laïcité ouverte* or *positive*); and *laïcité mouvement.*[31] The strongly assertive form, *laïcité du combat,* was in place just before and at the time of the 1905 law. As time passed, the public created its own social ecumenical catho-secular civil religion, a *laïcité plurielle.* This form of *laïcité* focuses on a benign neutrality toward religion in the public square. So long as one does not appear to be pushing a sectarian view, leave her alone. Individualization and tolerance became dominant. It became acceptable for political leaders to display their Catholic faith in a generalized manner as a demonstration of their morality in much the same way that American politicians did. The Catholic Church was no longer seen as a serious threat, and the church accepted its more restricted role, enabling the state to accept its presence as a useful component of society.[32] Williame has labeled this move from combative to pluralist *laïcité* as a "laicization of lacity" by redefining it as a "regulatory framework for a pluralism of world views [no longer as] a counter-system to religion."[33] *Laïcité mouvement* tries to take a middle road which recognizes that Islam does not fit the hierarchical model which the republic requires and that Muslims have practices that require some concessions in society.

The influential League of Education, a defender of the secular education system and traditional strict secularization, moved to *laïcité plurielle* in 1986.[34] This move brought the debate about retaining traditional *laïcité du combat* or moving to *laïcité plurielle* to the forefront of national debate.[35] The two camps are sharply divided and each contends it is true to French social norms. Jean Burdy and Jean Marcou observe that the *du combat/*

assertive secularism is "republican, monist, and anxious about the individual citizen's expression of his or her religious or communitarian affiliation in the public space," while the *plurielle*/passive secularism is "more democratic, flexible, and open to differences."[36]

Supporters of *du combat*/assertive secularism argue that the *plurielle*/passive will lead to disunity and communitarianism and ultimately destroy France. The assertive secularists view any loyalty toward any group other than the state as competition, which inevitably will weaken the state to a dangerous point. The allegiance to anything other than the state is the beginning of a slippery slope to chaos. One of the leading supporters of this view, Henri Peña-Ruiz, argues that in France religion must be confined to the conscience or home. Intrusions of religion in the public sphere are the same as the former Catholic ones and must be stopped.[37] Baubérot, a supporter of the *plurielle*/passive form, argues that the view in which one form of secularism must win is outmoded and secularization is an ongoing process that is changeable in time and place.[38] Williame agrees but puts the issue in the context of neutrality, arguing that "the state should become less assertive in a secularist ideology and by doing so it will recognize the contribution of religious groups to public life, thereby itself becoming more secular."[39] As will be seen below, the progressive universal human rights *laïcité plurielle* of modern France has been replaced by the strong *laïcité du combat* due solely to the increasing Muslim population.

COLONIES, IMMIGRANTS, AND MUSLIMS

Beginning in the nineteenth century immigration increased due to labor shortages associated with falling fertility rates, a trend that continues today. Unlike US immigrant populations with choices between moving to open land or remaining in cities, in France immigrants filled urban labor shortages which many French country peasants were not willing to fill. This refusal to move to the city was possible in France because most peasants owned their land and after 1848 constituted the largest electoral constituency, according them political power denied to rural populations in many other European countries. The pre–World War II (WWII) immigrants were from other parts of Europe, largely from Roman Catholic areas, so there was a measure of shared world view.[40] The government instituted two major tools to regulate immigration: the Card and the Code. The Card is the French identity card, which includes a card for all foreigners which identifies the individual, her work skills, and at times her ethnicity or religion. The notation of religion or ethnicity was practiced during Nazi occupation so there is a strong aversion to this type of identification being utilized by the government. The inclusion of work skills also categorizes the individual's socioeconomic status, enabling the state to regulate her agency in times of economic crisis.[41] The Code refers to the enactment of a naturalization code which permits any person born on French soil to become a citizen when she becomes an adult. The Code also initially loosened the requirements for naturalization.[42]

Post-WWII immigration can be divided into two types. First, government-encouraged labor immigration mostly from other European countries and French colonies in North Africa, chiefly Algeria, Tunisia, and Morocco.[43] This style ended in the 1970s. The second grouping flowed from the dismantling of an extensive colonial system. The dismantling of the French colonial empires (1953–1962) led the government to enter into bilateral trade agreements with the former colonies.[44]

Among other things, these agreements allowed the free movement of peoples from colonies to France, particularly from Algeria. Algeria demonstrates issues with the French notion of equality. In Algeria natives were long considered second-class persons, and when eventually accorded citizenship they were never accorded political rights in the colony. At the same time, immigrants to Algeria from other European countries were granted French citizenship with full rights.[45] The legacies of these colonial differences in treatment were brought to France with the end of colonialism, and ethnic differences remain an issue for the French state and the society at large.

The waves of immigrants to France post WWII led to a diverse society which includes peoples from a variety of geographical and cultural origins. Government immigration policies waxed and waned with economic needs. By the end of the 1970s immigration was slowed. Regulation steadily increased to the 1994 Pasqua laws, which sharply restrict immigration. Figures on population diversity largely come from private surveys, as French national statistics do not accumulate data on ethnicity, culture, or religion, reinforcing the attitude that any aspect of identity which is not viewed by the majority as French must be abandoned. The only classifications officially recorded are French by birth, French by naturalization, and foreigner. In 1999 the government began recording "previous nationality" of naturalized citizens. It is only nationality which matters to the French, and all other aspects of life formation are to be abandoned.

An increase in tension over immigration can be seen in the seesawing of the grant of automatic citizenship to children of naturalized French citizens upon turning eighteen. Until 1986 children of naturalized citizens were automatically accorded citizenship at eighteen. In 1986 a law was proposed which would end automatic citizenship, and in 1993 a law was enacted which required the children to declare they wanted to become French citizens to receive it. In 1998 the government abandoned enforcement of the declaration. In 2007 a new Ministry of Immigration and National Identity was created, but it was dissolved in 2010 when immigration issues were reassigned to the Ministry of the Interior.[46] Also in 2007, the Council of State implemented a New Reception and Integration Contract for immigrants.[47] The contract states that the individual must provide proof that she can meet four aspects of "assimilation into French society" that include language skills, "knowledge of the institutions and values of the French Republic," knowledge of daily life in France, and "good professional integration." Language training is provided if necessary.

It is nationality which is the axis around which all issues of equality and tolerance revolve in France. Adrian Favell explains that before the 1980s "there was no connection of immigration with the idea of republican citizenship" because before the 1980s immigrants were thought of by their socioeconomic status and after, by their perceived ability to integrate.[48] In 2010, following rioting in French cities by disgruntled Muslims, President Sarkozy threatened to strip of his citizanship any offender who had become a naturalized citizen within the last ten years.[49]

The relationship between Muslims and France has always been tense, beginning with the defeat of a Muslim invader in 732 by Charles Martel, grandfather of Charlemagne. During the Crusades (1095–1291), the French were so active that the Arabic word for crusader is *Al-Franki,* "The Franks." There is a growing Muslim population in France, but the numbers are still small, about 8–10 percent of the population; nevertheless, it is the largest in Europe.[50] Further, their religiosity varies widely from *athées musulmans* (atheist Muslims) to those who are devout practitioners. Olivier Roy observes that the lumping of all into one threatening category by the French national psyche adds to the feelings of alienation and lack of understanding between French natives and immigrants.[51]

Most Muslims in France are immigrants who emigrated from either Algeria or one of the other North African states. Many came at the invitation of the government for low-level jobs and, instead of returning home after their jobs ended, stayed and brought their families over. They are marginalized economically with an unemployment rate about twice the native rate. Also, most live in lower socioeconomic areas or government housing projects. They are marginalized politically, as only a few have achieved national political office.[52]

There was little public evidence of Muslims within France until the 1970s. Jocelyne Cesari observes, "The collective dimension of Islam was confined to the intimate space of the residences, the hearths, the provided places at hotels, or the backs of shops."[53] Evidence of the increasing population and public appearance of Islam can be seen in the increase in the number of mosques in France, from 5 in 1965 to 1,685 in 2004. This introduction of new cultures and points of view challenges the French communal cultural view of sameness.

In 1981, the Socialist Party won the presidential election on a platform advocating the right to be different. It did not promote immigrant differences, rather a strengthening of regional control and recognition of value in regional difference. However, this decentralization movement trickled over to immigrant issues and led to an acknowledgment that some ethnic diversity is palatable. In 1989, in response to the *affair du foulard* (discussed more fully below), the government created a *Haut Conseil à l'intégration.* The Council on Integration serves as a clearinghouse for statistical evidence about immigrant populations for the government and as an advisor to the government on proposed policies. Its stated mission is to preserve the values of the republic while being sensitive to the cultural traditions of immigrants. A review of its work shows it has dealt almost exclusively with issues of Muslims and religion in the public space. In one of its earliest reports concerning Islam in France, the *Haut Conseil à l'intégration* characterized the 1905 law as a "law of liberty" of individual first and a law of separation of church and state second, making accommodation the primary focus of state concern.[54] During the 1980s the Ministry of Culture adopted policies favoring expression of regional cultures, and the Ministry of Education developed strategies to address cultural needs of immigrant students.[55] Anti-racist organizations developed with the support of established political organizations.[56] In 2000, a socialist government created a French Muslim Council (CFCM). CFCM is legally a private nonprofit organization but was created by the government and holds special advisory status to the government. Under the initial agreement between the government and invited representatives of the participating Muslim organizations, the organizations declared their commitment to articles 10 and 11 of the French Declaration of Human Rights, article 1 of the constitution, and the 1905 law, and vowed to respect the public order, to preserve the neutrality of the republic, and to oppose all forms of discrimination. The organizations specifically agreed that they are bound by article 4 of the 1905 law which regulates religious organizations and prohibits them from engaging in politics. In the agreement the government pledged to assist the organizations in the building of mosques and private schools. While CFCM began under a socialist government, every government since has retained it. Although a private organization, it is seen as a government mechanism to deal with all of the Muslim community. This style of religion-state relationship works well with a religion which is hierarchically structured, such as Roman Catholicism, but not with diffuse ones, such as Islamism and Protestanism.[57] CFCM is seen by some Muslims as merely a government tool and not representative of all Muslim branches.

Another attempt to address the underlying immigration issues occurred after riots in the Parisian suburb of Clichy-sous-Bois in 2005. The precipitating factor in the riots was the accidental electrocution and death of two Muslim youth hiding from police. Local rioting by Muslims who felt the police were at fault in the deaths caused long-simmering dissatisfaction in the area and throughout Muslim populations in other parts of France to erupt.

Prime Minister De Villepin acknowledged that the underlying cause of the riots was France's failure to provide hope to the children of immigrants, who are mostly French citizens, and that they should have an equal opportunity to share in the promises of France, such as education and decent-paying jobs. De Villepin did propose some measures targeted to address economic inequalities but wider issues of discrimination and mistrust were not included. De Villepin acknowledged that the French model of integration, which does not allow for any co-cultural existence, is a point of contention with the immigrant and Muslim culture. Muslims in France expressed a desire to be considered equally French while at the same time maintaining their Muslim heritage. This balancing act would be so difficult for France to achieve that some believe it is so anti-French as to be impossible.

The softening of *laïcité* and opening of culture created a backlash through the formation of political parties dedicated to anti-multicultural/immigrant policies and laws. The largest is the National Front Party. It formed during the Algerian crisis with an emphasis on French nationalism but rose to prominence in the 1980s with an anti-immigrant rhetoric. Early on it called for the repatriation of immigrants and, while it no longer calls for deportation, it does continue to advocate strict immigration regulations and a public space devoid of all religious symbols. It has been a driving force behind changes to immigration policies and the *hijab* and veil laws.

AFFAIR DU FOULARD

In 1989 the principal of a public middle school (ages 11–15) in the lower-socioeconomic multinational Parisian suburb of Criel expelled three female students for wearing the *hijab*. Principal Cheniere was a black French citizen from Martinique who was unpopular with locals and was an aspiring right-wing politician.[58] The principal cited the 1905 law and a 1936 school regulation banning religious or political insignias from public schools. The headscarf issue was only one of many ethnic and religious issues over which the principal and community members differed.[59]

Previously, students had been allowed to wear the *hijab* on school grounds but were to remove it in the classroom. Some girls decided to wear the headscarf in the classroom. Three students were suspended but after community mediation, including the intervention of the king of Morocco, they agreed to revert to the practice of removing the headscarf in the classroom. By that point, the debate had moved well beyond the local community and had spawned a heated national debate encompassing foundational ideas of secularism/*laïcité*, equality of women, immigration, and fear of Islam. Perhaps the national debate occurred because 1989 was the bicentennial of the Declaration of the Rights of Man and Citizen, a time of celebration of the republic and French national values, or because the school has, since the time of the revolution, been a place of controversy regarding church-state relations. What we can be sure of is that this incident was a tipping point which started national political parties and prominent intellectuals and personalities to begin to voice their views on the issue of *laïcité*, French values, and Islam in France. France is a centralized political system, so the intervention of the national government was inevitable.

French minister of education Lionel Jospin announced that students who wore the *hijab* were to be allowed to attend school because suspension would hinder their ability to integrate and limit their socioeconomic development.[60] The policy did allow school officials to counsel students against wearing the *hijab* as un-French. Further, he prohibited any religious practice from being an excuse for an absence from any class. No one seemed satisfied with Jospin's approach. Jospin referred the matter to the Council of State, the highest administrative authority in France, to issue an opinion on three questions:

1. Was the wearing of the religious symbols compatible with the principle of *laïcité*?
2. If so, under what conditions was regulation of such wearing permissible?
3. Could refusal to follow such regulations result in the expulsion of the offending student from the school?[61]

The council's opinion held that wearing the *hijab* in public school was "not incompatible" with the French tradition of *laïcité*, the 1905 law, the constitution, or other relevant international treaties, including the ECHR or ICCPR, and was a constitutionally protected exercise of personal expression and religious belief. While the council held that the wearing of the scarf at school was not a per se violation of *laïcité* and was a protected freedom, it tempered the freedom with a limitation

> that freedom does not permit students to display signs of religious belonging which, by their nature, by the conditions which they are worn individually or collectively, or by their *ostentatious* or protesting nature, would constitute an act of pressure, provocation, proselytism or propaganda, would damage the dignity or liberty of the pupil or other members of the educational community, would compromise their health or safety, would affect the conduct of educational activities or the educational role of teachers, or would disturb order in the establishment or the normal functioning of the public service. (emphasis added)[62]

The Ministry of Education issued a circular which strictly interpreted the opinion.[63] The language of both the opinion and circular left many areas open for interpretation and called for a case-by-case approach, leading to inconsistencies in interpretation by school officials. From 1992 to 1999 the council reversed forty-one expulsions and affirmed only eight on the issue of the *hijab*.[64] In 1993, it was estimated that about two thousand students were wearing the *hijab* at school. In general, the council's decisions during this period reflected considerable deference to individual religious rights but not blanket approval. For example, in the case of *Kehorouaa* the council held that a school policy banning the wearing of all distinctive symbols was illegal; however, in *Moussaou* the council held that the student wore the *hijab* as a form of political protest, justifying its prohibition.[65] In the case of *Aoukili* the council held that a refusal to remove the headscarf during physical education classes, which the school said was necessary for safety, was improper as the refusal was disruptive of the order in school. The student's father's act of protest at the school weighed heavily in the decision that this case amounted to an improper disturbance of order.[66]

In 1993 a suspension of four students in the town of Nantua reignited the national debate. The new minister of education, Francois Bayrou, announced a policy banning the wearing of the *hijab* at school, effectively reversing the council's 1989 decision. His policy stated that

> [i]t is not possible to accept the presence and multiplication of ostentatious signs in school whose signification involves the separation of certain students from the rules of common life of the school. These signs are in themselves part of proselytization.[67]

Even after this change in policy, the Council of State continued to enforce its 1989 decision and use a more tolerant interpretation of *laïcité*, as evidenced in a series of cases in November 1996 when it confirmed twenty-three expulsions, all of which had aggravating circumstances, and reversed seven which emanated from blanket prohibitions of headscarves. Oddly, many of the expelled students and others who wished to wear the headscarf began attending private Catholic schools, which do permit them to wear the *hijab*.

Throughout this time the long-standing rule prohibiting public servants from wearing religious symbols at work remained in effect and was applied to all religions. In 2003 President Chirac reiterated the need for a religious free face of the state in stating

> We must forcefully reaffirm the neutrality and secularism of the public services. That of all public sector employees, serving the whole community and the general interest, who are forbidden to display publicly their own belies or opinions. For us, this is a rule of law, since no French citizens must be able to suspect a public official, because of his or her personal beliefs, of either according them special treatment or discriminating against them. Likewise, on

> no account must citizens be allowed to challenge a public sector employee on account of their beliefs.[68]

Any signal of individualism by anyone acting on behalf of the state is per se suspect in France. There is no assumption that the individual can separate their personal beliefs sufficiently to be able to properly carry out her duties. This political philosophy is also utilized by the courts as a legal philosophy. For example, in the case of *Abdallah*, a labor inspector was held to have committed a "particularly serious offense" when she wore a *hijab* to work. The court held the *hijab* was an improper, ostentatious expression of religion.[69]

The European Court of Human Rights (ECHR) was also asked to rule on the practices of the French schools. In the case of *Dagru v. France*, application no. 27058/05, the court was asked whether the expulsion of a student for refusing to remove her headscarf during physical education class was proper under article 9 of the ECHR. The court held that the administrative ruling did not violate article 9 because the school took the action in furtherance of order, sensitivity to the freedom of others, and safety during exercise. The case arose before the passage of the 2004 law but was issued after it was in effect. The court's decision implied that cases arising under the 2004 law would be decided in the same way.

In the midst of all this controversy an Algerian civil war in which Islamic hardliners who forced the wearing of the *burqa* sought control of the country began to impact French citizens. There was a series of bombings in the Paris and London transit systems, and the 9/11 attack occurred, all of which were attributable to Islamic extremists, which included some Algerians. In July 2003 President Chirac appointed a commission, headed by Bernard Stasi, to analyze the status of *laïcité* in France and to identify strategies for ensuring its protection. The main focus was on the education system, but the Stasi Commission interviewed a wide variety of people on the issue of Muslim immigrants in France.

The Stasi report recognized that the Catholic Church was no longer a threat to society as it had been perceived when the 1905 law was enacted. With religious diversification, the new challenge is to "forge unity while respecting the diversified society."[70] The commission drew fine lines in the debates. The commission drew a distinction between *signes religieux ostentoires* and *ostensibles*—religious symbols which are ostentatious and those which are visible. The 1989 council decision had held the headscarf was not per se improper proselytism. Each case is to be analyzed to determine whether the symbol is ostentatious (*ostentoire*) and used for proselytism. The Stasi Commission lessened the restriction of religious symbols which are merely visible (*ostensibles*).

The commission's decision was not unanimous. Jean Baubérot vetoed any call to ban visible religious symbols in schools because the obvious intent was to restrict Muslims, undermining access to public education by Muslim girls and also undermining *laïcité*, which ensures open access to public education for all. Baubérot referred back to the Debre laws of 1959, which allowed for a level of state support for private sectarian education. This support blurred the distinction between public and private education, resulting in an accommodationist stance by the state. Any new law restricting dress is exclusionary and contrary to the 1959 law. Another member of the commission, Patrick Weil, acknowledged that the report encourages Muslim girls to attend private schools.[71] In fact, the first private Muslim high school was approved in July 2003, the same month the Stasi Commission formed, and opened in September 2003. By 2004, the more radical Muslim French organization Union of French Islamic Organizations (UOIF) had under development about a dozen school building projects.

The public display of traditional Islamic dress, specifically the *hijab* and *burqa*, challenges the compromise of catho-secular ecumenical civil religion seen in *laïcité plurielle*. The display offends both the Catholic roots and the secular ecumenical compromise, reinforcing the apprehension that doctrinal religion leads to violence and that the retention of any immigrant religious tradition is a failure to properly integrate. "The majority of French intellectuals—on the left as well as the right—seem to feel the secular charter of the republic is under threat because of aspects of Islam that they see as being symbolized by the headscarf" and *burqa*.[72] The republican secularist is able to join with the feminist who sees the *hijab* and *burqa* as symbols of gender inequality.

Strict secularists see the veil as a symbolic gesture of religion threatening national integrity and harmony. Leftist secularists likened the policy of accommodation to that of appeasement to Nazi Germany by the British and French governments in 1938. To the leftist secularist,

> [t]his polemic shows the reinvigorated "laicity of combat" was not so much directed against the incriminated religious behavior itself as against its wrong-headed toleration by lax "new laicity." In other words, this time around it was not so much a conflict between the forces of laicity, on the one side, and the forces of religion, on the other, as in the nineteenth century battle of the Republican state against the Catholic church; rather, now it was a conflict between two different understandings of a laicity that, in principle, was shared and consented by all, but that in reality was given opposite interpretations. Republican versus liberal.[73]

Feminists see it as a sign of oppressive political cultures and claim that removing the veil is a victory for gender equality. French feminists also liken the scarf to Nazi oppression, referring to it as the female "yellow star."[74]

"French universalism insists that sameness is the basis for equality. To be sure, sameness is an abstraction, a philosophical notion meant to achieve the formal equality of individuals before the law. But historically it has been applied literally: assimilation means the eradication of difference."[75] This enables different interest groups to come together to attack anything which threatens the homogeneity of French society.

This political alliance proved too strong for the *laïcité plurielle* of the judiciary. This accounts for the dramatic shift from the 1989 decision finding the *hijab* was "not incompatible" with *laïcité* to the 2004 banning of the *hijab* in all public schools and the 2010 ban on the *burqa* in all public places.

In 2004 the French government passed, with overwhelming support of the public, a law prohibiting "[i]n public schools the carrying of signs or dress through which students *ostensibly* manifest a religious belonging."[76] The neutral tone of the statute prompted one commentator to opine that the new law "applies about as equally to all religions as the law that prohibits all people from sleeping under bridges applies to the homeless and the wealthy."[77] Supporters of the law assert that its acceptance proves that the girls did not really care about wearing the scarf or that they needed assistance from the state to be able to resist male family members forcing them to wear it. However, in a 2005 book entitled *Headscarved Girls Speak*, the authors included several interviews with Muslim students impacted by the 2004 ban who voiced feelings of being marginalized, now distrusting French authorities, and many said they have stopped their education because financial inability or geographical inconvenience did not allow them to attend private schools.[78] Some students who continue to attend public school replaced the headscarf with a bandana or headband but the courts ruled that because their motivation was religious these head coverings violated the law and had to be removed on school property.[79]

Additionally, the highest administrative court in France ruled that a private nursery school teacher was not wrongly terminated for wearing a headscarf at work because it violated an employer policy on *laïcité*.[80] In the case a lower court had ruled that the employer discriminated against the employee on religious grounds in violation of French employment anti-discrimination laws. An uproar immediately issued from the left and the right which claimed the republic and secularism were in danger.[81] The minister for women's rights said ministers would consider new legislation to impose secularism at private work places, claiming *laïcité* "does not stop at the door of a crèche [nursery school]." President Hollande created a commission to study the enactment of a new law. The commission decided a new law was not needed about the same time as the appellate decision ruling that the private school could ban the headscarf was issued. The main argument used to justify restrictions on the headscarf in schools is for inculcation of *laïcité* and to foster republican values in children. Defenders of the school restrictions argue this is their only motivation and that they are not anti-Islam. However, this defense is being proven false in the *burqa* ban.

THE BURQA BAN

In 2005, Fazia Silmi, a woman who had lived in France for many years and who was married to a French citizen, had her application for citizenship denied because she wore the face veil. On appeal from a lower court, the Council of State affirmed the denial of citizenship on the grounds that Silmi was a radical practitioner of her religion, which is "incompatible with the essential values of the French community and notably the principle of the equality of the sexes [so she] cannot be considered to be fulfilling the requirement of assimilation." The court also concluded that Silmi "lives in total submission to the men in her life . . . to the point that it has never occurred to her to contest that submission."[82] In response Silmi asserted, "Don't believe for a minute that I am submissive to my husband. . . . It is me who pays the bills and deals with the paperwork."[83] Calls for banning all face veiling by women immediately ensued and were quickly named *burqa* bans. The fact that few women in France wear the *burqa* was ignored and it became the new symbol of imminent, overwhelming, extreme danger to the republic.[84]

The *burqa* ban was first proposed in June 2009 by President Sarkozy in the first presidential address to a joint session of Parliament in 136 years. He asserted that the *burqa* is not a religious sign, rather it is "a sign of subjugation [and] of debasement [which] is not welcome in France."[85] The next day a parliamentary commission was formed, under the leadership of Communist Party representative Andre Gerin, to "review the practice of wearing the *burqa* and the *niqab* by certain Muslim women" in France. The mission of the commission was to "better understand the problem and to find ways to fight against this *affront to individual liberties*."[86] Mr. Gerin's impartiality in leading the investigation is questionable because previously he referred to Muslim women covering themselves as being in "mobile prisons" and as wearing a mark of Islamic fundamentalism, which is not proper in France.[87] The commission became known as the *Burqa* Commission even though Gerin, after having been informed that the wearing of the *burqa* was essentially nonexistent in France, relabeled the commission as an investigation of the integral veil (*voile integral*), a made-up umbrella term which could include any clothing worn only by Muslim women. In addition to the official commission hearings there was an open web forum, and local town hall meetings were held. The postings and local meetings became vitriolic and were terminated.[88]

There was never any pretense that the issue concerned face covering by anyone other than Muslim women. Joppke and Torpey refer to the *burqa* ban as occurring as part of a "backdrop of thorough institutionalization, if not nationalization, of Islam in France . . . [t]he transition of Islam in France to French Islam."[89] Joppke and Torpey argue that the commission's hearings were carefully orchestrated for testimony from only supporters of restricting the practice. In his testimony, Tariq Ramadan, a frequent supporter of French government policies, called the face veil "an attack on the rights of women," "a restriction on their liberty," and "contrary to human dignity."[90] The director of the CFCM referred to it as "an extreme practice that we do not wish to see gaining ground in the national territory," and the leader of the Grand Mosque in Paris called it ridiculous in France because the practice was actually for life in the desert environment and not religious.[91] The proponents of a ban were selling it not as a matter of religion but as a perpetuation of gender inequality—they were acting in the best interest of the oppressed woman. The leader of the feminist group *Ni Putes Ni Soumises* (Neither Whores Nor Submissives) exclaimed before the commission that "the *burqa* is the most violent symbol of the oppression of women and has nothing to do with the Muslim religion, my religion."[92] Anthropologist Dounia Bouzar argued that the *burqa* is part of Salafist discourse, not a general Muslim practice; therefore it is sectarian. By virtue of being a sectarian practice she reasoned it is not religious because the word "religious" comes from the Latin word meaning "to gather together" and "sectarian" from the word "to separate." She asserted that France should "treat these factions as if they are not Muslim."[93] This gave the commission a way out of the accusation that they were attempting to dictate religious practice, which a secular state is not supposed to do.

It is interesting to note the response of President Sarkozy to the Swiss minaret ban, which occurred at the same time the commission was investigating banning the *burqa* in France. Sarkozy asserted the Swiss ban was a misguided attempt at national identity in an increasing globalized world that demonstrated a lack of respect for people by requiring them to "practice their religion in cellars or garages."[94] Sarkozy utilized a need for national identity to support his own call for the *burqa* ban, so he was drawing a fine line between state-allowed development of communal worship space as not threatening national identity and an individual's choosing to practice a discretionary act of piety that threatens national unity. Sarkozy admonished French Muslims to practice their religion "in humble discretion" because France had a Christian heritage and is a place "where the values of the republic are an integral part of our national identity." He argued that any action seen as disrespectful to this heritage or values will "condemn to failure the establishment of Islam in France that is so necessary."[95] He placed the burden on the Muslim woman to restrict her exercise of individual liberty so as not to upset the majority, even when that majority claims to protect individual liberty. To his thinking, the individual woman is misguided in her individualism and is, regardless of her independence of choice, submitting to gender inequality, which France cannot tolerate.

In January 2010, the *Burqa* Commission issued its report, which states the evidence

> shows with precision how the wearing of the full veil infringes upon three principles that are included in the motto of the Republic: liberty, equality and fraternity. The full veil is an intolerable infringement on the freedom and the dignity of women. It is the denial of gender equality and of a mixed society. Finally, it is the will to exclude women from social life and the rejection of our common will to live together.[96]

The commission concluded the evidence proved that wearing the full veil is a practice that is contrary to French values:

> Several witnesses testified that freedom to wear clothing of their choice did not exist in some Parisian suburbs, as the social pressure to wear the full veil is so strong that they have to conform. It is feared that if the wearing of the full veil is normalized, the number of women wearing it will increase, as this practice will be forced on them by their communities. Social services reported several cases near Paris of eight-year old girls fully covered by veils. In a high school near Lyon, a group of Muslim students asked the headmaster to provide them with a room where they could change their clothes to wear clothes similar to those worn by other students, as their parents were forcing them to wear clothes hiding all signs of femininity.[97]
>
> The practice of the wearing of the full veil is an infringement of the principle of freedom. One cannot liken it to the simple will to be noticed, because it is very often worn as a result of varying degrees of inexplicit pressures or of explicit ones. The full veil is the symbol of subservience, the ambulatory expression of a denial of liberty that touches a specific category of the population: women. In this it also constitutes a negation of the principle of equality.
>
> [The full veil is] a regression of the rights and the dignity of the woman in our society. . . . A form of sexual apartheid with on one side the world of men that is open and on the other side the world of women, constrained and closed . . . a uniform that reduces the woman to anonymity . . . [it results in] the disappearance of the woman in her specificity. . . . It takes her away from the public place.[98]

The commission also concluded that the full veil violates the French principle of fraternity because the face is "the mirror of the soul" and covering it creates an unequal position in the social context, which is an infringement of the social code for living together in our society.[99] The report admits that the committee is not unanimous on the need for a complete ban on wearing the full veil, but all do feel it is an indication of a larger problem of Islamic fundamentalist influence in France.[100] In response the Prime Minister asked the Council of State to render an opinion on the legal grounds for a ban on the full veil that would be as wide as possible and to do so quickly so that a draft law could be submitted to Parliament no later than the end of March.[101]

In July 2010, Parliament, by an overwhelming vote, passed a law making it a criminal offense to cover one's face in public, except for compliance with safety and health regulations or for limited holiday celebrations.[102] "Public" is defined as any space "open to the public or used for provision of public services." The penalty for covering the face in public is a fine of 250 euros or required attendance at cultural education classes, and any person forcing another, by means of menace, violence, constraint, abuse of authority, "because of her sex" to cover her face is subject to a fine of 30,000 euros and a one-year prison term, with the fine doubling if the person imposed upon is a minor.[103] The cultural classes may be imposed on any person, citizen or not, and are part of the French Criminal Code as possible punishment for criminal activity in France.[104] The course content is set by the Council of State, and its purpose is to "remind the offender of the republican values of *tolerance, respect of personal dignity* upon which society is based."[105]

The Constitutional Council has held the law "conforms to the constitution," as it does not impose a disproportionate punishment or restrict free exercise of religion in places of worship.[106] A case challenging the law was filed with the European Court of Human Rights, *S.A.S. v. France*, application no. 43835/11, on allegations of violation of ECHR article 9 (freedom of religion), article 8 (private life), and article 14 (discrimination based on religion or sex).

Justification for the Ban

France claims it is protecting its values with the ban. Let's review its arguments through the national motto: liberty, equality, and fraternity/solidarity. Proponents of the law assert they are protecting women's liberty because the veil "clearly negates the freedom of choice of women."[107] This is only true if the evidence shows that women are wearing the veil as a result of external pressure.

The Open Society Foundation conducted interviews with thirty-two women who live in the Paris area shortly before the *burqa* ban came into effect to give a better understanding of why women veil and to give them a voice, which the society asserted had been marginalized in the debate.[108] Twenty-nine of the respondents were born in France and thirty are French citizens. The society found that many of the women experienced discrimination that included inability to finish school or find a job. The practice of wearing the veil for these women was an individual spiritual choice and did not signal a social seclusion, and any isolation was because of harassment when they went out in public. None of the women interviewed voiced any problem with complying with removal of the veil for security checks by police, hospitals, government offices, banks, etc. The only request they made was that a woman be the identifier. The Open Society found the wearing of the full veil was not a new phenomenon in France, as claimed by proponents of the ban, for some of the women had been wearing it for more than ten years. The respondents felt they were being made into scapegoats for broader socioeconomic issues. The women felt that the ban would make them more likely to retreat further from society, and "their feelings of belonging had recently been overtaken by feelings of alienation."[109] Evidence gathered by the Open Society study indicates that the respondents made an independent choice to veil as an act of piety. The evidence does not appear to support the assertion that women who choose to wear the face veil are oppressed or forced to do so.

Further, even the *Burqa* Commission report found that less than twenty women who veil are minors, so any argument that there is a mass need for state intervention is false. Existing laws on domestic abuse can be utilized in those cases where there is actual evidence of violence or excessive coercion. The wearing of the veil is an expression of liberty while the prohibition of veiling is an improper restriction on individual liberty because it is not necessary to address issues of abuse; the only other restrictions on dress are for health and safety and narrowly tailored to the situation.

The veil is viewed as a threat to national cohesion and republican values. With public schools, one can argue the ban on religious dress is about inculcation of the young with a particular view of the place of religion in society, which is within the state's authority. However, this argument fails with a ban on the sartorial choices of adult women on the public street. *Laïcité* cannot be utilized because no other religious dress is restrained, and the conduct is individual to individual—not state to individual. Further, the targeting of women is clearly the motivating factor because the commission of inquiry specifically researched the wearing of the *burqa* and *niqab*, articles worn by women only. On the other hand, the French enjoy an expansive liberty in all other areas of sartorial choice as a part of the right of a private life, free movement, and free expression. If the woman had chosen to walk down the street in a bikini, even as a political protest, she would be legally protected, and French society would applaud her exercise of individual freedom.[110]

Fraternity can be translated as solidarity. Unlike liberty and equality it has "never been considered a legal principle."[111] "This omission is astonishing in the land of Durkheim, which has forever been obsessed by the 'integration' of society."[112] It can only be justification for a law if one accepts it as a threat to national cohesion, and republican values are usually protected thorough liberty or equality, which are legal principles. The commission concluded that the veil is a violation of solidarity because the woman can see without being seen, signaling a failure to communicate/interact and committing a symbolic violence against all exposed to the veil.[113] Feminist Elisabeth Badinter argued to the commission that it creates "all-powerfulness" because the woman wearing the veil "arrogates to herself the right to see me but denies me the right to see her."[114] While this is true, how does this differ from any other person's decision not to communicate in the public realm? The *Burqa* Commission focused on the open face, which has become the tag line for the debate, with the president declaring that France has an "open face." The commission cited passages from philosopher Emmanuel Levinas about the face being "the mirror of the soul" and claimed the open face is a mark of Western civilization.[115] To cover the face is to render one an object robbed of humanity.[116] The views of Badinter and Levinas show this justification is a matter of personal opinion. Badinter views it as a violent capture of power by the veiled person over the unveiled, while Levinas views it as a signal of loss of power and identity of the veiled person. How can the veiled woman be at the same time the authority and the submissive party? Is it merely that the veil makes one look different so society is uncomfortable?

The commission sought the advice of several lawyers and judges in determining what ban it could legally impose, demonstrating the judicialization of politics. The legislature was concerned from the beginning about the legality of restricting dress in the public space. In fact, the concern over the judiciary's reaction became so great that one exasperated legislator proclaimed the Parliament needed to liberate itself from the "dictates of justices."[117]

The lawyers and judges were as muddled about the legality of a ban as were the philosophers about the ills underlying the practice. The legal arguments generally invoke three concepts: *laïcité*, human dignity, and public order. As discussed before, *laïcité* was quickly deemed inadequate as a justification for a general ban. Human dignity and public order became the focus of argument.

Human dignity is not specifically mentioned in the French Constitution but is viewed as an underlying principle at its foundation. The Kantian conception of dignity underlies Enlightenment thinking. Kant defined dignity as an end in itself, a condition of being, not of value in relation to another thing or purpose. It has a value of its own, not a relative value. It arises out of being human with an ability to reason right and wrong and means that each person, by mere virtue of being human, is equal in value and in dignity.[118] This view was adopted in the Enlightenment concepts of free and equal.

However, two styles for implementation of this concept arose out of the ambiguity of whether dignity is objective or subjective. If it is objective an idealized human exists by which all is measured, and an individual can be in violation of this ideal, even if no one else is obviously harmed by the action. The community needs to protect the individual from straying too far from the ideal. This was adopted in the Rousseauian vision of the collective (state) being placed first as necessary to emancipate the individual, even if they do not know they are not free. In subjective dignity, there is a wider freedom of choice. Only if the larger community can be visibly harmed is the individual restrained in conduct. This became the Lockean view.

We can see the different styles in the school ban because one of the main arguments was that the girls were being forced to wear the scarf. Even if they said they wanted to wear it, their minds needed to be freed of the contagion of the religious group which was preventing them from seeing the harm to their dignity. Further, the state needed to protect the other children from being pressured into improper conduct by merely observing the wearing of the scarf. Thus, an objective standard of dignity was utilized in the school setting.

The objective standard becomes difficult to apply to the general adult population in the public space because previous French law and liberal democratic theory adopted the subjective, freedom of choice standard. To declare the choice of adult women illegitimate would call into "question the capacity for self-determination that modern thinking has posited as a foundation of our democratic system."[119] Only if the French interpretation changed to an objective one could the practice legitimately be restricted. Objective dignity focused through the lens of equality allowed for the restriction; the woman was violating equality by placing herself subservient to a man and/or God. The French divided on the pursuit of this line of reasoning, as some saw in it the proper role of the state while others became concerned about the slippery slope designating the state as ethical arbiter for all of human conduct. The divide was not left-right French politics but what is the state's duty, and persons from all sides of the political debate joined the arguments. Those advocating a ban and objective view of dignity argued that "[p]ublic authority is founded on protecting the dignity of the person, if necessary against the person herself."[120] Conservative UMP politician Francoise Hostalier argued that "society must protect its members, even if they voluntarily torture themselves, mutilate themselves, or impose upon themselves an undignified appearance."[121] Radical leftist Pierre Forgues argued that "freedom itself must be organized and it is up to the legislator to protect the citizen, even against her- or himself."[122] Conversely, conservative politician law professor Guy Carcassone argued that to take this stance causes "the legislator to cease being democratic precisely if it superimposes itself over liberty, telling the citizen under the cover of dignity what to do or not to do . . . [the ban] acts as a formidable signal to the virtue leagues to prohibit also pornography, prostitution, or piercing."[123]

The dignity debate had been simmering in France since 1995. In the case of *Commune de Morsang-sur-Orge* a dwarf made a living selling himself to be used as a projectile for public amusement at a nightclub. The commune authorities alleged violation of a community code of decency. The Council of State upheld a conviction under the code by holding that the dwarf's dignity was violated. Protection of dignity was a proper area of concern for the state, and consent did not excuse the conduct. The council held that public morality and order permitted the state to regulate even voluntary conduct.[124] The precedent immediately raised alarm in legal circles and has not been applied to another case.

In 2008 a French legislative committee was formed to analyze whether the word "dignity" should be added to article 1 of the constitution. The Veil Committee, named after its chair, Simone Veil, recommended amending article 1 of the constitution to include the term, despite conceding its ambiguity and that the state would have to ensure that dignity remain "a matter of choice, of liberty, in a word, or autonomy."[125] The amendment did not occur.

It appears that the majority of legal testimony before the *Burqa* Commission agreed with the subjective view of dignity. However, this would mean that the *burqa* ban was legally questionable. In the subjective view dignity is only harmed if a third party is harmed, which is questionable with an individual sartorial choice. Bertrand Mathieu and Denys de Bechillon argued that if dignity exists in the relationship of self to others and not in an internal relationship, then it is a protection of liberty to allow the wearing of the *burqa*. "The heart of the dignity of the woman is precisely the exercise of her free judgment, of her liberty, including the liberty to wear the *burqa* if she so intends."[126] In this line of reasoning a paradox arises. If you tolerate all personal action as an expression of dignity, then you tolerate intolerance. If you restrict intolerance in the name of tolerance, then you are acting in an intolerant manner, violating your own conception of tolerance and dignity. In the context of the French *burqa*, adopting the view of subjective dignity, prevalent in the legal system in France and European Court of Human Rights, would deny the imposition of a ban, not what the legislature was seeking. They wanted legal analysis to justify the ban, not thwart it.

Parliament moved to use the public order as justification and found a more accommodating vessel. French public law often rests on a justification of public order with a range of meanings that includes health, safety, tranquility, and morality. The *Commune de Morsang-sur-Orge* decision had recently reiterated the state's right to regulate public morality. While the decision had been quickly and loudly criticized, it now proved useful. Until that decision, the upholding of laws on the basis of public morality had been on the decline for years in deference to broadening individual freedoms; the definition of morality had to be strengthened.[127]

They tried a security argument but that is limited in time and place. There already exist laws and regulations on the removal of face and head coverings for government identification, and there was no supporting evidence of a specific threat in all public spaces. Further, other dress would fall under the restrictions, so the government would now be regulating all clothing and accessories to see if they were loose or large enough to pose a real threat by containing a bomb. The only portion of the *burqa* which could be justified on any security ground is covering the face. Regardless of the fact that few women do cover their face, this was latched onto as a threat to public order.

Interestingly, Carcassonne, proponent of the subjective dignity, latched onto this argument to assert that Western society required revealing the face and covering the genitals in public. Everyone just had to accept that this is the social norm so the state could intervene to prohibit face covering. He reasoned dignity is still a subjective idea of personal freedom, but the face covering ruptured the social fabric, causing harm which must be remedied—it is not a victimless crime. Carcassone argued that face covering was a signal to the seer that he was not worthy to see the face, so there was harm to the third party. Carcassone's analysis is not from the perspective of the wearer but from the viewer and external society; thus, it is a violation of subjective dignity and also a violation of article 4 of the constitution ("freedom is the power to do anything which does not harm another"). In making this assertion Carcassone ignored a long-standing French law that regulation of expression or individual conduct is from the viewpoint of the individual restrained, not the other. This view was used to justify the first ban proposal, but it was rejected by the Council of State, which asserted that a general ban would mean the creation of a "new concept of public order . . . in which public order rests on a minimal foundation of reciprocity and of essential guarantees of life in society." The Council of State held this was not in keeping with French legal doctrine and opined that the Constitutional Council would likely conclude that any law on this basis is unconstitutional. Remy Schwartz voiced the concern of many at this point: "Even if it is true that public order requires the power to identify people, this authority cannot be permanent. One cannot impose on citizens a state of permanent surveillance."[128] Legal analysts seemed to be stuck. As Denis de Bechillon put it, "I don't like the *burqa*, it disgusts me, but I don't believe that we have the tools and the political culture of prohibiting the wearing of such dress on the territory of the Republic."[129] Thus, the commission did not recommend a complete ban but made a number of recommendations to narrow its allowance, including restricting immigrant entry or naturalization if the veil is worn and education of immigrants as to its unacceptability in society. It also recommended more active measures of integration, including economic ones, and steps to create a more acceptable French Islam.

The government was not happy with the report and still pursued a complete ban by forwarding a new request to the Council of State to find a way to do so legally. The government would be disappointed because the Council of State came to the same conclusion, although it rested its acceptance of a limited ban on security grounds only. The president was not deterred and asserted that the veil is an "assault on *laïcité*, on equality between men and women . . . [t]he response must be the complete prohibition of the integral veil."[130] The political side wanted a complete ban regardless of what the legal side regarded as acceptable.

The issue became a political talking point in regional elections in early 2010. Politicians drew sides and sought to gain votes by pledging they would stand up against the tyranny of the judiciary in denying this ban which the majority of the public now supported. Anger at the perceived juristocracy exploded during the campaign, and support for politicians who would vote for the ban against the tyranny of the judiciary became a new populist revolution. Candidates who vowed to stand up to the judiciary were elected and the revolution carried on.

Another proposed law was submitted to the Council of State in May 2010 and rejected. Parliament was now in a fit of pique. A proposal made in July 2010 included references for its support on every ground imaginable, and the Council of State was bypassed. This version passed Parliament on July 13, 2010, and was passed to the Constitutional Council as required. The Constitutional Council is made up of political appointees and former presidents of the republic—not jurists as in the Council of State. The Constitutional Council concluded, in their normally succinct manner, that the law was "in conformity with the constitution" and said little else about the justification for the law. However, the council did add a provision that the law was not to apply in places of worship. This reopened the question of whether this was a religious or a social practice. By including the worship space exception the council was rejecting Parliament's assumption that the *burqa* was not a religious exercise but was a political and social threat. As Patrick Weil observed, the lawmaker had been careful to remove the religious aspect and the council reinserted it.[131] This reinsertion made it more possible for European Court of Human Rights intervention and is a ground in the *S.A.S.* case.

Prior to the French *burqa* ban and *S.A.S.* case, the European Court of Human Rights had already held that restrictions in the wearing of religious dress inside public institutions was legal, while restricting the wearing of religious dress on the public street was a violation of article 9 (freedom of religion) of the ECHR.[132] French politicians aware of the age of judicialized politics quickly argued that their law was different because it did not specify any religious dress—just a general covering of the face. The justification of the law was public order, not regulation of religion.

The *S.A.S.* case involves a French national who voluntarily wears a *burqa* as a sign of her personal religious devotion.[133] She removes her face covering when visiting the doctor or friends and acknowledged the need to remove it for security/identity checks. Prior to the *S.A.S.* case, the European Court of Human Rights had ruled in *Arslan* that generalized bans on the wearing of religious dress in public violated article 9 (religious freedom) of the ECHR. In *Arslan* and other cases the European Court of Human Rights had upheld bans on religious dress in public schools (teachers and students) and government workers. In *S.A.S.*, the court retreated from the protection of state neutrality and legal equality of religious practitioners, approving France's return to strict *laïcité* even though France is a signatory to the ECHR, which provides at a minimum for an accommodating style of *laïcité*.

The *S.A.S.* opinion reads as a strong case against a ban on face coverings, but a twist in the reasoning at the end of the opinion upholds the ban. The court recognized that the *burqa* ban is a breach of the ECHR, European, and international standards and laws. The court also recognized that the French ban is the most extensive in Europe, a factor frequently considered by the court. Further, the court rejected France's claims that the ban was needed for public safety, gender equality, or human dignity. Thus, the court rejected all of the reasons expressed by politicians in enacting the ban, except one. The court found the ban furthered the interest of "living together." There is no standard of living together expressed in the ECHR. The judges found it in the penumbra of the convention as a document encouraging community and respect for interaction. The dissenting opinions point out numerous examples where face coverings are permitted in public and which have not been found to endanger communal feelings. The dissenting judges assert that mere covering of the face is not what is engendering social discomfort; it is that the covering is being done by women of a minority religion of which many are afraid.

In addition to upholding France's burqa ban the European Court of Human Rights upheld termination of a public sector employee for wearing a hijab at work in the case of Ebrahimian v. France, no. 64846/11. Christiane Ebrahimian, a French national, worked on a contract basis for a City of Paris public hospital service. Her contract for employment was not renewed due to her refusal to remove her hijab following complaints from patients. Human Resources advised Ebrahimian that wearing the hijab violated the secular character of the state and its right to restrict her religious expression at work. French courts upheld the non-renewal because the state was acting in accordance with its principles of secularism and neutrality in public services. At the European Court of Human Rights, Ms. Ebrahimian asserted violation of her article 9 right to free expression of religion, the court agreed but found the interference necessary for the protection of freedom of others. The court concluded the restriction was part of guaranteeing equality in treatment of patients even though no evidence of breach of actual care occurred. The only breach was to the sensibilities of those objecting to Ms. Ebrahimian practicing her religion. The court concluded the state's action fell within the margin of appreciation granted to states to act outside the norms of the ECHR due to local social mores. The court did not follow its own reasoning in the Eweida case requiring "evidence of [a] real encroachment on the interests of others" before the individual right of exercise could be restricted. We can conclude that just as in *S.A.S.* the European Court of Human Rights acknowledges

France's actions towards Muslim women violate their rights under the ECHR but the court permits France to do so because the state holds its own right to disregard the protections of the Convention when they do not comport with local cultural mores. This leaves us wondering, just what does the ECHR protect if it is not to establish a European-wide standard for non-discrimination and human rights.

These events in France demonstrate a shift in the balance of democratic boundaries of state neutrality and legal equality. Prior to the *burqa* ban legal opinion in France made clear, regardless of personal feelings about the veil, that it is a violation of accepted principles of liberal democracy to ban it in all instances in the public space. French politicians narrowed the boundary of liberal democracy and exerted greater state restriction on individual choice. The Constitutional Council, with its close ties to the political, agreed with the narrowing of democratic rights; however, it recognized that this narrowing could only be legitimated through the local church-state style. Thus, it narrowed the concept of religious freedom in the state but not general individual choice. The allowance of restrictions on wearing the scarf in private employment further blurs the democratic public/private distinction. As discussed in chapter 4, France attempted to impose this view at the international level at the Council of Europe but lost. However, it was able to get legal approval of the narrowing of individual rights at the Court of Human Rights through the *S.A.S.* case on a ground not expressed in the ECHR and Ebrahimian's wide margin of appreciation standard. Thus, while a European-wide legislative body rejected France's narrowing of rights, a European-wide judicial body engrafted a standard onto a document enacted by that same legislative body in order to uphold France's restrictive treatment of Islamic women.[134] The French influence is also being felt in the enactment of *burqa* bans in other nation's at various government levels.[135] One state which has wrestled with the issue and is wavering in its decision is the Netherlands.

NOTES

French national motto: Liberty, Equality, Fraternity.

1. President Chirac claimed in a speech at Elysee Palace on 17 December 2003, proposing the ban on religious clothing in schools that "[e]verywhere in the world France is recognized as the homeland of human rights." http://www.cesnur.org/2003/fr_veil.htm (accessed June 4, 2012). Hereafter, Chirac Speech.

2. Gérard Noiriel, *The French Melting Pot: Immigration, Citizenship, and National Identity* (Minneapolis: University of Minnesota Press, 1996); Amy Chua, *Day of Empire: How Hyperpowers Rise to Global Dominance and Why They Fall* (New York: Doubleday, 2007); Bhikhu Parekh, *Rethinking Multiculturalism: Cultural Diversity and Political Theory*, 2d ed. (New York: Palgrave, 2006).

3. See Adrien Wing and Monica Smith, "Critical Race Feminism Lifts the Veil: Muslim Women, France and the Headscarf Ban," *U. C. Davis L. Rev.* 39 (2006): 755.

4. For an overview of French history see Georges Duby, *France in the Middle Ages, 987–1460: From Hugh Capet to Joan of Arc* (New York: Wiley,1993); Georges Duby and Robert Mondrau, *Histoire de la Civilisation francaise* (Paris: A. Colin, 1984); Michel Troper, "Religion and Constitutional Rights: French Secularism, or *Laïcité*," *Cardozo L. Rev.* 21 (February 2000): 1267–84; Jeffrey Merrick, *The Desacralization of the French Monarchy in the Eighteenth Century* (Baton Rouge: Louisiana State University, 1990).

5. Edward James, *The Origins of France: From Clovis to the Capetians, 500–1000* (New York: St. Martin's Press, 1982).

6. Brian Tierney, *The Crisis of Church-State, 1050–1300* (Toronto: University of Toronto Press, 1988); Yves Renouard, *The Avignon Papacy, 1305–1403*, trans. Denis Bethell (Hamden, CT: Archon Books, 1970).

7. Jeremy Gunn, "Religious Freedom and *Laïcité*: A Comparison of the United States and France," *BYU L. Rev.* 2004 (Summer 2004): 419.

8. http://www.avalon.law.yale.edu/18th_century/rightsof.asp.

9. Gerard Noiriel, "Immigration and National Memory in the Current French Historiography," *IMIS-BEITRÄGE* 10, no. 46 (1999), http://www.imis.uni-osnabrueck.de/pdffiles/imis10.pdf.

10. http://www.elysee.fr/elysee/anglais/the_institutions/founding_texts/preambule_to_the_27th_of_october_1946_constitution/preambule_to_the_27th_of_october_1946_constitution.20243.html.

11. http://www.assemblee-nationale.fr/english/8ab.asp.

12. http://www.conseil-etat.fr/en; John Bell, "What Is the Function of the *Conseil D'État* in the Preparation of Legislation," *The International and Comparative Law Quarterly* 49, no. 3 (July 2000): 661–72.

13. http://www.conseil-constitutionnel.fr/conseil-constitutionnel/english/homepage.14.html; Michael Davis, "The Law/Politics Distinction, the French Conseil Constitutionnel, and the U.S. Supreme Court," *The American Journal of Comparative Law* 34, no. 1 (Winter 1986): 45–92; FL. Morton, "Judicial Review in France: A Comparative Analysis," *The American Journal of Comparative Law* 36, no. 1 (Winter 1988): 89–110.

14. Eugene Weber, *Peasants into Frenchmen: The Modernization of Rural France, 1870–1914* (Stanford: Stanford University Press, 1976).

15. Cecile Laborde, *Critical Republicanism: The Hijab Controversy and Political Philosophy* (New York: Oxford University Press, 2008), 4, citing Dominique Schnapper, *La Communauté des Citoyens* (Paris: Gallimard, 1994).

16. Jules Ferry Laws of 1881 and 1882, Goblet Law of 1886, and a number of others. See Gunn, *BYU*, 439–42.

17. Gunn, *BYU*, 433, 440.

18. Gunn, *BYU*, 440. French laws refer to religions as sects and cults. "Cult" does not carry the same pejorative meaning as in American English. "Sect" does.

19. Law of December 1905, http://www.journelofficiel.fr.

20. Jean Baubérot, "Existe-t-il une religion civile republicaine?" *French Politics, Culture, and Society* 25, no. 2 (Summer 2007): 3–18, http://www.EBSCOhost.

21. Baubérot, "Existe-t-il,"15.

22. Gunn, *BYU*, 420; T. Jeremy Gunn, "Under God but Not the Scarf: The Founding Myths of Religious Freedom in the United States and *Laïcité* in France," *Journal of Church and State* 46, no. 1 (2004): 7–24; Jennifer Selby, *Questioning French Secularism* (New York: Palgrave, 2012); Joel Fetzer and Christopher Soper, *Muslims and the State in Britain, France, and Germany* (New York: Cambridge University Press, 2005); John Bowen, *Why the French Don't Like Headscarves* (Princeton: Princeton University Press, 2007).

23. Emile Poulat, *Notre Laïcité Publique* (Paris: Editeurs Berg International, 2003), 116.

24. Paul Robert, *Le Grand Robert de langue francaise*, 5: 915 (2d ed., 1992).

25. Jean-Paul Williame, "The Paradoxes of *Laïcité* in France," trans. Allyn Hardyck, in *The Centrality of Religion in Social Life: Essays in Honour of James A. Beckford*, ed. Eileen Barker (Burlington, VT: Ashgate, 2010), 41–54.

26. Gunn, *JCS*, 8–9.

27. Bowen, 14–15.

28. Chirac Speech.
29. Gunn, *JCS*, 9.
30. Poulat, 106.
31. Jean Baubérot, *Histoire de la Laïcité Francaise* (Paris: Pressses de Universitaires de France 2000), 119.
32. Pierre Birnbaum, *The Idea of France* (New York: Hill and Wang, 2001).
33. Jean-Paul Williame, "The Cultural Turn in the Sociology of Religion in France," *Sociology of Religion* 65, no. 4 (2004): 373–89.
34. Jean Baubérot, "Two Thresholds of Laicization," in *Secularism and Its Critics*, ed. Rajee Bhargava (New York: Oxford University Press, 1999), 130–36; Alain Seksig, Patrick Kessel, and Jean-Marc Roirant, "Ni Plurielle ni de combat la laïcité," *Hommes and Migrations* 1218 (March–April 1999): 64–75, http://www.hommes-et-migrations.fr/index:php?12=2340.
35. Jocelyne Cesari, "L'unité républicaine menace par les ideologies multiculturelles," in *La laïcité une valeur d'aujourd'hui? Contestations et renégociations de modéle francais*, ed. Jean Baudouin and Philippe Portier (Rennes: Presser Universitatat de Rennes, 2001); Jean-Paul Williame, *Europe et religion: Les enjeux du XXIe siècle* (Paris: Fayard, 2004), 328–38.
36. Jean-Paul Burdy and Jean Marcou, "Laïcité /Laklik: Introduction," *CEMOTI (Cahiers d'etudes sur la mediteranee orientale et de le monde turco-iranien)* 19 (1995): 13–14, http://www.cemoti.reves.org/1677.
37. Henri Peña-Ruiz is one influential leader of this view. For example see Henri Peña-Ruiz, *Qu'est-ce que la laïcité?* (Paris: Gallimard, 2003).
38. Jean Baubérot, "Secularism and French Religious Liberty: A Sociological and Historical View," *BYU L. Rev.* 2003, no. 2: 451–64.
39. Jean-Paul Williame, "L'Union europennee est-elle laique," in *Les entriens d'auxerre: De la separation des eglises et de l'etat a l'avenir et la laïcité*, ed. Jean Baubérot and Michel Wieviorka (Paris: L'aube, 2005), 350.
40. Noiriel, *Melting*, 79–89.
41. Noiriel, *Melting*, 60–66.
42. Noiriel, *Melting*, 66.
43. Gerard Noiriel, *Le Creuset francais: Histoire de l'immigration XIXe–XXe siècle* (Paris: Seuil, 2006).
44. Independence came to Cambodia in 1953; Vietnam in 1954; Tunisia and Morocco in 1956; Benin Burkina Faso, Cameroon, Chad, Congo-Brazzaville, Cote d'Ivorie Gabon, Mai, Senegal, Mauritania, Niger, Togo, Central African Republic, and Madagascar in 1960; and Algeria in 1962.
45. Patrick Weil, *La France et ses étrangers* (Paris: Gallimard, 2004).
46. http://www.immigration.interieur.gouv.fr.
47. http://www.conseil-etat.fr/en. For an explanation of the contract in English, see http://www.expat.com/doc/78.Elan_Art_CAI_050107_EN.pdf (accessed June 10, 2012).
48. Adrian Favell, *Philosophies of Integration: Migrants, Minorities, and Citizenship* (New York: Palgrave, 1998), 46.
49. http://www.telegraph.co.uk/news/worldnews/europe/frnce/7919011/Nicolas-Sarkozy-threatens-to-strip-citizenship-from-immigrants-who-target-police.html (accessed June 16, 2012).
50. http://www.state.gov/g/drl/rls/irf/2010. The largest single immigrant population in France is from other European countries. This group correlates to about 40 percent of the total immigrant population.
51. Olivier Roy, *Vers un Islam Européen* (Paris: Espirit, 1999).
52. Ahmet Kuru, *Secularism and State Policies toward Religion* (New York: Cambridge University Press, 2009), 121.
53. Jocelyne Cesari, "Demande d'islam en banileue: Un défi a la citoyen-néte?" *CEMOTI (Cahiers d'études sur la Mediterranée orientale est le mond turco iranien)* 19 (1995): 180–81, http://www.cemoti.revues. org/1677.
54. http://www.hci.gouv.fr/.

55. H. Giordian, *Democratic culturelle et droit a la difference* (Paris: Ministere de la Culture, 1982); J. Berque, *Les enfants de l'immigration a l'ecole: Rapport au Ministre de l'education Nationale* (Paris: La Documentation Francaise 1985).

56. Riva Kastoryano and Angeline Escafre-Dublet, "Tolerance and Cultural Diversity Discourses in France," Accept Pluralism Project of the COE (San Domeinco di Fiesole, Italy: European University Institute, 2010), http://www.accept-pluralism.eu/Home.aspx.

57. This problem occurs in several European countries due to laws requiring religious groups to register or be officially recognized to legally exist within the state. In nonhierarchical religions there is no one body to license or recognize and variations under an umbrella name may vary widely.

58. Cheniere served as National Assembly representative for the Oise district from 1993 to 1997 on a platform arguing that France is not a collection of individual rights but a community and that community must reflect the French identity. Joan Scott, *Politics of the Veil* (Princeton: Princeton University Press, 2007), 26.

59. For a fuller discussion of these issues see Joel Fetzer and Christopher Soper, *Muslims and the State in Britain France and Germany* (New York: Cambridge University Press, 2005), and Dominic McGoldrick, *Human Rights and Religion: The Islamic Headscarf Debates in Europe* (Portland, OR: Hart, 2006), 64–66.

60. *Journal Officiel*, 25 October 1989, 113–15, http://www.journelofficiel.fr.

61. *Conseil d'Etat*, avis no. 2466.893–2, 7 November 1989, http://www.conseil-d'etat.fr.

62. Avis rendus par l'assemblée générale du Conseil d'Etat, 1989, www.conseil-etat.fr/content/download/635/1933/version/1file/346893.pdf.

63. Circular of 12 December 1989, "Laïcité, port de signes religieux par les eleves et caractere obligatoire des enseignements," *Journal Officiel*, 15577, 15 December 1989, http://www.journelofficiel.fr. Circulars from administrative agencies are not themselves binding law. They are interpretations of law by the agency which is tasked with enforcing the law and are therefore considered a strong indication of what conduct is expected.

64. Haut conseil a l'integration, *L'Islam dans la Republique* (2001), http://www.ladocumentation francaise/fr/rapports-publics/014000017. It is interesting to note that the number of cases steadily declined from 1994 to 2003. Further, the Education Ministry set up a *hijab* mediator who assisted in settling many disputes before they were formally filed.

65. Conseil d'Etat, avis no. 130.394, 2 November 1992 (Kherouaa); Conseil d'Etat, avis no. 170207, 27 November 1996 (Moussaoui).

66. Conseil d' etat, avis no. 159.981, 10 March 1995.

67. F. Bayrou, "Le texte du minister de l'education nationale," *Le Monde*, 21 September 1994, http://www.lemonde.fr/ (accessed June 10, 2012).

68. Chirac Speech.

69. Cour administrative d'appel de lyon, 03LY01392, 27 November 2003, http://www.eur-lex.europea.eu or http://www.legifrance.gouv.fr.

70. Commission de Reflexion sur L'Application du Principe de Laicite dans la Republique, *Rapport au President de la Republique* (11 December 2003), 38–40, http://www.ladocumentationfrancaise.fr/ var/storage/rapports-publics/034000725/0000.pdf. Hereafter, Stasi Commission.

71. Patrick Weil, "A Nation in Diversity: France, Muslims and the Headscarf," *Open Democracy*, 25 March 2004, 4, http://www.opendemocracy.net/faith-europe-islam/article_1811.jsp.

72. Talal Asad, "Trying to Understand French Secularism," in *Political Theologies: Public Religions in a Post-Secular World*, ed. Hent de Vries and Lawrence Sullivan, (New York: Fordham University Press, 2006), 497.

73. Joppke, "State," 320.

74. http://www.npns.fr.

75. Scott, 12.

76. Law 2004–2, 28 March 2004. http://www.assemblee-nationale/fr. Emphasis added.

77. Ahmet Kuru, *Secularism and State Policies toward Religion* (New York: Cambridge Press, 2009), 104, no. 9, quoting Jeremy Gunn.

78. Pierre Tevanian, Ismahane Chouder, and Malika Latreche, *Les filles voilles parlent* (Paris: Lafabrique 2008).
79. Conseil d'Etat req. no. 285394 and no. 295671.
80. Cour de Cassation, Chambre Sociale, nos. 536 and 537, judgment 19 March 2013, http://www.Courdecassation.fr/jurisprudence_2/chamber_sociale_576.
81. http://www.thelocal.fr/page/view/a-dark-day-for-secularism-in-france (accessed June 10, 2012).
82. Conseil d'etat, req. no 286798, 27 June 2008.
83. Vivre en France avec le niqab, *Le Monde*, 24 June 2009, 3, http://www.lemonde.fr/ (accessed June 10, 2012).
84. The number of women wearing the face veil in France is in contention, with figures ranging from about four hundred to about two thousand, including overseas territories. Open Society Foundation, "Unveiling the Truth: Why 32 Muslim Women Wear the Full Veil in France" (2011), http://www.scros.org/initiatives/home/articles_publications/publications/unveiling the truth. The Parliamentary Commission formed to analyze the need for a ban found that 1,900 women wear the face veil (*niqab*) and none wear the *burqa* in France. Assemblée Nationale, *Rapport d'information au nom de la mission d'information sur la pratique du port du voile intégral sur le territoire national*, January 26, 2010, http://www.assemblee-nationale.fr/13/pdf/rap-info/i2262.pdf. Hereafter, *Burqa* Report.
85. Liberation 22 June 2009, http://www.Liberation.fr; http://www.mirror.co.uk/news/uk-news/franch-president-nicholas-sarkozy-calls-401816 (accessed June 10, 2012).
86. Assemblee Nationale, Proposition de resolution, no. 1725, 19 June 2009. Emphasis added.
87. http://www.telegraph.co.uk/news/worldnews/europe/france/5580732 (accessed June 10, 2012).
88. http://www.debateidentitenationale.fr.
89. Christian Joppke and John Torpey, *Legal Integration of Islam* (Cambridge, MA: Harvard University Press, 2013), 23.
90. Minutes of the sixth meeting of the commission on 29 September 2009, http://www.assemblee-nationale.fr/13/cr-miburqa/09–10/index.asp. Hereafter, Commission hearing and date.
91. Commission hearings, October 14, 2009, and October 28, 2009.
92. Commission hearing, September 9, 2009.
93. Commission hearing, July 8, 2009.
94. Nicols Sarkozy, "Respecter ceux qui arrivent, respecter ceux qui accueillent," *Le Monde* 9 December 2009, 1, http://www.lemonde.fr/ (accessed June 10, 2012).
95. Sarkozy, "Respecter," 20.
96. *Burqa* Report, 13.
97. *Burqa* Report, 97–100.
98. *Burqa* Report, 107.
99. *Burqa* Report, 116–22.
100. Burqa Report, 13; The report defines the full veil as being either, the *niqab*, which covers all the body and the face with the exception of the eyes; the *sitar*, an additional veil that covers the eyes so no part of the woman's body is visible, the hands being covered by gloves; and the *burqa*, which entirely covers the body and has a mesh grille in front of the eyes. *Burqa* Report, 25–26.
101. *Le Premier Ministre demande au Conseil d'Etat d'étudier les solutions juridiques pour interdire le port du voile intégral* (29 January 2010), http://www.gouvernement.fr/premier-ministre/le-premier-ministre-demande-au-conseil-d-etat-d-etudier-les-solutions-juridiques-po.
102. National Assembly, 335–1; Senate, 246–1 with 100 abstentions.
103. Law 2010 of 13 July 2010, http://www.assemblee-nationale/fr.
104. Penal Code article 131–16. All laws are available in French at http://www.Legifrance.gouv.fr. Criminal laws are available in English at http://www.legislationonline.org/documents/section/criminal-codes.
105. Penal Code article 13–5–1 (emphasis added), http://www.legislationonline.org/documents/section/criminal-codes.

106. http://www.conseil-constitonnel.fr.
107. *Burqa* Report, 95.
108. Open Society Foundation.
109. Open Society, 18.
110. This type of political protest against gender discrimination and violence is done by women, as seen in the Slutwalk protests. http://www.slutwalktoronto.com.
111. Testimony of Remy Schwartz, Member of Council of State, Commission hearing 7 October 2009.
112. Joppke and Torpey, 30.
113. *Burqa* Report, 118–19.
114. Testimony of Abdennour Bidat, well-known French philosopher, Commission hearing 9 September 2009.
115. *Burqa* Report, 118.
116. *Burqa* Report, 118.
117. Testimony of Jacques Myard, UMP delegate, Commission hearing 25 November 2009.
118. Immanuel Kant, "Metaphysics of Morals (1797)," in *Practical Philosophy: The Cambridge Edition of the Works of Immanuel Kant*, ed. and trans. Mary Gregor (New York: Cambridge University Press, 1999), 353–604.
119. Testimony of Xavire Darcos, Minister of Work, Commission hearing 16 December 2009.
120. Testimony of Eric Besson, Minister of Immigration, Commission hearing 16 December 2009.
121. Testimony of Francois Hostalier, UMP politician, Commission hearing, 25 November 2009.
122. Testimony of Pierre Forgues, leftist politician, Comission hearing 25 November 2009.
123. Testimony of Guy Carcassonne, Commission hearing 25 November 2009.
124. Conseil d'Etat, *Commune de Morsang-sur-Orge*, no. 136–270, judgment of October 27, 1995.
125. *Redecouvrir le Preamble de la Constitution—Rapport du Comite Preside par Simone Veil* (2008), http://www.ladocumenataionfrancaise/fr/rapports-publics/084000758/index/shtml.
126. Testimony of Bernard Mathieu, Commission hearing 25 November 2009; Testimony of Denys de Bechillon, Commission hearing 14 October 2009.
127. Testimony of Remy Schwartz, Commission hearing, 7 October 2009. Examples include the striking of laws in towns along the French Riviera prohibiting the wearing of bathing suits on city streets and requiring wearing of trousers and shirts.
128. Testimony of Remy Schwartz, Commission hearing 7 October 2009.
129. Testimony of Denis de Bechillon, Commission hearing 4 October 2009.
130. Nicolas Sarkozy au Congress de Versailles, June 22 2009, youtube.com.
131. Patrick Weil, "La Loi sur la Burqa Risqué l'Invalidation par l'Europe," *Le Monde*, 24 November 2010, 23, http://www.lemonde.fr/politique/patrick-weil. (accessed June 10, 2012).
132. *Arslan and Others v. Turkey*, application no. 41135/98, judgment of 23 February 2010.
133. *S.A.S. v. France*, application no. 43835/11, judgment of July 1, 2014.
134. France has lost cases involving religious groups' right to exist, such as Jehovah's Witnesses and Mandarom. France tried to close these groups using its tax laws. The European Court of Human Rights rejected the attempts, further demonstrating the court's interest in protecting group rights rather than individual religious rights.
135. Belgium has enacted a state-wide *burqa* ban; Germany, provincial; Spain, one municipality. The Spanish municipal law was held invalid as Spanish law does not grant this authority to the municipal level of government.

Chapter Six

The Netherlands

Ik zal hand haven

The Netherlands has a long history of being a center of international trade. The quintessentially Dutch product the tulip is an import from the Ottoman Empire, likewise porcelain making, another Dutch specialty, came from China. Consequently, their culture, while exposed to many others, did not absorb many non-Europeans until the 1960s. The Netherlands is often called "the tolerant society," but that tolerance becomes murky when one looks below the surface. The Dutch expression "*Hoge bomen vangen veel wind*" (Tall trees catch the most wind) expresses the overarching social attitude of the Netherlands: you should not expect special treatment, it is best if we are all equal.[1] The official motto "I will stand firm" also shows that while the Dutch are tolerant there is a limit to that tolerance, and actions perceived as un-Dutch will not be tolerated. The deep social-psychological need for egalitarianism, neither expecting nor receiving special treatment, is so ingrained that it moves the Dutch tolerance from acceptance of difference to an attitude which is more syncretist than integrationist or multicultural, regardless of proclaimed policies of multiculturalism. This syncretism can be seen in how the Dutch treat Muslim women.

The Netherlands has a long history of coexistence among various European Christian and Judaic religious groups. The manner in which the state and religion interact has seen marked changes, and the recent wave of Islamic immigrants is causing some to advocate a shift in Dutch religion-state relations. The Dutch pillarized (*verzuiling*) scheme, in place from the 1800s to 1960s for dealing with state and religion questions, utilized vertical separation to achieve a concept of equality which was highly restrictive in practice, even though its rhetoric made it appear to be a robust tolerance. The "separate but equal" pillarized system contemplated that no one social group would be large enough to dominate the others. However, the system has been largely dismantled institutionally. A group has entered Dutch society which some fear has a population growth rate that positions it to overtake the native groups. In the modern, nonpillarized system this forces the Dutch to face the issue of true diversity for the first time. As the "separate but equal" institution of pillarization no longer exists, Dutch society must find a new balance to equality, tolerance, and liberal democracy.

HISTORY

The Netherlands is a lowland delta area in northwestern Europe. Most of the land area has been reclaimed from the sea.[2] Sometimes referred to as the golden delta, the area consists of crossing river valleys and sea coasts; trade routes have crossed the area at least since the Iron Age.[3] The geographical location causes the area to be one of cultural and economic interchange.

The geography of the area forced the early independent duchies to work together to establish a network of dikes and canals for flood control, land reclamation (*polders*), and economic trade routes. The extensive *polder* system led to the expression "God made the world but the Dutch made Holland." The Dutch are proud of this sentiment and see it as part of their culture that they, not nature, made them what they are in land and in culture. Early on, a pragmatic approach to relations (*poldermodel*) among peoples developed to aid in creation of this land and culture; working together to solve problems became a basic characteristic of the Dutch.[4] This led to a strong sense of shared space, public and semipublic, and a desire that the maximum number of people feel comfortable in that space. It rests on a belief that humans working together can conquer all problems, but it also leads to an overly optimistic assumption that the sensibility of the Dutch view is unassailable.

When the area fell under the rule of the Roman Empire and later the Holy Roman Empire, it was largely left alone to create independent duchies. The area eventually fell under Spanish control as part of the Habsburg Empire. With the Protestant Reformation catching fire in northwestern Europe, the area sought freedom from Catholic Spain beginning in 1568. In 1579 several of the area's provinces united under the Treaty of Utrecht to aid each other in the fight for independence.[5] While independence was not fully achieved until the 1648 Peace of Westphalia, the Netherlands considers the Treaty of Utrecht as the foundation of the modern nation-state.[6] Throughout the war for independence from Spain, the Dutch economy flourished and began what is called its Golden Age. In the period before and during the war Renaissance humanism flowered in the Netherlands. The highly influential philosopher

Desiderius Erasmus advocated a level of tolerance for various religions in the area, and religious refugees from other areas, particularly France after the repeal of the Edict of Nantes (1685), settled in the Netherlands.[7] The Netherlands was also a place of refuge for dissenting British Protestants, including the Puritans. As a place of refuge with a robust economy, the area also attracted independent thinkers in science and philosophy, including Englishman John Locke. Thus, the area has long been influenced by ideas of social and political coexistence.

After independence, a confederation of autonomous states governed the area through a loose confederation of regional parliaments all under the regional leadership of a member of the House of Orange and a national States-General. This republic was noted for its policy of tolerance by allowing the coexistence of Protestants, Roman Catholics, and Jews. During this Dutch Golden Age the confederation rose to be an economic world power, establishing colonies and trade throughout the world, and is often considered the first truly capitalist country. Part of their seafaring trade led to emigration to the American colonies/United States as well as Dutch colonies for economic pursuits.[8]

By the mid-eighteenth century, wars with England and France, along with internal unrest, caused a severe economic downturn. In 1795 a republic fashioned after the new French Republic formed and eventually fell under Napoleonic control.[9] This republic centralized political control in a national government with the provinces having limited authority. This centralized system remains today.[10] After the collapse of the French Empire in 1813, the House of Orange returned as sovereign but after a few years was forced to accept a limitation of authority under the constitutions of 1815 (unitary state, constitutional monarchy) and 1848 (parliamentary democracy).[11] The 1848 constitution made government accountable only to the elected proportional parliament, protected civil liberties, including religion, and made the monarch a largely ceremonial position. The 1848 constitution also laid out the unique pillar system of religion-state relations (*verzuiling*), a structure which will be discussed more fully below.

The Netherlands remained neutral in the First World War but even after declaring neutrality was drawn into the second by German invasion and capture. Blom observes that "Dutch political institutions triumphantly withstood the test of the war. Though during the war most of them were temporarily suspended they appeared virtually unchanged at the end of the war."[12] In the postwar world, the Netherlands has built itself into a modern, industrialized, liberal democratic country. The current constitution was ratified in 1983.[13]

The executive branch of the Dutch government consists of the monarch and the Council of Ministers. The monarch is the head of state but has little political authority. The Council of Ministers consists of the appointed heads of the national ministries and the prime minister. All serve in equal power, with the prime minister usually being the leader of the largest party in the coalition government. The Council of Ministers initiates policies and proposes legislation. Once the council has adopted a policy or proposed a law all members of the council must support it. The Council of Ministers and State secretaries make up the cabinet.

The Dutch Parliament, the States-General, is bicameral, with most power in the lower House of Representatives. Laws may be proposed by individual members of the House of Representatives, but this is rarely done. The Senate may not propose or amend laws; it may only reject ones put before it for a vote. The House is directly elected, while the Senate is elected by provincial legislatures.

All proposed laws must be reviewed by the Council of State for constitutionality and compliance with binding international law, such as the ECHR. The Council of State's advice is not binding but is usually followed. The Council of State is also the highest administrative court, an important function because the Netherlands is a civil law country. The administrative decisions are binding law. There is an independent judiciary interpreting and applying civil and criminal law without ruling on its constitutionality. Another important advisory body setting policy and enacting law is the Socio-Economic Council. The Socio-Economic Council is made up of labor and employer organizations and advises the government on all actions impacting the economy.

The 1983 constitution made no substantial change to the institutional framework; however, it did make extensive changes to the statement on religion. The prior constitution dedicated an entire section to church-state relations and freedom of religion. The 1983 constitution has only one article directly addressing freedom of religion but does include religion in its lists of protected civil rights.[14] Article 1 provides that "[a]ll persons in the Netherlands shall be treated equally in equal circumstances. Discrimination on the grounds of religion, belief, political opinion, race, or sex or on any other grounds whatsoever shall not be permitted." Article 6 provides:

1. Everyone shall have the right to profess freely his religion or belief, either individually or in community with others, without prejudice to his responsibility under the law.
2. Rules concerning the exercise of this right other than in buildings and enclosed places may be laid down by Act of Parliament for protection of health, in the interest of traffic and to combat or prevent disorders.

These provisions are put into effect chiefly through the General Equality Act of 1994, which provides that individuals may bring claims of religious discrimination to the Equal Treatment Commission, now known as the Institute of Human Rights. The institute also advises the government on all proposed policies and laws as to whether they comply with the General Equality Act of 1994 and all other binding human rights laws, including the ECHR. The tone of the institute is set by its enacting law, which does not use the term "discrimination," rather it refers to "differentiation." This is not mere semantics as it signifies a legal standard which does not require proof of intent to treat another differently in a protected area. The mere fact of unequal treatment constitutes a violation of law unless the violator can prove a legitimate justification for the unequal treatment. Decisions of the commission are non-binding but are usually followed by parties and courts.

POLDERMODEL

Poldermodel underlies all forms of political and economic action in the Netherlands. In the *poldermodel* parties come together to jointly solve a specific problem in a manner beneficial to the collective.[15] Different political parties set aside philosophical differences to form coalition governments, a common necessity due to the large number of political parties. In times of economic crisis, unions, businesses, and government usually come together to negotiate compromises, with all seeking what is best for the national collective, not advancement of the self-interest of each.[16]

Compromise is rarely seen as a bad thing in the Netherlands, and *overleg* (discussion-meeting) remains the chief means of dealing with any issue. There is pressure at these meetings to put forth a public appearance of consensus. This consensus may be thin, however, and coalitions are easily broken. The *overleg* is not a mutual conversation, as it is directed by a leader, often political, who directs the discussion to support the existing national structure. In the *overleg*, not all voices carry equal weight. Strong criticisms are discouraged and emotional outbursts considered irrational are to be dismissed. Appeals to individual choice or freedom are incorporated only if the collective agrees they do not pose a threat, real or imagined, to national unity.[17]

This striving for consensus is interpreted as tolerance by both the Dutch and outsiders. The Dutch practice of tolerance has been utilized through history to foster economic peace. The major area of Dutch tolerance in the modern era involves sexual identity, sexual relations, and drugs. While much of the rest of the West continued to restrict sexual practices and drug use, the Netherlands became tolerant of both so long as it was done discreetly. For example, prostitution is legal but no one can be a street walker. It is tightly regulated and advertising is discreet. The same applies to homosexual conduct. One is not questioned about it, but one is also not expected to flaunt it in public. The Netherlands was the first country to legalize same-sex marriage. Drugs also are regulated and limited. The use of hashish is legal at specific businesses. Its sale and use is regulated but stronger drugs are illegal. The tolerance of the Dutch system, however, reaches only as far as to what the majority has agreed is permissible. Traditionally, it has not been a broad tolerance of individualism.

Since the 1960s there has been both a growth of the social welfare system and an individualization of conduct. The social welfare state is seen as forming a common base guarantee of assistance (elder and child care, education subsidies, generous unemployment and welfare benefits), freeing individuals to pursue their *zelfontploozing* (personal development). The state is expected to ensure a certain quality of life, including regulation of public conduct to the level least objectionable to the majority. Thus, there is a tension between the individual and the collective in public space. An example of the Dutch desire to solve all problems by collective consensus is seen in the large amount of government resources dedicated to social policy research through government agencies or grants. Government funding for research means that the government will identify which issues need attention, thereby restricting independent problem-solving. One observer of Dutch society likened this style to that of a school of fish moving together to meet alterations in the government current.[18] Acceptable cultural difference is limited and thin, and currently concern that cultural differences are too deep to be overcome has increased. Dutch tolerance is a style of "non-intervention to regulate the differences between its large minorities."[19] The cultural differences are fixed, and the institution is merely seeking a means of keeping them in check for the common good. The style of discipline may change—pillarization, multiculturalism, integration—but the goal remains the same: limited public individuality with emphasis on the common space implementing the majority view. Hoving observes that Dutch tolerance is "based on the radical differentiation between self and other . . . a strong sense of superiority, from which stems the authority to tolerate or evade others."[20] Hoving believes that the Dutch have still not fully addressed issues of race, colonization, and slavery and that in one sense the multicultural society with tolerance and openness is "[n]othing but a strategy to maintain exploitative power hierarchies, and to silence all critical counter-discourses." She concludes that ethnic minority knowledge of cultural habits and values will not aid in understanding or overcoming political differences.[21]

VERZUILING

From the 1600s to the 1970s the Dutch version of religious tolerance relied on a system of pillarization, *verzuiling*.[22] After the Peace of Westphalia, Calvinism became a quasi state religion, and the tolerance of non-Calvinists waxed and waned. Calvinism itself broke into many forms, and religious disagreements in the Netherlands during the early years rested on which style of Calvinism was in political control, with the country largely divided between north and south. Usually the larger population of the north was able to push through laws restricting the southern form, and southerners were not able to openly practice until the late nineteenth century with the installation of the formal pillar system of religion-state relations. This early intra-Calvinist and intranative disagreement over religious freedom led to a strong desire on each side for freedom to practice its theology with minimal hindrance and a desire for a political compromise which enabled each theology to be independent while maintaining a unified nation.

The pillar system recognized certain religions as favored and allowed them to form separate vertical social communities. The communities existed in separate but equal vertical components within all aspects of society—religious practice, education, business, and political. Even the media was divided according to pillar, with the government assisting in the funding of radio and television channels. The school you attended, the newspaper you read, the trade union or political party you belonged to telegraphed to the wider society which pillar you were born into; further, you were expected to stay within your pillar even if you did not identify with its theology or ideology. One could go through life with little if any contact with someone from another pillar.

In the beginning there were two pillars, Catholic and Protestant. The Catholic pillar, being largely directed by church hierarchy, exercised tighter control over all aspects of society within the pillar than the Protestant pillar.[23] The Protestant pillar sometimes split into two, *Gereformeerd* (conservative and now the ARP political party) and a more reformed pillar which included several Protestant theologies.[24] As is common in religious-political debates, the initial issue was education. The pillars allowed a means for establishing religious schools funded through the state. Using the *poldermodel* eventually resulted in equal state funding for all schools, secular and faith based, which is still in effect today.

The two initial religious pillars, Protestant and Catholic, were later joined by a socialist pillar. Citizens were not required to join a pillar but found it socially beneficial to declare allegiance to a pillar. Consequently, many who did not fall within the denominational theology of the Catholic and Protestant pillar or the politics of the socialist joined together to form their own general liberal pillar.[25] There are social exceptions and nuances to these pillars; however, their importance to the development of Dutch society until the 1960s cannot be overemphasized. "As the minorities were not just political groupings, the political parties were not autonomous political agents, but rather the embassies of subcultures in the Hague. . . . Political strife was exacerbated by the depth of the subcultural cleavages and the animosity that existed between the pillars. The minorities were introverted, isolated and hostile toward one another, and at times emotions ran high."[26]

There is an important distinction between the early political mobilization (1870–1920) led by Abraham Kuyper which resulted in the denominational pillars and the later socioideological political pillars after 1920.[27] The *poldermodel* and pillarization created a stable, homogenous nation-state with

> a stagnant economy and stable society, in which the cleavage between the political and cultural elite and the common people was by far the most important social distinction. . . . When the Netherlands entered its period of industrialization and societal differentiation in the 1870s and 1880s the country seemed poised to follow a course which would see the broad consensus of the elite on national identity challenged by the emergence of socialism and of a Catholic subculture.[28]

In the post-1920s political structure the pillars led to the creation of consociationalism, power sharing among elites within a segmented society. The system of delineation is the means to implement the *poldermodel* of elite compromise as a reaction to social division or ideological conflict. Governance under pillarization was a long-term process with a widespread awareness that power should be shared and individual autonomy need not impair practical cooperation among groups.[29] This system meant that socialism and Catholicism could not mount a serious challenge to the existing Protestant elite due to their permanent minority position.[30]

The cleavage of pillarization limited the development of any class-based political movement which might challenge the structure. The separation of the pillars by denomination (Catholic and Protestant) and political ideology (socialist and liberal) caused Catholics and Protestants to have to choose their identification—political, economic, or religious. This had "the effect of minimizing radicalism and withdrawal from the political process, and it prevented a strong left-right polarization."[31]

Until 1960 lives were arranged around the pillar to which you belonged, with rare crossing of pillars. The separation is viewed as a form of tolerance: a separate but equal form of life. This does not mean approval of other pillars, just an agreement not to interfere. Pressure to conform to the ideas and practices of your pillar was strong. With the dismantling of the pillars a backlash against the imposition of social cohesion became popular to such an extent that it was referred to by the popular name of *spruitjeslucht* (the smell of brussels sprouts), conjuring up an image of a closely confined space with an unpleasant odor.

Pillarization and *poldermodel* demonstrate that the Dutch tolerance is not one of openness and acceptance to difference. Rather, they demonstrate a long psychological history of managing conflict through social pressure to conform and elite power consolidation being framed for the common good.

Public displays of difference, whether political or religious, have long been discouraged and are rewarded with the wind of disapproval. Forbearance in the Dutch manner should not be confused with openness. Tolerance is a form of conflict management and avoidance rather than recognition of the right to individual difference.

After World War II (WWII), the pillar system was slowly dismantled under an ideology of universal human rights and unity of the Dutch people. The integrated economics of post World War II led to greater interaction between pillars. Additionally, the realization that national segregation based on racial, ethnic, or religious grounds could lead anyone to the horrors witnessed during the war resulted in people beginning to see that persons in other pillars were not so different.

ONTZUILING

By the 1960s the political pillars had morphed into ideological parties, and many restrictions, such as broadcast access, had been removed. By the dawn of the twenty-first century the formal institutional pillars had disappeared, but voluntary remnants can still be seen, particularly in the education system.[32] The 1960s saw the final institutional dismantling of pillars, *ontzuiling*. Throughout the 1950s Dutch leaders urged modernization of the social and political world that had existed before WWII. While working inside their pillars, these leaders sought a pragmatic progressive direction for the country, which included the dismantling of the pillars. Political and religious leaders embraced this social opening, even reforming theological doctrine to a more liberal theology. Political action rejected the former isolationist and neutral foreign policy, and domestic policy emphasized social welfare solutions.[33] Joris Voorhoes, former minister of defense, identifies the three phases of Dutch foreign policy as maritime commercialism, neutralist abstentionism, and internationalist idealism.[34] In the current international idealist phase, the Netherlands seeks to be a leader of strong liberal democracy with broad civil rights and an example of a successful multiculturalist state.

The Dutch economy boomed throughout the 1960s, with educational levels and salaries increasing. From 1959 to 1962 salaries increased 21 percent; in 1964, 17 percent; and during the rest of the 1960s they rose at least 10 percent each year.[35] The economic boom and the desire to throw off any ideas associated with WWII led to an optimism which made the pillars seem old-fashioned and restrictive of progress. Additionally, more women began working outside the home, albeit at a lower percentage than in most other Western countries.[36] Also, for the first time peaceful political demonstrations became tolerated and were even seen as a beneficial means of defusing tensions and fostering discussion.[37] The major changes came in the area of social issues, particularly sexual practices, sexual identity and drug use, and a sharp decrease in religiosity.

Even though many religious leaders embraced the social changes, religiosity steadily declined. James Kennedy argues that the new ecumenism was partly to blame for the decline in religiosity. In an attempt to remain relevant by becoming more ecumenical, the churches removed themselves from being places to find one stable belief system. The dismantling of the pillars and decreasing strict theological principles made the churches less essential to one's life.[38] In the mid-1960s 18 percent of the population stated that it did not belong to a church; today it is about 50 percent.[39] Of those who do identify as members of a religion, Roman Catholic is the largest group (25 percent), followed by all Protestant denominations (16 percent), Islam (4–6 percent), and Hindu and Buddhist each about 1 percent. From 2004 to 2011 the number of persons identifying themselves as belonging to a religion declined 3 percent overall.[40] However, this self-identification still does not mean that they actively practice their religion. For example, only about 1.2 percent of those who identify themselves as Roman Catholic attend mass weekly, while 38 percent of Muslims regularly attend services. "The downward trend is observed across the board and applies to all levels of education, both genders, and people with a native Dutch background and a foreign background."[41]

Religious ideology is now separated from political and most aspects of social identity. One may vote for a political party identified by a religious or social philosophy (Christian Democrats, Christian Union, Socialist, Labor Party), but this rests more on party platform than theology or social network. Broadcast and print media are largely devoid of ties to their past pillar. They are now identified by their liberal or conservative leanings, just as media in the United States and France. The government announced the end of the last vestige of state support for religious broadcasts by withdrawing funding for religious programming on the public broadcasting system.[42] In fact, pillarization is seen as a negative relic of the past. Only some small, conservative religious groups still organize their social and political lives around a voluntary pillar-type system, which is criticized by wider society.

One such group, *Gereformeerden*, restricts the role of women to their biblical interpretation, forbidding them from running for political office. Dutch courts ruled the political party violated Dutch law on equality. In 2007 the Council of State, the highest administrative court in the Netherlands, ruled that the party's view of women's place in society was not a violation of equality because the women were free to join or form another political party. In 2010 the Dutch Supreme Court ruled that the Political Reformed Party's (*Staatkundig Gereformeerde Paritj* [SGP] refusal on biblical grounds to allow women to stand for or serve as elected government representatives was contrary to Dutch laws of equality and that religious freedom rights did not take precedence over equality laws. The SGP appealed to the European Court of Human Rights (ECtHR), alleging the decision violated the European Convention on Human Rights' protections of freedom of religion, assembly, and expression. The ECtHR rejected the appeal. The court reiterated that "the Convention was designed to promote and maintain the ideals and values of a democratic society. . . . Democracy . . . is the only political model contemplated in the Convention and the only one compatible with it." The court held that the wording of the convention makes the only "necessity" capable of justifying an interference with any of the rights enshrined in the convention to be one which springs from a "democratic society."[43] The court then applied ECHR articles on the prohibition of discrimination and guarantee of free elections through appliction of the "very weighty reasons" standard to hold that the states in the Council of Europe are prevented from supporting any view which sees the "man's role as primordial and the woman's as secondary." The court concluded that the religious freedom interests of the party were subordinate to the state's and women's rights of equality.[44]

WOMEN

Women were granted universal suffrage in 1919, just two years after it was granted to men.[45] The number of women in politics is less than that of the neighboring Scandinavian countries but is higher than the United States. Some political parties voluntarily use nomination quotas to ensure they put up women candidates, and women are generally given higher positions on party lists. In each Parliament since the early 1980s, about 35 percent of the members have been women. Since the turn of the century the number of non-Western immigrant women in Parliament has increased to about 8 percent of the seats.[46]

Laws on the equality of women date back at least to post World War II, but full-time work outside the home remains low among women. Visser and Hemerijck attribute this to Nazi occupation during the war. While in the US women joined the workforce to assist in the war effort, in the Netherlands they stayed home to avoid appearing to support the occupation.[47] In the 1970s about 30 percent of women worked outside the home and, while it is now 55 percent, it remains lower than in the US and France.[48] Even now most women are part-time workers, with 75 percent of all part-time workers being women.[49] Further, women are not equally represented in higher management or professional positions. Of the country's largest 250 companies only 13.1 percent of upper management positions and only 9 percent of full professorships are held by women.[50]

While some equal employment laws followed World War II, it was not until 1973 that it was illegal for an employer to terminate a woman for getting married or pregnant.[51] As part of the EU Lisbon Strategy to decrease reliance on the social welfare state in EU countries, the Netherlands passed a Childcare Act (2007) providing for government assistance toward the cost of childcare and requiring school boards to provide aftercare for students.[52] The government now officially encourages employers to implement equal pay and promote women to senior positions.[53] Many current efforts on behalf of women focus on emancipation of ethnic minority immigrants (*allochtoon*), arguing that such will aid in their integration.

IMMIGRATION

The Netherlands is ethnically diverse with about three million of its inhabitants classified as born outside the country or within three generations of those born outside the country. Dutch colonies in Indonesia, Suriname, Antilles, and Aruba existed for hundreds of years and have shaped Dutch ideas about the non-Dutch. The first trade colonies began in 1602. The presence of the Dutch in the colonies varied during time and place, but some Dutch workers were assigned to protect and manage assets in all. Interaction with local peoples was limited as needed to achieve economic goals. It was not until the independence of the colonies that migration to the Netherlands became common. Immigration from Indonesia (independence in 1945), Suriname (independence in 1975), Aruba (1985), and Curacao (1985) was particularly strong.[54] From 1960 to 1973 guest workers were imported to take on lower-skilled and lower-paying jobs during the economic boom. Workers were chiefly from Spain, Italy, Portugal, Greece, Yugoslavia, Turkey, and Morocco. Initially they were males expected to return to their home country after a short time, but they stayed and brought their families to join them. Additionally, the Netherlands admitted a large number of asylum seekers during the 1990s. However, since 2001 the Netherlands has had some of the strictest asylum policies in Europe. An example of the Dutch change in openness that has occurred is many natives feeling that there are too many foreigners and the place is too crowded.[55]

During the early rise in immigration, the authorities established policies seen as sensitive to ethnic differences and allowing the greatest room for individual cultural differences. However, as immigrant numbers continued to grow, widespread concern about integration of some ethnic groups began to rise. While there are skill-level issues, the problem is usually discursively linked to cultural attributes of certain groups. Extreme right-wing groups have become more vocal and have grown in influence. In their work, Lucassen and Penninx thoroughly reviewed the last four hundred years of immigration to the Netherlands and show that multiple factors affect how each group is received. Some of the more important factors include the size and visibility of the group, its ability to succeed in the economy, and the national economic situation in the early years of absorption.[56] Immigration has occurred in three waves: postcolonial, guest workers, and *allochtonen*.

Postcolonial

The first wave of migration was from the East Indies. After the independence of Indonesia, those of mixed Indonesian and Dutch parentage (Indis) were given a choice of settling in the Netherlands, and about thirty thousand largely educated, middle-class persons accepted from 1946 to 1962. These people were generally accepted by society, and the government instituted several assistance programs.[57] Today persons of Indonesian descent are not counted as an ethnic minority.

In contrast, the exodus from the Moloccas (Maluku) Island of Ambon, a section of islands in the Indonesian chain, was not well received. About 12,500 Moluccas received permission to immigrate, but little government aid for settlement was given. Everyone, government and people, thought the stay would be short and that the Moluccas would return to establish an independent republic of Moluccas. The immigrants were set up in isolated housing markets and restricted from job opportunities. The immigrants included Dutch soldiers who had served on the island and, upon immigrating home, were dismissed from the military and prevented from seeking other employment.[58] Ambon was reconquered by Indonesia in November 1950 after only a few months of independence, closing off any chance of return.[59] In the 1970s many Moluccas youth became disenchanted and turned to violence. The Dutch government took a hard line against the acts of violence and demands of the Moluccas and implemented policies geared toward integration.[60] Today, Moluccas are not counted in ethnic statistics by the government and are considered Dutch.

West Indies immigration followed a similar trajectory. Early immigration was of educated, middle-class people from Surinam, prior to its independence, during the 1960 economic boom and was generally viewed as a good thing for the Netherlands.[61] However, immigrants in the 1970s entered a troubled economy and came after Surinam's independence. These immigrants were not welcomed. "The increasing immigration and the will of the government to end it were the most important factors contributing to the Dutch government's decision to realize the independence of Suriname in 1975."[62] Today the total Surinamese population is about 330,000 with unemployment rates about twice that of white Dutch.[63]

A larger wave of immigrants from the Antilles arrived under even less welcoming circumstances. In 1985 oil refineries were closed in the Antilles and large numbers of lower-class blue-collar workers immigrated to the Netherlands.[64] Prior immigration around the time the colony became an autonomous member of the Kingdom of the Netherlands in 1954 was a slow but steady stream of the educated middle class.[65] From 1985 to 1992 the immigrant population from the Antilles tripled. Van Hulst notes this immigration came at a time of economic downturn and the colonial history of the Antilles had created a sharp class/education split in population, leading to long-term poverty of those who made up the second wave of immigrants.[66] Even today the unemployment rate remains two to three times higher than for white Dutch but less than for Turks and Moroccans.[67]

Guest Workers

Guest workers also came in two waves. The first wave from southern and eastern Europe came in the 1960s at a time of high employment. Most brought over their families shortly after arriving and settled into Dutch society. Reception varied according to education, skill level, and Dutch relations with their home countries.[68] Additionally, established Dutch Catholic groups provided support for fellow Catholic immigrants. Lindo notes that some animosity existed against these groups but the arrival of large groups of Turks and Moroccans distracted public attention away from Italian and southern European immigrants.[69] Additionally, many of the guest workers eventually returned home, so now there are only about 150,000 people who identify themselves as of southern European and Yugoslavian descent in the Netherlands.[70]

Immigrants from Turkey and Morocco came to the Netherlands in small numbers as guest workers in the 1960s with their peak migration just before the closure of the program in 1973. In general Turkish workers were better educated than Moroccans, many of whom lacked any schooling.[71] Most waited a few years before bringing their families, so there was a second surge many years later as part of the family reunification program. Further, as many of the children of these immigrants reached marriage age in the 1980s they brought spouses from their home countries, spiking immigration figures.[72] In 1971 there were about 22,000 Moroccans and 30,000 Turks in the Netherlands. There are about 400,000 Turks and 315,000 Moroccans today.[73]

Allochtonen

Dutch population statistics count the number of nonnationals and *allochtonen* (foreign born)—residents who were born elsewhere or who are the child of one parent born elsewhere.[74] The Central Bureau of Statistics calculates the *allochtonen* as about 20 percent of the population.[75] *Allochtonen* fails to account for ethnic differences except for Western and non-Western. While statistically *allochtonen* can refer to Westerner and non-Westerner, in common speech it is used to refer to a foreigner who is a non-Westerner. Japanese and Indonesian are counted as Westerners, which Vermeleun and Penninx attribute to the fact that many of them come to the Netherlands as employees of corporations that the government wants to attract.[76] In recent years the term "ethnic group" has become popular to refer to immigrants who are seen as poorly integrating and therefore at social and economic disadvantage.[77] Since the 1960s there has been a substantial increase in nonnationals and *allochtonen*. The percentage of Western nonnationals and *allochtonen* has remained steady while the number of non-Western has quadrupled but is even now only about 12 percent of the population.[78] Even though the number remains a small percentage, it is the public perception of the foreigners and of government policies implementing this perception which has changed. Ethnic groups have become concentrated in neighborhoods with low education levels and high unemployment rates.

Part of this reaction is due to the high population density of the Netherlands. The Netherlands is one of the most densely populated countries, 398 inhabitants per square kilometer, much denser than France (117) and the United States (32).[79] UN rankings place the Netherlands as thirty-ninth largest in population and thirty-fourth in land mass while France is twenty-first in population and forty-second in area, and the United States is third in both categories. Additionally, just as in the United States and France, the graying of the baby boomer generation means more people are relying on social welfare benefits. Low birth rates of white Dutch and higher birth rates for non-Western migrants means that distribution by population age is skewed, with white older and decreasing in numbers, while non-Westerners are younger and increasing in numbers.[80]

The low white birth rate is accompanied by a concern for overcrowding via the increase in the immigrant nonwhite population. The numbers suggest that the real anxiety in the traditional population is more about the changing face of the Netherlands rather than the overall population density. Dutch population tripled from 1850 to 1950, from 3 million to 9.5 million, and from 1950 to 2000 to 16.3 million.[81] State statistics show that the population increase since 1980 has remained steady at 0.8 percent, and overall growth has declined about 50 percent over the past fifty years. However, the decline in birth rate is statistically matched by an increase in immigration rate. The overall population is expected to begin decreasing around 2030.[82]

Much of the rhetoric about Dutch social ills focuses around the changing face from white to ethnic, a perception that Dutch traditional identity is disappearing and that immigrants strain the social welfare system. The Netherlands has a history of being a place for refugees, particularly religious ones. However, these were European Sephardic Jews, French Huguenots, and other Europeans. Whether it is statistically true that the new immigrants are less able to integrate and "qualitatively" different is not the issue. The problem arises because the public perception is that there is a qualitative difference that will prevent the immigrants from ever integrating and that threatens Dutch identity and values.

During the early years of the increase in immigration from Muslim countries, public debate focused on assistance and the level of welcoming to the ethnic culture. As time passed and the non-Western population increased, the talk became less politically correct. In 1983 a Ministers Memorandum was issued in which the government expressed resignation to the fact that immigrants were not returning home after work programs concluded, as originally planned by the government. The memorandum expressed a policy of inclusion of the minority cultures by active government preservation.[83]

In the 1990s Liberal Party leader Frits Bolkestein and Social Democrat activist Paul Scheffer began to voice concerns about the dilution of Dutch societal norms and values by the introduction of large numbers of people who do not share those values.[84] The focus was on the Enlightenment or liberal democratic values of free speech and press following the Rushdie affair. Quickly issues of gay and women's rights were added to the discussion. After the Iranian Revolution there was an increase in concern about oppression of women in the Middle East, which some began to see as an integral part of Islam.[85] In 1994 a new policy paper was issued which expressed the view that communities, not government, were responsible for preservation of culture and shifted government focus to economic inclusion. Under the 1997 Newcomers Integration Act, mother-tongue classes were removed from the schools and civic integration classes became mandatory for immigrants.[86] On June 16, 2012, the government announced it was abandoning its policy of multiculturalism. In a press release the government stated:

> The government shares the social dissatisfaction over the multicultural society model and plans to shift priority to the values of the Dutch people. In the new integration system, the values of the Dutch society play a central role. With this change, the government steps away from the model of a multicultural society.
>
> A more obligatory integration is justified because the government also demands that from its own citizens. It is necessary because otherwise the society gradually grows apart and eventually no one feels at home anymore in the Netherlands. The integration will not be tailored to different groups.[87]

Four persons have been leaders of the movement away from multiculturalism: Pim Fortuyn, Theo Van Gogh, Ayaan Hirsi Ali, and Geert Wilders.

ISLAMAPHOBIA AND NATIONAL IDENTITY

The Dutch seem to be at a crossroads in their approach to religion—will it continue to be accommodationist, allowing a public place for religious expression, or move to a segregationist style, removing religious manifestations from public eyes? Thus, it sits between France and the United States. The political debates are tied with broader issues of immigration and wax and wane as individuals and political parties are able to build the symbolic myth of the veil. The judiciary, including quasi-judicial bodies, has largely avoided the political winds. It has become a proponent of human rights, neither privileging nor narrowing religious expression. The Dutch veiling debates revolve around individual politicians and political parties. Two events ark the points of sharp break in Dutch political feelings toward Muslims: the assassinations of Fortuyn and Van Gogh.

Pim Fortuyn

Pim Fortuyn was a politician and outspoken critic of open immigration policies.[88] He declared a "cold war" on Islam in the Netherlands due chiefly to Islam's stance on homosexuality. He advocated assimilation, not multiculturalism, which was the government policy until early 2012. Fortuyn sought attention and established a political party named after himself to carry out his ideas.[89] He argued that Islam was backward and intolerant. Therefore, Islam could not be tolerated in the Netherlands regardless of individual concessions to Dutch values. Fortuyn focused on anti-immigrant sentiment and Islamic rejection of homosexuality. He flaunted his own homosexuality in contrast to Dutch circumspection of sexuality and claimed a special insight into the Muslim threat due to his sexual preference.[90] He was able to move a marginalized view of immigration and Islam in the country to the limelight and stoke the fires of fear to advocate eradication in lieu of *poldermodel* for Muslims.

Just before the elections of 2002 Fortuyn was assassinated by a non-Muslim animal rights advocate who claimed he committed the murder to stop Fortuyn from using Muslims as both a scapegoat for social ills and as a means to achieve political power.[91] The assassin even went so far, in a speech to the court during his murder trial, as to compare Fortuyn to Hitler and claimed he was saving Dutch society from Nazism.[92] This political assassination, only the third in Dutch history, shocked the nation.[93] In a poll before his death Fortuyn's party was not expected to do well in the election, but with his death his party picked up enough seats to become a member of the coalition government. However, internal problems and an inability to successfully navigate the business of government led to their and the government's downfall less than a year later. Fortuyn's party lost a large number of seats and was no longer a factor in Dutch politics. Anti-immigrant voters moved their allegiance to new leaders, particularly Theo Van Gogh.

Theo Van Gogh

The second shock which solidified the fear of Islam in the minds of the Dutch public occurred in 2004 with the assassination of Theo Van Gogh.[94] Van Gogh was a filmmaker and vocal critic of all of traditional society, particularly religion. Van Gogh was assassinated by an extremist Dutch Muslim claiming to act to protect Islam. The assassination occurred after Van Gogh had worked with politician and Somali refugee Ayaan Hirsi Ali in making a film critical of Islam.[95] Van Gogh's assassin's note claiming responsibility stated that he would have preferred to murder Ali but she was too difficult to reach. Even though Van Gogh was an unpopular lightning rod for controversy before his assassination, his death granted him martyrdom in the name of Dutch values. Van Gogh's assassin was born and raised in the Netherlands but was of Moroccan descent. The public perception became that the tolerant, peaceful oasis of the Netherlands was under siege, and the enemy was the intolerant, violent religion of Islam. Ayaan Hirsi Ali and Geert Wilders took up this fight against the enemy.

Ayaan Hirsi Ali

Ayaan Hirsi Ali is a strident critic of Islam, particularly regarding women's rights. Her rhetoric focuses on her early years in Somalia and claims of being a victim of abuse. Feminist groups use her as proof that Islam is abusive to women to argue that no part of it can be tolerated in the Netherlands.

She is the author of the film *Submission* that she made with Theo Van Gogh. The film superimposes quotes from the Quran about women's need to submit to men and restrictions of their rights in society over images of women wearing see-through *burqas* and veils. The sole purpose of the film is to show that Islam is misogynist and not compatible with Western norms of human rights. She also argues that shari'a law is "as inimical to liberal democracy as Nazism" and is inherently violent.[96]

Ali served as a member of Parliament until her downfall, which also indirectly led to the downfall of the government in 2006.[97] Her claims of abuse in Somalia began to be challenged, and she was forced to admit exaggerations in her application for asylum.[98] She left the Netherlands, claiming fear of assassination, but by the time she left her power had been largely degraded. Even though her individual power has lessened, the feminist critique of Islam has not abated. While Ali's voice has left the Netherlands, the mantle was taken up by many others. Most successful recently is Geert Wilders.

Geert Wilders

Geert Wilders was already politically active when the issue of immigration became the focus of his dissatisfaction. His hardening of position caused him to leave the large Liberal Party (VVD) to form his own Freedom Party (PVV). He takes a hard line against Islam and wants a complete ban on all immigration from Islamic countries.[99] His party was able to garner enough seats in the States-General in the 2008 elections to influence the policies of the ruling coalition. In this position he was able to force abandonment of the official multicultural policy and reintroduce a bill to ban the *burqa* and a tax on women wearing the headscarf.[100] A backlash due to changes in multicultural policy, immigration reforms seen as racist, and his proposed *burqa* ban, along with Wilders's refusal to join proposed economic reforms, led to the fall of the coalition government and elections in 2012.[101]

In the 2012 elections and all elections since, the PVV has been steadily losing seats and is no longer part of the coalition government.[102] However, Wilders's international celebrity continues to give him a platform for anti-Islamic and anti-Dutch egalitarian rhetoric. He advocates abandonment of broad egalitarianism because it offers tolerance to the intolerant, among whom he includes Islam in any form. While Wilders himself is outspoken and flamboyant, he sells himself as an ordinary, unassuming patriot trying to return the country to its pure Dutch roots.

THE VEILING DEBATES

After September 11, the London and Madrid bombings, and the assassinations of Van Gogh and Fortuyn, political correctness was abandoned by many. Debates focused on Islam and whether there was any way the immigrants could be *made* to fit into Dutch society. One example seen by some as proof that Islam cannot fit into Dutch society is women's religious dress. Others see the allowance of religious dress as proof that Dutch society is holding to its values. The debate over the headscarf and veil in the Netherlands is delineated in three ways:

1. by the dress being worn: headscarf (*hijab*), full body covering with or without face veil (*burqa*), and just the face covering or veil (*niqab*); and
2. by the institution the debate is before: policy, legislation, judicial decision; and
3. context: employment, education, public areas.

In the Netherlands many of the judicial issues have occurred in the employment context and have been heard by the Equal Treatment Commission

(ETC). In general the commission has ruled that the headscarf is allowed under anti-discrimination laws and that freedom of religion as provided for in the constitution is a fundamental right. Following precedent, the commission has held that restrictions of freedom of religion must be narrowly tailored to achieve a "legitimate goal" (important and neutral) which cannot be achieved in another manner.[103] The context in which the covering is considered is of primary concern. The European Court of Human Rights observed in the landmark headscarf case of *Sahin v. Turkey* that in the Netherlands "[t]he question of the Islamic headscarf is considered from the standpoint of discrimination rather than of freedom of religion, it is generally tolerated."[104]

Issues in the Netherlands over the headscarf and veil arose first in the context of education in 1985. In 1985 the school board of the town of Alphen aan de Rijn forbade Muslim girls at the local public secular primary school from wearing a headscarf, and local public faith-based Christian schools also enacted prohibitions.[105] Local parents protested, claiming infringement of religious liberty. A question was put to the Ministry of Education to respond to the issue in the weekly parliamentary debates. The minister responded that the practice of wearing headscarves is protected religious freedom. The local public school authorities complied. Faith-based school cooperation has been mixed.[106]

In another early case, in the town of Helmond a public Roman Catholic school forbade the wearing of the headscarf and denied students' requests to be excused from coed swimming classes and to wear tracksuits in other mixed physical education classes.[107] The city court of justice ruled that the private school was not required to follow the same rules as public schools, so the prohibitions were allowable. The court also rested its decision on the fact that there were public schools available to the children. In December 1993 several private Christian schools in Amsterdam prohibited the wearing of the headscarf.

The Equal Treatment Commission also ruled against a public faith-based Roman Catholic school in Volendom, the Don Bosco secondary school, in a case challenging a headscarf ban at the school.[108] The school argued that it had a right to make its religion the only one recognized on school grounds. In 2011 the commission ruled that the ban discriminated against Muslim students because consistent identity was not essential to the school. The school refused to comply with the decision, which it was not legally obligated to do because commission rulings are advisory only. However, refusal to obey a commission ruling is rare and viewed by the general public as improper conduct. The student appealed to the Harleem district court. The court ruled against the student, agreeing that a faith-based school's right to make its religion the only one visible on school grounds overrode her right of individual religious freedom.[109]

In the context of employment of a teacher in a public (nonfaith) school, the commission has held that the wearing of a headscarf cannot be banned.[110] In 1998 a public primary school teacher trainee wore a headscarf to school. The school board ordered her to remove it, arguing that the public school is to be neutral and needed to protect liberal Islamic girls from pressure to conform. The commission viewed state neutrality not on the student's perception of the teacher but rather whether the school was treating the trainee neutrally because this was an employment discrimination case. The commission held that the trainee was being discriminated against because the restriction would limit her job opportunities to religious schools only, while other teachers could seek employment both in public and religious schools. Further, the alleged pressure on students to copy the act was not proven. Just because the trainee wears a headscarf does not mean that the trainee does not "hav[e] an open attitude and . . . is not capable of teaching in accordance with the character of the school as a public educational institution."[111] Precedent allowed other religious displays in schools, thus the same standard applied to Islamic schools, an equal treatment standard. Accordingly, there was no infringement on the neutral space of the school.

The *ETC* has ruled against wearing the face veil but did so applying existing legal standards.[112] In 2003 two students in training to become kindergarten teachers began wearing face veils to classes. The school ordered them to stop. The student teachers brought a case to the Equal Treatment Commission. The trainees conceded that in the future while teaching or when working with only women or children they would remove the veils. The commission applied an existing two-step analysis utilized in all discrimination cases. First, the court determines if discrimination as provided in the law has occurred. If so, then the court determines if the discrimination is in furtherance of a legitimate goal and is narrowly tailored to meet that goal. If so, the restriction is permitted. In this case, the commission held that a rule which prohibits covering the face disproportionately affects one religious group, so it is discriminatory; however, expert evidence proved the prohibition is legitimate and narrowly tailored. Expert testimony showed that uncovering the face is necessary for effective communication between teachers and pupils, is necessary for public safety and identification, and covering impairs the school's task of preparing student teachers to fulfill the social service job of teaching children. Therefore, the requirement that everyone have an open face at school is legitimate in that it is narrowly tailored, only applies in class, and meets an important goal, proper training of teachers.

In 2003 the Equal Treatment Commission approved a regulation proposed by the Regional Center for Occupational Education (ROC) to prohibit the wearing of face veils by students and teachers. The ROC reasoned that face-to-face communication was essential to the learning process, outweighing the general right of religious liberty.[113] The Board of Governors of Leiden University implemented a similar rule the same year, also arguing that proper identification is necessary for examinations. Following suit, the Association of Dutch Universities (VSNU) adopted a nonbinding prohibition for all Dutch universities. Few adopted the rule. The policy statements by government have also utilized this case-by-case approach but have become more generous to individual school interpretation of the need to restrict the scarf or veil. A 2003 Ministry of Education clothing directive, which is advisory only, held that a general ban was improper as religious discrimination. However, if there are safety concerns (physical education classes), it can be restricted. Additionally, faith-based schools may only restrict it if such has been consistently and strictly enforced by the school on all religions. Face veils can be restricted on the basis of open communication. The same rules apply to teachers.[114]

The commission applied the same reasoning in cases in which employers require employees to wear the headscarf. A Muslim teacher applicant to an Islamic college which required Muslim women to wear a headscarf on school grounds alleged improper denial of employment because she refused to wear a headscarf. The applicant alleged the rule was discriminatory because non-Muslim teachers were not required to wear a headscarf. The commission agreed and ruled that employees were being treated unequally based on religion and that the rule did not fulfill a legitimate goal. The college refused to comply with the decision.

Similar reason has been applied in other public employment cases. In 2000 a local court refused to hire a woman to act as a court clerk because she refused to take off her headscarf while in court sessions. In the Netherlands court personnel wear a uniform black toga or robe with a white front. The employer court argued that the appearance of a headscarf on a court staff member threatened the public's trust in the neutrality of the court. The commission ruled that in this context the appearance of impartiality was a major component of public trust, but in a multicultural society it was not necessary for public employees to hide all personal religious beliefs, and the head scarf is not per se a signal of a lack of impartiality.[115] As allowed under Dutch law, the national justice minister intervened and ordered all court personnel to remove all clothing which manifests personal religious beliefs while in courtrooms to eliminate questions about partiality that might impair trust in the system.[116] The proponents of the ban cited Lady Justice's blindfold as evidence that all personal views must be scrubbed from the system to ensure impartiality. The balance of neutrality in this situation requires a cleansed public space that takes precedence over individual religious freedom.[117] Additionally, the National Board for Jurisdiction, the administrative body for court operations, entered a decree that no religious symbols of any kind may be visible in any courtroom.[118]

Another controversy with public employees arose about police officers in uniform wearing the headscarf. The National Board of Police Commissioners initiated a plan for developing a uniform headscarf which policewomen would be allowed to wear on duty, except, for safety reasons, in the Mobile Force (SWAT).[119] The plan was part of a desire to attract more ethnic police officers and improve relations in ethnic communities. The police union agreed, adding that it protected the religious freedom of officers.[120]

A boisterous public protest resulted. The protest again focused on neutrality in public space. Paul Scheffer argued that accommodating the headscarf would be yielding space to an ideology wanting to abolish Dutch separation of church and state and asserted that the Dutch way required restriction of religious symbols to the private sphere. This need for a cleansed public space overrides individual religious freedom as well as the police force's need for personnel and desire to improve relations with ethnic communities.[121]

The board reversed course and issued a recommendation that all officers in uniform strive for a "lifestyle neutral" appearance when dealing with the public. Lifestyle neutral precludes wearing all clothing which demonstrates a religious or personal belief, body piercings, and long hair on males. The PVV came to greater power with the coalition government and proposed making the restriction on court personnel and police a law. The proposed law was forwarded to the Ministry of Interior Affairs and Kingdom Relations, asking for its implementation as a national regulation for all police forces. The ministry forwarded the request to the Equal Treatment Commission for analysis. The commission ruled that police officers, like court personnel, must appear impartial to all persons; however, this does not necessarily preclude expression of any personal religious belief, and it recommended against implementation of the restriction due to its indirect discriminatory effect. The commission specifically cited the possible deleterious effect on Muslim women who might want to join the police force and those observing police officers.[122] The police union also objected, calling for a code of conduct rule only. The government fell while the proposal was still pending in Parliament. The ban was ultimately implemented via a code of conduct. The rule prohibits all religious symbols, piercings, tattoos, and unusual hairstyles.[123]

Private employers have also faced discrimination claims from Muslim women regarding the headscarf. Two notable cases involve a doctor's assistant and a supermarket employee who were fired for wearing the headscarf. The employers argued they were employed in a position which presented the face of the office so the employer had the right to regulate that appearance. The employees agreed the employer had a right to a professional appearance and work but argued that the headscarf did not violate professionalism and that religious freedom entitled them to wear the scarf. The commission held these were cases of discrimination and ordered the employees to be reinstated. The commission and courts have generally ruled in favor of employees in other cases, holding that, except for safety reasons, employers should accommodate the headscarf and other religious dress. It has recommended that private employers who require uniforms work with employees to find a means of accommodation for headscarves, Sikh turbans, and beards. For the most part private employers have been more accommodating to employee requests than public employers.

In local government contexts, some cities have prohibited employees from wearing the face veil even when no one has worn it or expressed a desire to do so. In 2005 the issue hit the national States-General when Geert Wilders proposed a ban on the *burqa* and *niqab* in public during debates on legislation for the prevention of terrorism. The minister of integration, Rita Verdonk, appointed a commission to study the proposal's legal and social consequences.[124] In its report the commission found that a ban specifically prohibiting the *burqa* and *niqab* would violate the Dutch Constitution's clauses on and Dutch principles about nondiscrimination, freedom of religion, and freedom of choice.[125] The commission did recognize that the practice of veiling emanates from a view of women's inferiority and can be scary to some people; however, these concerns did not outweigh the protection of constitutional rights and Dutch liberal principles. The commission also concluded that rewording the ban to general face coverings would not remedy the discriminatory effect because the only group affected by the ban would be Muslim women. The commission did conclude a limited ban, such as in public transportation or government offices, could be appropriate due to site-specific safety and identity concerns. The Parliament began voting to enact the bill before the report was received. The government fell before the ban could be fully enacted.[126]

In the new government another ban was proposed. In response to this proposal the Council of State asserted it is improper because it targeted *burqas*, which it held to be religious dress. Thus, the law was a violation of religious freedom and equality under Dutch and international norms.[127] Additionally, the argument that the ban is needed for safety is inadequate because the ban applies to *burqas* only and not other face coverings.[128] Both private bills remained pending when the PVV made the issue one for the government.[129]

Geert Wilders's party (PVV) made significant gains in the 2010 elections to the point that its agreement to a coalition government was necessary. In forming the coalition government the leading party agreed to change the official multicultural policy and to propose a *burqa* ban. The 2012 version of the Dutch *burqa* ban provides:

1. The wearing of the *burqa* in public spaces is prohibited.
2. For the purposes of this law the term "public space" includes places or settings open to the public and in which a public service takes place.

3. In case of violation of the prohibition as provided for in Article 1, there will be a sanction of imprisonment up to 10 days or a penalty of 3000 Euro.
4. Those who encourage or force others to wear the *burqa* will be sentenced to one year in prison and 10000 euro.
5. Articles 1–3 of this law will enter into force 6 months after its publication in the official journal, whereas Article 4 will enter into force immediately after its publication in the official journal.
6. This law shall not apply to persons in international travel transit terminals and places of worship.

The Council of Ministers passed the proposal to Parliament, with supporters arguing that requiring women to cover their face hinders open communication and violates gender equality.[130] Because the Council of Ministers accepted the proposal, all members of government were required to publicly voice support for the ban and encourage Parliament to pass it.

In a policy paper addressed to the Dutch government considering the 2012 ban, Elena Bossi opposed the proposal as violating ECHR article 9 (freedom of religion) because it is not limited in time and space.[131] Bossi concludes that "the draft law is very risky for the Dutch government, who could be charged with a pecuniary compensation by the ECHR." She did theorize that, under current ECtHR rulings, restrictions limited to public primary school teachers may be permissible. Mauritis Berger, professor at Leiden University, stated that "[t]hese policies [*burqa* ban and strong anti-immigrant] were driven by PVV but also by the government in order to maintain their relationship with PVV. They have turned Holland into a pariah. . . . These are the legacy of the PVV. Face veils, dual nationality—both these proposals have not been really thought through."[132] Wilders was blamed for the fall of the government in 2012, and the PVV lost a significant number of seats to the point that it is not a member of the new government. After the elections, the Christian Democrats stated that they would no longer support the proposed *burqa* ban, removing majority support for the ban. In addition, Dutch immigration minister Gerd Leers announced the government would no longer push anti-immigration issues, in part due to the public relations nightmare created by Wilders's inclusion of Polish immigrants in his anti-immigrant rhetoric.[133]

On May 22, 2015, the Dutch cabinet voted to place a proposal for a limited ban on face coverings before the National Assembly. The new ban applies to all face coverings and does not specify the *burqa*. Further, the ban is limited to educational and health care facilities and public buildings and transportation. This proposal must be sent to the Council of State for constitutional review. It is believed that the proposal will be held to be constitutional because it does not specify the *burqa*, is limited in time and space, and is less broad than the French ban, which the ECtHR upheld in *S.A.S.*

Another signal that political forces are moderating on immigrants can be seen in the Amsterdam city council's announcement that it will no longer use the terms "*allochtoon*" and "*autochtoon*."[134] They conclude the term "*allochtoon*" is divisive because it is primarily used to refer to non-Western immigrants. First-generation immigrants will be referred to by their country of origin hyphenated with *Amsterdammer* (Turkish-*Amsterdammer*) and second-generation as foreign *Amsterdammer*. Later generations will not have any designation other than *Amsterdammer*. The national cabinet's advisory group on social development has recommended that the government stop the categorization of persons according to ethnicity or parental birthplace.

Dutch tolerance is still challenged with regard to the treatment of Muslim women, but the judicial branch is holding firm to the liberal principle of equal treatment underlying Dutch society. The only exceptions have come when communication and safety reasons provide an overriding justification. In the political arena there is a strong voice that is anti-immigrant, which mythologizes the headscarf and face veil as emblematic of a clash of civilizations, but other voices seem to be practicing *poldermodel* in an attempt to reach a balanced consensus. The emphasis on women's equal rights and nondiscrimination in the Netherlands appears to be aiding the attempt to include Muslim immigrants, even with their cultural differences, so long as they too join in the liberal vision of nondiscrimination and women's equality.

NOTES

The official state is the Kingdom of the Netherlands. The kingdom consists of Aruba, Curacao, St. Marteen, and the Netherlands. The Netherlands includes the Caribbean islands of Bonair, Saba and St. Eustatius, and the Netherlands area in Europe. This discussion only involves the European portion of the Netherlands.

National motto: I will hold firm.

1. Erin Martineau, "'Too Much Tolerance': Hang-Around Youth, Public Space and the Problem of Freedom in the Netherlands" (PhD diss., City University of New York, 2006), 35–38.
2. http://www.government.nl; http://state.gov/r/pa/ei/bgn/3204.htm.
3. Paul Arblaster, *A History of the Low Countries*, 2nd ed. (New York: Palgrave, 2011), 111–49.
4. William Shetter, *The Netherlands in Perspective: The Dutch Way of Organizing a Society and Its Setting* (Utrecht: Nederlands Centrum Buitenlanders, 1997); Jonathan Israel, *The Dutch Republic: Its Rise, Greatness, and Fall, 1477–1806* (Oxford: Clarendon Press, 1995); Rudy Andeweg and Galen Irwin, *Governance and Politics of the Netherlands,* 3rd ed. (New York: Palgrave, 2009); J. C. H. Blom and E. Lambert, eds., *History of the Low Countries* (Amsterdam: Berghahn, 2006).
5. John Lothrop Motley, *The Rise of the Dutch Republic* (1856; Project Gutenberg, 2004), http://www.gutenberg.org/ebooks/4836.
6. The Peace of Westphalia is a series of treaties. The part known as the Peace of Munster is the treaty which deals with the independence of the Dutch Republic.

7. The Edict of Nantes (1598) was a French truce in its war on French Protestants (Huguenots). The edict permitted them to live in France under restriction or to leave peacefully. After its repeal by the Edict of Fontainbleau (1685) there was a mass exodus of Huguenots to Great Britain, the Dutch Republic, Switzerland, Prussia, South Africa, and the American colonies.
8. Glenn Ames, *The Globe Encompassed: The Age of European Discovery, 1500–1700* (New York: Prentice Hall, 2005).
9. Israel.
10. Andeweg and Irwin, 21.
11. There have been fifteen revisions to the constitution but only the 1815 and 1848 altered the basic government structure. English versions of the Dutch constitutions may be found at http://www.sevat.unibe.cn/icl/nl100000.html.
12. J. C. H. Blom, "The Second World War and Dutch Society: Continuity and Change," in *Britain and the Netherlands VI: War and Society*, ed. A. C. Duke and C. A. Tamse (The Hague: Nijhoff, 1977), 228–48, 227 quoted in Andeweg and Irwin, 20.
13. Arblaster, 211 et seq.
14. Article 1, prohibition of discrimination; article 3, right of all Dutch nationals to be eligible for office; article 23, freedom of association and expression; article 23 continues equal funding of all schools, public (secular) and faith-based. http://www.sevat.unibe.cn/icl/nl100000.html.
15. Shetter.
16. Andeweg and Irwin, 33–38, 176–79.
17. See Shetter and Andeweg and Irwin.
18. J. E. Ellemers, "The Netherlands in the Sixties," *The Netherlands Journal for Sociology*, 17 (1981): 132, http://www.webdoc.ubn.kun.nl/tijd/n/nethjoofs/; Marineau, 20.
19. Isabel Hoving, "Circumventing Openness: Creating a New Sense of Dutchness," *TRANSIT: Migration, Culture and the Nation-State* 1, no. 1 (2005): 2, https://escholarship.org/uc/item/1g62t/wx.
20. Hoving, 3.
21. Hoving, 6.
22. Peter Van Rooden, "History, the Nation and Religion: The Transformation of the Dutch Religious Past," in *Nation and Religion: Perspectives on Europe and Asia*, ed. Hartmut Lehmann and Peter van de Veer (Princeton: Princeton University Press, 1999), 96–111.
23. Andeweg and Irwin, 30–31.
24. Andeweg and Irwin, 31–32.
25. Andeweg and Irwin, 31–32.
26. Adeweg and Irwin, 32–33.
27. Van Rooden, 99–102.
28. Van Rooden, 103–4
29. Hans Daalder, "On the Origins of the Consociational Democracy Model," *Acta Politica* 19 (1984): 97–117.
30. Van Rooden, 104.
31. Shetter, 115.
32. Paul Dekker and Peter Ester, "Depillarization, Deconfessionalization, and De-ideologization: Empirical Trends in Dutch Society, 1958–1992," *Review of Religious Research* 317, no. 6 (June 1996): 325–241, http://www.jstor.org.stable/3512012.
33. James Kennedy, *Building the New Babylon: The Netherlands in the Sixties*, 3d ed. (Amsterdam: Boom, 1999), 25. For example, see the works of Abraham Kuyper.
34. Joris Voorhoes, *Peace, Profits and Principles: A Study of Dutch Foreign Policy* (The Hague: Nijihoff, 1979).
35. Kennedy, 46; Andeweg and Irwin, 208–25.
36. Kennedy, 82; Andeweg and Irwin, 218–19.
37. Kennedy, 136–45.
38. Kennedy, 15–16.
39. US State Department, *International Religious Freedom Report*, http://www.state.gov/j/drl/rls/irf/religiousfreedom/index.htm?dlid=192845; Statistics Netherlands, http://www.cbs.nl/en-GB/menu/themes/vrije-tjid-cultur/publications/artiken/archief/2012/2012–3759-wm.htm.

40. http://www.cbs.nl/en-GB/menu/themes/vrije-tjid-cultur/publications/artiken/archief/2012/2012–3759-wm.htm. Hereafter, CBS.

41. CBS.

42. "Public Broadcasters to Cut Sport, Amusement and Human Interest Shows," DutchNews.nl, 1 January 2013, http://www.dutchnews.nl/news/archives/2013/01/public-broadcast-ters-to-cut-spo.php (accessed January 3, 2013).

43. *Staatkundig Gereformeerde Partij v. Netherlands*, application no. 58369/10, 10 July 2012, Third Section, http://www.hudoc.echr.coe.int/sites/eng/pages/serach.aspx?i=001–112340. It is interesting to note that the number of *Geer* and the number of Muslims in the Netherlands are about the same.

44. *Staatkundig Gereformeerde Partij v. Netherlands.*

45. The age for voting has been lowered from twenty-five to eighteen. Appearing at the polling place on election day was compulsory until 1970.

46. Andeweg and Irwin, 164.

47. J. Visser and A. Hemerijck, *"A Dutch Miracle": Job Growth, Welfare Reform and Corporatism in the Netherlands* (Amsterdam: Amsterdam University Press, 1997), 33.

48. "Work and Health Statistics in the Netherlands," European Foundation for the Improvement of Living and Working Conditions, http://www.eurofound.europa.eu/ewcol/surveys/NL0403SR01/ NL0403SR01.pdf.

49. "Women's Labour Force Participation," http://www.governemnt.nl/issues/gender-equality/womens-labour-force-participation.

50. Wil Portegijs, Annemarie Boelens, and Linda Olsthorn, *Emancipatiemonitor 2004* (Report on emancipation 2004), ed. Sociaal en Cultureel Plaanbureau (Social and Cultural Planning Office). http://www.scp.nl/dsresource?objectid=20863andtyp e=org.

51. "The Netherlands: Gender discrimination in the Field of Employment," report contains links to specific statutes, http://www.equalrtstrust.org/ert/documentbank/microsoft%20Word%20-%20Netherlands-gender-employment.pdf.

52. "The Netherlands."

53. "Women's Labour Force Participation," no. 42.

54. Indonesia declared independence in 1945. The Netherlands recognized it in 1949.

55. Willem Maas, "Citizenship and Immigration in the Netherlands," in *Migrant and Minorities: The European Response*, ed. Adam Luedtke (New York: Cambridge Scholars Publishing, 2010), 226–43.

56. Jan Lucassen and Rinus Penninx, *Newcomers: Immigrants and Their Descendants in the Netherlands, 1550–1995*, trans. Michael Wintle (Amsterdam: Het Spinhus, 1997).

57. Hans Vermeulen and Rinus Penninx, Introduction to *Immigrant Integration: The Dutch Case*, ed. Hans Vermeulen and Rinus Penninx (Amsterdam: Het Spinhus, 2000), 6–7.

58. Henk Smeets and Justus Veenman, "More and More at Home: Three Generations of Moluccans in the Netherlands," in *Immigrant Integration: The Dutch Case*, ed. Hans Vermeulen and Rinus Penninx (Amsterdam: Spinhuis, 2000), 38–39.

59. The Republic of Molucca continued on another island until its leader was executed by the Indonesian government in 1966. A government in exile still exists in the Netherlands.

60. Smeets and Veenman, 40–41.

61. Mies van Niekerk, "Paradoxes in Paradise: Integration and Social Mobility of the Surinamese in the Netherlands," in *Immigrant Integration: The Dutch Case*, ed. Hans Vermeulen and Rinus Penninx (Amsterdam: Spinhuis, 2000), 64–92.

62. Vermeleun and Penninx, 7.

63. Vermeleun and Penninx, 13.

64. Hans van Hulst, "A Continuing Construction of Crisis: Antilleans, Especially Curacaoans, in the Netherlands," in *Immigrant Integration: The Dutch Case*, ed. Hans Vermeulen and Rinus Penninx (Amsterdam: Spinhuis, 2000), 93–122.

65. Van Hulst, 92.

66. Van Hulst, 93–100.

67. Vermeleun and Penninx, 12.

68. Flip Lindo, "The Silent Success: The Social Advancement of Southern European Labor Migrants in the Netherlands," in *Immigrant Integration: The Dutch Case*, ed. Hans Vermeulen and Rinus Penninx (Amsterdam: Spinhuis, 2000), 129.

69. Lindo,132.

70. Vermeleun and Penninx, 12.

71. Anita Bocker, "Paving the Way to a Better Future: Turks in the Netherlands," in *Immigrant Integration: The Dutch Case*, ed. Hans Vermeulen and Rinus Penninx (Amsterdam: Spinhuis, 2000), 156.

72. Bocker, 155.

73. Vermeleun and Penninx, 12.

74. Children with one Dutch-citizen parent and one born elsewhere may apply for citizenship after the age of eighteen.

75. About 12 percent of the population has a non-Western background and about 9 percent Western foreign background. The non-Western has increased from about 2 percent in 1972. http://www.cbs.nl/en-GB/menu/themas/dossiers/allochtonen/nieuws/default.htm and http://www.cbs.nl/en-GB/menu/themas/dossiers/allochtonen/publicaties/artikelen/archief/2012/2012-b72-pub.pdf (accessed June 10, 2012).

76. Vermeleun and Penninx, 20–21.

77. Lucassen and Penninx, 21–22.

78. See note 66.

79. UN Economic Commission for Europe, http://www.unece.org/stats/social-demographics; unece.org/pxweb/quickstatistics/readtableasp?qs_id=22.

80. UN world population report, http://www.un.org.esa/population/publications/worldageing19502050/esa.un.org/wpp/country-rpofiles/pdf528.pdf.

81. CBS, n. 41.

82. CBS; UN World Population Statistics.

83. Han Entzinger, "Changing the Rules while the Game Is On: From Multiculturalism to Assimilation in the Netherlands," in *Migration, Citizenship, Ethnos: Incorporation Regimes in Germany, Western Europe and North America*, eds. Y. Michal Bodemann and Gokce Yurdakul (New York: Palgrave, 2006), 121–44. Also available as a pdf at http://migrationeducation.org/fileadmin/uploads/HanEntzingerNL.pdf.

84. Andeweg and Irwin, 45–46; Justus Uitermark, *Dynamics of Power in Dutch Integration Politics: From Accommodation to Confrontation* (Amsterdam: Amsterdam University Press, 2012), 77–92; Ian Buruma, *Murder in Amsterdam: The Death of Theo Van Gogh and the Limits of Tolerance* (New York: Penguin Press, 2006), 29–37.

85. Uitermark, 77 et seq.

86. Entzinger, 121–44; Maas, 226–43.

87. http://www.eutimes.net/2011/06/the-netherlands-to-abandon-multiculturalism/; The cover letter and policy plan can be found at http://rijksoverheid.nl.Aanbiedngsbrief-integratienota.pdf.

88. Peter Jan Margry, "The Murder of Pim Fortuyn and Collective Emotions: Hype, Hysteria and Holiness in the Netherlands," *Etnofoor: Antropologiseh tijdschrift* 16 (2003): 106–31, http://www.jstor.org/ stable/ 25758060.

89. Margry, 10.

90. Andeweg and Irwin, 23–22; Uitermark, 92–100.

91. http://www.telegraph.co/uk/news/worldnews/europe/netherlands/1425944/Fortuyn-killed (accessed June 8, 2012).

92. Andeweg and Irwin, 22–24; Uitermark, 97; http://www.telegraph.co.uk/news/worldnews/europe/netherlands/1425944; http://www.nytimes.com/2002/05/07/news/07iht-dutch_ed3
.html (accessed June 8, 2012).

93. The other two assassinations were Willem van Oranje in 1584 and Johan de Witt in 1672.

94. Buruma.

95. http://www.news.bbc.co.uk/2/hi/Europe/3974179.stm (accessed June 10, 2012).

96. http://www.aei.org/scholar/ayaan-hirsi-ali (accessed June 10, 2012).

97. "Dutch MP to Step Down," 30 June 2006, CNN, http://www.cnn.com/2006/WORLD/europe/06/29/ netherlands.index.html (accessed June 10, 2012).

98. http://www.independent.co.uk/news/world/europe/dutch-uturn-over-passport-for-somal-iborn-MP-465771.html (accessed June 10, 2012).

99. Maas 226–43.

100. http://www.Geertwilders.nl; http://www.groep.wilder.com.

101. "Dutch PM Says Government Austerity Talks Collapse," *Washington Post*, http://www.washingtonpost.com/business/reports-dutch-government-austerity-talks-collapse-possibly-paving-the-way-for-fresh-elections/2012/04/21/gIQAR.html (accessed January 12, 2013).

102. http://www.dutchnews.nl/news/archives/2012/09/the-election-massive-win-for-VVD.php (accessed January 12, 2013).

103. Commissie Gelijke Behandeling (Equal Treatment Commission), judgment 2003–40, previously at http://cgb.nl, now at http://mensenrechten.nl; hereafter, I will cite Equal Treatment Commission judgments as ETC Judgment [case number]. See also Sawatri Saharso, "Headscarves: A Comparison of Public Thought in Germany and the Netherlands," *Critical Review of International Social and Political Philosophy* 10, no. 4 (December 2007): 519, http://dx.doi.org/10.1080/13698230701660204.

104. *Leyla Sahin v. Turkey*, Grand Chamber, application no. 44774/98, judgment of 10 November 2005.

105. In the Netherlands, state funding is provided to secular and faith-based schools. There can also be privately funded schools. W. Shadid and P. S. van Koningsveld, "Muslim Dress in Europe: Debates on the Headscarf," *Journal of Islamic Studies* 16, no. 1 (2005): 35–61, 49, http://dx.doi.org/10.1091/jis/eti002.

106. Brigit Sauer, "Headscarf Regimes in Europe: Diversity Policies at the Intersection of Gender, Culture and Religion," *Comparative European Politics* 7, no. 1 (2009): 82, http://ezproxy.baylor.edu/login?url=http://search.proquest.com/docview/222264753?accountid=7014.

107. Shadid and Van Koningsveld, 50.

108. Catholic school ban on headscarf, http://www.cgb.nl/nieuws/bericaht/1000000743/verbod_ hoofddoek_op_katholieke_school; the court's opinion is available at http://www.njcm.nl/site/jurisprudentie/show/60.

109. Catholic school ban on headscarf.

110. ETC Judgment 99–18:3–4, http://www.mensenrechten.nl. See discussion in Saharso.

111. ETC Judgment 99–18:3–4.

112. ETC Judgment 2003–40. See discussion in Saharso, 520–521.

113. Saharso, 513.

114. *Leidraad Kleding op Scholen* (June 11, 2003), WJL/2003/23379; Saharso, 513.

115. ETC Judgment 2001–53; see discussion in Odile Verhaar and Sawitri Sahraso, "The Weight of Context: Headscarves in Holland," *Ethical Theory and Moral Practice* 7, no. 2 (2004): 185–88, http://www.jstor.org/stable/27504308.

116. M. Kuijer, "Vrouwe Justitia: Blinddock of Hoofddoen?" *NJCM Bulletin* 7 (2001): 890–903, http://www.njcm.nl/site/bulletins/bulletin_info.

117. Verhaar and Saharso, 188.

118. Verhaar and Saharso, 189.

119. Verhaar and Saharso, 181.

120. Verhaar and Saharso, 182.

121. Verhaar and Saharso, 182.

122. ETC Judgment 2008–123.

123. http://www.Dutchnews.nl/new/archives/2011/07/police-to-be-barred-from-wearing-crosses-and-headscarves, 13 July 2011 (accessed June 14, 2012).

124. "Dutch Government Backs Burqa Ban, 17 November 2006, BBC, http://www.news.bbc.co.uk/2/hi/Europe/615–9046.stm (accessed June 13, 2012).

125. Gerhard van der Schyff and Adriaan Overbeeke, "Exercising Religious Freedom in the Public Space: A Comparative and European Convention Analysis of General Burqa Bans," *European Constitutional Law Review* 7 (2011): 433–34, http://dx.doi.org/10.1017/

S1574019611300041.1. The report in Dutch is available at http://www.justitie.nl/images/rapport%Overweigingen%.20bij%20een%20boerka%20verbod_ 6651_tem34–28821.pdf.

126. Van der Schyff and Overbeeke, 433–34.

127. Parliamentary paper 2007/08, 31108 no. 4, http://www.overheid.nl.

128. Parliamentary paper 2007/08.

129. Private bills are ones proposed by individual members of the House of Representatives. Government-proposed bills are those approved and put forward by the Council of Ministers. Because the Council of Ministers is the voice of the government, these bills are perceived of as having a better chance of passing Parliament.

130. "Government Approves Ban on Clothing that Covers the Face," January 27, 2012, http://www.government.nl/news/2012/01/27/government-approves-ban-on-clothing-that-covers-the-face.

131. Elena Bossi, "The Burqa Ban: An Insight into Its Compatibility with Human Rights," http://www.academia.edu/338326/The_burqa_ban_law_an_insight_into_its_compatibility_with_human_rights.

132. "Dutch 'Burqa Ban' May Go after Government Falls," Reuters, 25 April 2012, http://www.reuters.com/assets (accessed Janaury 6, 2013).

133. Ibid.

134. "Amsterdam Dumps the 'A' Word," February 13, 2013. http://www.dutchnews.nl/news/archives/2013/02/Amsterdam-dumps-the-a-word.php (accessed February 15, 2013).

Chapter Seven

The United States of America

E Pluribus Unum *and In God We Trust*

The historical mythology of the United States of America (US) paints it as an open land where people seeking to escape religious and cultural oppression came to be free. Although the truth may be driven more by economic than ideological issues, the settlers of the US did bring with them a variety of religions and cultures. While not always welcoming to new immigrant groups, the US has long been accustomed to their presence. The recent influx of Muslim immigrants has been largely viewed as another wave to be added to the mix. The American way, in which a variety of ethnicities and religions are married in spirit but not in appearance, is reflected in two national mottos: "*e pluribus unum*" (out of many one), which was used from the founding until 1956, when Congress replaced it during the height of the Cold War with "In God We Trust."[1]

HISTORY

Immigration: Overview

While indigenous populations did exist on the North American continent at the time of European settlement, they were scattered and overtaken by the settlers. Immigration can be divided into four periods by major immigrant group: colonial (British); mid-nineteenth century (northern Europe); early twentieth century (southern and eastern Europe); and post-1965 (Latin America and Asia).[2] Immigration can also be divided by sheer numbers. Prior to the mid-1800s it was a trickle, but from 1820 to the early 1900s it was a deluge that peaked in 1907 with 1.3 million. From the 1920s to 1965 it was severely restricted, and since 1965 it has again burgeoned.

The current nation-state originated with the British colonies of the 1600s.[3] There were scattered French and Spanish settlements on the continent, and the Dutch initially settled the area which became New York, but it is the British influence which set the tone for the formation of the US. The first permanent British colony was at Jamestown, Virginia, in 1607. These settlers came for economic pursuits. The Puritans followed a few years later and settled in the Massachusetts Bay area.

American church-state relations begin with the Puritans of New England. It is true that they came to the open land of America seeking to escape religious and economic oppression, but it is not true that they sought to create a land free for all religions.[4] They sought to create a specific society which followed their views.[5] Because many colonists had been persecuted for their religion, there was some degree of separation of authority, but it varied widely by colony and time from state executions for religious heresy in Massachusetts in the 1600s to complete separation in Rhode Island.[6] Eventually thirteen colonies under control of the British government were established along the East Coast. These colonies largely self-segregated by religion.

Soon after the enactment of the Constitution in 1789, the nation began regulating entry and citizenship of persons. Laws regulating naturalization began in 1790 with naturalization restricted to "free white persons." Immigration from western Europe began to increase after 1830, with most people coming from Ireland and Scandinavia. The Louisiana Purchase and end of the Mexican-American War in 1848 added large amounts of territory to the West, enabling new immigrants to spread out across the continent. The Civil War amendments to the US Constitution granted citizenship to all former slaves but did not ensure full property and political rights. An amendment to the 1790 naturalization act in 1870 and a new immigration act in 1875 limited entry of most nonwhites and prohibited entry of "undesirables," generally meaning Asians.[7] Additional laws excluding Chinese immigrants were passed in 1882, 1884, 1886, and 1888. Other South Asian groups were also excluded by laws of 1917 and included in the exclusions of 1921 and 1924. Laws enacted in 1913, 1920, and 1923 barred Asian immigrants from owning property by naming them nonwhite and, thus, ineligible for citizenship.

Two major restrictive laws were enacted in 1921 and 1924 establishing national origin quotas that severely limited ethnicities deemed undesirable, including Irish Catholic, Italians, and southern and eastern European Jews. Entry for any group was limited to 3 percent (1921 Act) and 2 percent (1924 Act) of their US population as of 1890. Another act in 1934 specifically limited Filipino immigration to fifty persons per year. During the Great Depression the US went so far as to establish a program of repatriation for

Mexican immigrants. The program was revived in the late 1950s under the unfortunate name of Operation Wetback.[8] All of these laws remained in effect during World War II, preventing many people escaping Nazi and Japanese invasions from finding refuge in the US.

Laws with racial or ethnic quotas severely restricting non-Western, non-Protestant immigration continued to be the norm with the exception of intermittent refugee accords and a 1952 act permitting entry for persons holding special skills as part of the Cold War strategy.[9] A major overhaul of the immigration system occurred in 1965 when the basis for quotas was changed from national origin to hemisphere, Western or Eastern. This act enabled overall immigration flows to increase, particularly from Latin America and Asia.

Immigration restrictions are now based on economic factors such as possession of needed skills. The 1986 and 1990 statutory revisions also focus on the skill of the immigrant as the determining factor for admittance. By far the largest immigrant group is from Mexico, with most settling in the border states.[10] Muslim immigration falls within the strictures of nonwhite, non-Western immigration and can be divided into two major periods.

Muslims in America

It is estimated that a significant number of African slaves were Muslim.[11] In addition, from 1880 to the fall of the Ottoman Empire in World War I, several thousand Muslims immigrated to the United States, with most assimilating into wider society. Communities, which still exist today, settled in Dearborn, Michigan; Quincy, Massachusetts; and Ross, North Dakota. Due to the restrictive quotas there was little Muslim immigration between WWI and 1965. Unlike the Netherlands and France, there were no specific governmental programs for the importation of labor or for housing immigrants in isolation from the general population. Muslim immigrants today tend to be middle class and college educated.[12] The Muslim population in the US is largely dispersed and estimated at 2–3 percent of the overall population.[13]

From the beginning the US has been a place of *e pluribus unum*, with an increase in recent years in the variety of ethnicities in the mix. In the early years, the ethnic makeup was largely British, and there were disparate groups based on religion that had to find a way to work together. The desire to establish a democracy and the need to find a way for the disparate religious adherents to coexist are major factors contributing to the origin of the United States.

ORIGIN OF THE NATION

The US does not have the lengthy history of monarchy of France or the Netherlands, so reformation to a democracy was not a result of civil turmoil—it is *ab ovo*. At the time of the American Revolution nine of the thirteen colonies had a dominant religion which the state promoted to some extent. It is a recently invented myth that America was founded seeking religious freedom for all. Most of the early colonies instituted laws allowing the government to punish, unto death or banishment to the wilderness, anyone who disobeyed religious laws that included mandatory church attendance and prohibited voicing a dissenting view on the colony's accepted doctrine.[14]

There was no single *ancien regime* of one church and monarchy. The only religious group seen as tied to the British rulers was the Anglican Church, the state Church of England, which was the established church in only six of the thirteen colonies.[15] Even in these colonies the Anglican establishment in England only had limited control over the American practitioners. With the revolution these states disestablished their churches because of the Anglican Church's tie to the British government.[16] Congregational religions were the established church in three colonies, and there was no established denomination in four.[17] Many churches took an active role in promoting the Revolution lest they be viewed as an enemy of the cause.[18] As the colonies achieved independence, the British government, military, and church were evicted; thus, there was no ongoing quarrel.

Two underlying philosophies came together at the founding and the adoption of the First Amendment, a Lockean style of Enlightenment philosophy and the attitude of the First Great Awakening (c. 1730–1740). A Lockean style of Enlightenment philosophy includes an attitude that religion is beneficial to society. Locke also emphasized individualism and negative freedom; restriction on government is beneficial.[19] Locke's view of religion fit well with the philosophy of the First Great Awakening, which swept the colonies just before the revolution. The Great Awakenings are periods of widespread religious revival in the US which also impact social morés and attitudes toward church-state relations. The religious philosophy of the First Great Awakening emphasized the inward experience of faith and a separation of the spiritual and temporal spheres. State power, as part of the temporal, should not interfere in religious matters.[20] These two philosophies, coupled with the absence of an *ancien regime*, meant that rational Enlightenment followers did not have to justify their new political institutions with anticlericalism. The Declaration of Independence invoked this religion-friendly rationalism with its appeals to God, creator, supreme judge, and divine providence.[21] When it came time to set up the institution of government, the rationalist religion-state separation attitude took control and was incorporated into the Constitution's First Amendment.

As the US formed from independent colonies, the founders realized that pluralism on a national level was necessary to hold the new nation together. The failed loose confederation under the first governmental structure of the United States showed that a stronger national government was necessary. The states wanted to retain substantial authority over local issues but were willing to entrust meaningful power to the federal government.[22] Since many had left England expressly to escape the state church, the idea of a new national church was anathema. Absent from the US Constitution is the establishment of a national state church. The only mention in the original Constitution of religion was the prohibition of a religious oath for officeholders.[23] At the Constitutional Convention the delegates debated the need to include specific provisions related to nonestablishment and freedom of religion, but this was felt to be a state (local) matter for which laws already existed.[24] During the ratification process states made it clear they wanted specific provisions for nonestablishment and freedom of religion included along with restrictions on national government action.[25] After ratification and the formalities of setting up business, Congress quickly adopted the first ten amendments to the Constitution, known as the Bill of Rights, as a package. These amendments were quickly ratified by the states and came into effect in 1791.

The First Amendment sets the tone for church-state relations in the United States, as well as individual freedoms. It is written as a negative liberty, a check on the state:

> Congress shall make no law respecting an establishment of religion, or prohibiting the free exercise thereof; or abridging the freedom of speech, or of the press; or the right of the people peaceably to assemble, and to petition the Government for a redress of grievances.

But American's celebration of religion as the "first freedom" is a recently invented myth. There is no mention of religious freedom in the original Constitution. It is contained in the First Amendment; however, this place is by default, not design. The congressional debates leading to the adoption of the Bill of Rights did not assert that religious freedom held any primacy over other rights. In fact, the First Amendment is numerically first simply because the first two proposed amendments were not ratified by the states. Accordingly, the third proposal upon ratification became the First Amendment.[26]

What is clear from the beginning of the First Amendment is that a formal legal separation on the national level existed *ab initio*. There were no restrictions on ceremonial comingling at the national level, and each administration set its own level of religious rhetoric. While there was a national restriction, there was no restriction on the state level until after the Civil War, and states frequently based laws on religious grounds.[27]

The diversity of denominations, while almost exclusively Protestant, meant that no one group could take national control. There were Catholics and Jews in America, but their numbers were small. This Protestant pluralism also began to filter into states, and each group sought to protect its position, which many believed was best accomplished by the disestablishment of all religion.[28] An inherent Protestant preferentialism would remain until the late twentieth century, with some arguing it is still in effect. The Second (1790–1840) and Third (1880–1900) Great Awakenings ignited Protestant preferentialism, creating a "de facto establishment of Protestantism," particularly in the fields of education, media, and social reforms.[29] Government neutrality was interpreted as neutrality toward and among Protestant denominations, not neutrality to all religions or to nonreligion.

A major challenge to the Protestant establishment began when Catholic immigrants from Europe began arriving in large numbers in the mid-1800s. In 1910 the Catholic population reached sixteen million. A strong Protestant and native backlash, called "nativism," ensued. Some nativists resorted to fabricated stories of Catholic atrocities and others to violence.[30] The new public schools were a major target of anti-Catholic rhetoric, and the King James Bible was used as a teaching tool.[31] The well-known McGuffey's reader consisted largely of Protestant religious appeals as the topic of reading exercises for young children.[32] Catholics responded by opening private parochial schools, which at the time were allowed to receive direct assistance from the state. In 1876 President Grant called for an amendment to the US Constitution prohibiting the use of public money for faith-based schools and called for the church and state to be forever separate.[33] Shortly thereafter Representative James Blaine (Maine) proposed an amendment to the Constitution prohibiting any state from using state funds to support any activity of a "religious sect."[34] The House passed the proposal, but it failed in the Senate. Nevertheless, thirty-seven states passed Blaine amendments.[35]

Not just Catholics were targets of Protestant preferentialism; Mormons also suffered its restrictions. The Supreme Court entered the fight over state control of religion and began using the "wall of separation" as the metaphor for church-state relations as early as the case of *Reynolds v. U.S.*, 98 U.S. 145 (1878). The use of the wall metaphor in a Protestant-majority society in America is not surprising. Martin Luther had advocated a paper wall between the spiritual and temporal world, and Roger Williams had advocated a hedge or wall separating church and state in Rhode Island.[36] President Jefferson had used this metaphor in response to a request from a group in Connecticut to use his influence in state-level religious issues. Jefferson declined, claiming a wall of separation between church and state.[37]

The *Reynolds* case involved polygamy in the Mormon settlement of the Utah territory, a practice which had been banned under the federal act creating the territory in 1862. The Supreme Court rejected the Mormon argument of complete free exercise of religion. Instead, it found authority to regulate "barbarous practices" which are "an offense against society" and a "blot on our civilization" that is contrary to Christianity. The court held that complete freedom exists in belief and conscience but not in religious practice. The exercise of a religious belief cannot be superior to the law; to do so would "in effect permit every citizen to be a law unto himself."[38] Court approval of the US as a Christian nation, whose Constitution permits state nudging toward Protestantism, remained until the 1960s.

In addition to Supreme Court rulings on the First Amendment, four other major events affected American church-state relations between the Civil War and the 1960s and ultimately impacted Muslim women's right to wear religious dress today: laws on religious garb in the classroom, anti-masking laws, secularization, and civil rights law.

Religious Garb in the Classroom

By the 1900s thousands of Catholic nuns were teaching in public schools that were fully or partially supported by public funds.[39] The nuns were required by Canon law to wear the full habit at all times. Americans at first accepted this practice from trained schoolteachers but later began to object on two grounds. First, impressionable Protestant schoolchildren should not be exposed to the dangerous Catholicism represented by the habit, and second, children should not be exposed to sectarian religion at all in the classroom, an influential place for the inculcation of American democracy.[40] The habit, like the *hijab* and *niqab* today, was viewed as a mark of the unhealthy subjugation of women. "For its mid-century opponents, the habit was a piece of propaganda; it was dangerous because of the lessons it broadcast to children who saw it every day."[41]

Through WWII Christian expression in the classroom waned as patriotic symbolism increased.[42] State decisions on the propriety of religious garb in the classroom had been mixed when in 1948 the New Mexico case of *Zellers v. Huff* brought the controversy to national attention. The nun teachers wearing the habit in the classroom allegedly served as a constant reminder of their faith, "thereby exerting a sectarian or denominational influence in the class room at all times" in violation of the New Mexico Constitution's Blaine Amendment.[43] Shortly after issuance of the US Supreme Court decision in *Everson*, discussed below, the New Mexico Supreme Court held that not only does the garb "have a propagandizing effect for the church, but by its very nature it introduced sectarian religion into the school." Therefore, it was prohibited under the state constitution.[44] By 1949 states were split on whether religious garb in the classroom was permissible, with twenty-three allowing and twenty-five prohibiting it.[45] All but three states have since repealed these laws. A fourth, Oregon, only recently repealed its law, which will be discussed more fully below in the context of the headscarf.

Anti-masking Laws

The rise of the Ku Klux Klan (the "Klan") had a significant impact on minority religion and ethnicities in the US that even today influences laws affecting Muslim women's right to wear religious dress. The Klan's activities in the US can be divided into three periods: Civil War and Reconstruction, the 1920s, and post World War II. Each edition of the Klan used face covering for anonymity in conducting violence against minorities and political opponents.[46] The first use was during the 1868 election campaign. The US Congress enacted a law which made it a felony for "two or more persons . . . [to] go in disguise upon the highway with the intent" of depriving another of his civil rights.[47] This version of the Klan died out soon after the election.

The Klan was resurrected a few years later and again committed violent acts against minorities, particularly blacks, Catholics, Jews, and political opponents, while wearing white hoods. At this time, states and municipalities acted to prohibit the wearing of masks in public to undermine the Klan's efforts to remain anonymous. Most of these statutes did not include an intent clause and simply made it unlawful to appear in public masked, excepting only certain enumerated purposes, usually associated with health, safety, and specified holiday celebrations.[48] The third incarnation of the Klan, post World War II, prompted more states and municipalities to pass anti-masking laws.

The anti-masking statutes vary widely as to style (criminal or general), intent requirements, and permissible exceptions. Most of the criminal laws, as criminal laws usually do, contain an intent clause which prohibits masking only if one intends to commit another illegal act. These are rarely constitutionally problematic and not applicable to the Islamic women's situation. General laws prohibiting covering the face in public are more problematic constitutionally and for Islamic women, which will be discussed below.

Secularization

By the 1920s states began to divide on how much pressure in favor of Protestantism was acceptable, ushering in a second disestablishment period.[49] This second disestablishment is marked by the failure of Prohibition and the Scopes trial of 1925. Prohibition lasted from 1920 to 1933, beginning and ending with the ratification of the Eighteenth and Twenty-First Constitutional Amendments. Its origin lies in the reform-minded social gospel of the

Second and Third Great Awakenings. Its utter failure marked a failure of conservative Protestantism in the minds of many.[50]

Another challenge to fundamentalism was occurring with the increase in industrialization and scientific progress. The Scopes trial was the watershed event in the tug-of-war between modernists (science) and fundamentalists (strict biblical adherents). In *State of Tennessee v. John Scopes*, teacher John Scopes was charged with teaching evolution in violation of Tennessee law. It was viewed by the public as a trial between science and the Bible. Scopes was found guilty so the Bible triumphed, at least in court.[51] A perception arose among the educated elite that the fundamentalist view was holding back scientific progress and should be rejected for the betterment of all.

Christian Smith explains the public shift by asserting that the "historical secularization of the institutions of American public life was not a natural, inevitable, and abstract by-product of modernization; rather it was the outcome of a struggle between contending groups with conflicting interests seeking to control social knowledge and institutions."[52] Smith identifies one of these contending groups as the evangelicals, who were trying to preserve Protestant preferentialism. Smith characterizes the opposition as a coalition of three groups: (1) religious minorities, including Catholics and Jews; (2) secularists, including scientists embracing Darwinism and scientific inquiry; and (3) educated professionals who regarded Victorian and Protestant restrictions as barriers to social and economic advancement.[53] A fourth group, mainline Protestants, soon joined these forces in opposing evangelical fundamentalism as backward and detrimental to the future of America.[54] These religious, ideological, and professional groups encompassed all aspects of society and were able to make a concerted attack on all levels of open Protestant preferentialism, including education and the courts.[55]

US Supreme Court

Throughout the nineteenth century the rhetoric of Protestant preferentialism was pervasive at the state level, manifesting itself in discriminatory laws and unprosecuted violence.[56] Anti-Catholic politicians served in the US Congress and were a major political force in nine states under the Know Nothing Party.[57] The Know Nothings painted themselves as protectors of American values and ideals. They targeted immigrants and minority religions as grave threats to the American way of life.[58]

> At the turn of the twentieth century and increasingly thereafter, local officials began routinely denying Roman Catholics their school charters, Jehovah's Witnesses their preaching permits, Eastern Orthodox their canonical freedoms, Jews and Adventists their Sabbath-day accommodations, non-Christian pacifists their conscientious objection status. As State courts and legislatures

> turned an increasingly blind eye to their plight, religious dissenters began to turn to the federal court for relief.[59]

The turn to the federal courts was possible because of the Civil War amendments—thirteen, fourteen, and fifteen. The Fourteenth Amendment provides, in part, that

> [n]o State shall make or enforce any law which shall abridge the privileges or immunities of citizens of the United States; nor shall any State deprive any person of life, liberty, or property, without due process of law; nor deny to any person within its jurisdiction the equal protection of the laws.

Beginning in 1925, the court began holding that the Bill of Rights applied to the states via what is called the incorporation clause—the Fourteenth Amendment's specification that states must provide due process means they must adhere to the Bill of Rights because to not do so would be a deprivation of due process of law.[60] Beginning with *Cantwell v. Connecticut*, 310 U.S. 296 (1940), and *Everson v. Board of Education*, 330 U.S. 1 (1947), the Supreme Court began setting the tone for what is religious freedom throughout the US, and minority religion rights greatly expanded.

The First Amendment religion clause divides into two parts, acting as a type of yin and yang for the legal boundaries of religion in the US. The establishment clause restricts government involvement in religion. The restriction includes not only official government pronouncements but also includes individuals acting as government employees advocating a particular religion. The second clause, free exercise, is the individual citizen's ability to act on a religious belief alone or in concert with others. The first religion clause emanates from a restrictive position, limiting governmental action from inception, while the second presumes total individual freedom with boundaries imposed as the practice of that freedom extends outward and impacts others. Whether a law falls within the establishment or free exercise clauses largely depends on whether it aids (establishment) or hinders (free exercise) religion.[61] The religious law has evolved in tandem with other constitutional rights so that expansion in one area spills over into other areas.

The establishment clause is a restrictive clause. Official government policies and laws, as well as government actors, are bound by its strictures. The establishment clause affects the veiling debate through setting boundaries on what laws can be enacted and in what religious practice a government actor may engage. The first case in which the establishment clause was applied to state action was *Everson v. Board of Education*, 330 U.S. 1 (1947). In *Everson* a state public school provided bus transportation to all students, including those attending parochial schools. Suit was filed alleging the practice was a violation of the establishment clause because it amounted to support for religion. The court held that bus transportation for parochial school students did not violate the Constitution. Even though the result in *Everson* permitted state assistance to a religious school, the dicta of Justice Black and his style of interpretation marked a change in precedent. Justice Black, writing for the majority, opined:

> Neither a State nor the Federal government can set up a church. Neither can pass laws which aid one religion, aid all religions, or prefer one religion over another. . . . No tax of any amount, large or small, can be levied in support of any religious activities or institutions whatever they may be called, or whatever form they may adopt to teach or practice religion. Neither a State nor the Federal Government can, openly or secretly, participate in the affairs of any religious organization or groups and vice versa. In the words of Jefferson, the clause against establishment of religion by law was intended to erect "a wall of separation" between Church and state.

The dissenting justices' opinion agrees with this reasoning; it just differs in its application to the facts of the case in holding that "separation means separation, not something less." Relying on Jefferson's metaphor in describing the relation between church and state, the dissenters found it "speaks of a 'wall of separation,' not of a fine line easily overstepped." Therefore, they would build an even higher wall and find the transportation a violation of the First Amendment. This use of the wall metaphor echoed back to the *Reynolds* decision and telegraphed that the same level of restriction which had been applied to the federal government would now be applied to the states.

A year later strict separation reached its peak in *McCollum v. Board of Education*, 333 U.S. 203 (1948), in which Justice Black described the wall as "high and impregnable," and Justice Frankfurter referred to public schools as the "symbol of our secular unity."[62] Robert Wuthnow asserts this turn is possible post WWII because of the states' increasing role in society, particularly education. Prior to WWII parochial schools provided much of higher education, health care, and other social services.[63] It is the timing of the separationist legal trend which made it possible. However, this strict separation did not last long due to national and international events.

Conservative religious practitioners from many denominations began to push back against strict separation, and the Supreme Court softened its stance. The major influence on the softening was the rise of communism worldwide. In an effort to distinguish the US from the atheist communists, the federal government began pursuing American ideals, including religion. This can be considered a ceremonial deism or national monotheism, which was watered down enough to include most Christians and sometimes Jews. These actions include a national day of prayer, the inclusion of the phrase "under God" in the Pledge of Allegiance, and the adoption of "In God We Trust" as the national motto to be officially placed on currency.[64] The mood was succinctly declared by President Eisenhower: "Our government makes no sense unless it is founded on a deeply held religious belief—and I don't care what it is."[65]

Justice William Douglas signaled the court's turn to this style of accommodation when he wrote in the majority opinion of *Zorach v. Clausen*, 343 U.S. 306 (1952), that "we are a religious people whose institutions presuppose a supreme being," and when the state accommodates religious practices, "it respects the religious nature of our people and accommodates the public service to their spiritual needs."[66] He opined that the First Amendment does not require total separation in all situations. To do so would lead to hostility between state and religion. He retreated from the impregnable high wall of separation as impractical and contrary to American traditions. Finally, he equated an impregnable wall with a "callous indifference," and such a stance amounts to an atheist preferentialism that itself violates the Constitution.[67] This accommodationist position reinterpreted neutrality to a passive monotheism, a ceremonial deism.

As pluralism increased, the trend to define state neutrality as noninterference, and equality as equal treatment expanded. The case of *Lemon v. Kurtzman*, 403 U.S. 602 (1971), established a test used for determining whether government action violates the establishment clause: first, the statute must have a secular legislative purpose; second, its principal or primary effect must be one that neither advances nor inhibits religion; and finally, the statute must not foster "an excessive government entanglement with religion."[68] The court has utilized this standard or variations of it in determining the constitutionality of laws impacting religion and the use of religion in a variety of government settings with a variety of results. I will discuss each of these scenarios with the headscarf and veil more fully below.

We also need to consider the development of the second prong of the religion clause, free exercise. In *Cantwell v. Connecticut*, 310 U.S. 296 (1940), a Jehovah's Witness alleged a violation of the free exercise clause because he was required to obtain a solicitor's license, the granting of which was left completely to the discretion of a clerk, in order to proselytize door-to-door. The state justified the licensing requirement by asserting that it had an interest in maintaining order. The court found a need to balance the state interest in order and the individual's interest in fulfilling what he perceived to be a necessary religious practice, a constitutionally protected freedom.[69]

The court has been balancing these interests ever since. In *Sherbert v. Verner*, 374 U.S. 398 (1963), the court established a test of strict scrutiny. The court first determines if a law imposes a substantial burden on a religious practice. If so, the state must show that the law or practice is important to the accomplishment of a compelling secular objective and that the manner in which this is done is the least restrictive means to accomplish the task. The state must prove the motivation for the burdening law is secular, which means the expressed motivation for the law is not to promote or hinder religion.

The court has heard many requests for relief from laws by those claiming a wide variety of religious affiliations, requiring the court to establish some definition of what is a religion. The court has set some boundaries without ever specifically defining religion, and there is a good argument that any exact definition would violate the establishment clause. In *Thomas v. Review Board of the Indiana Employment Sector Division*, 450 U.S. 707 (1981), the court recognized that defining what is religion is a "difficult and delicate task [and that] the resolution of [the] question [should not turn] upon a judicial perception of the particular belief or practice in question."[70] Protection extends to even unconventional beliefs so long as they rise to the level of a religious belief. The court has held that a religious belief must affect all areas of life, be sincerely held, and have some level of existence beyond the one individual claiming its protection.[71]

Faced with increasing pluralism the court retreated from the *Sherbert* test to a legally neutral stance. In *Employment Division v. Smith*, two Oregon State drug counselors failed drug tests and were fired. They claimed that they ingested the drugs as part of a religious ritual, so they were protected under the *Sherbert* test. The court rejected their claims and ruled that the First Amendment

> does not relieve an individual of the obligation to comply with a law that incidentally forbids (or requires) the performance of an act that his religious belief requires (or forbids) if the law is not specifically directed to religious practice and is otherwise constitutional as applied to those who engage in the specified act for nonreligious reasons.

The court moved from a standard of a state burden to prove compelling interest to restrict a religious practice to one which requires the state to carefully enact laws which are generally applicable and motivated on neutral, secular grounds. A law will be deemed unconstitutional if it does not meet the broad rule of law standards of neutral motivation, neutral on its face, and neutral in effect. With this development there was no longer a Protestant or even religious preferentialism in law.

The exception to this neutral standard occurs when another constitutional right is also impinged.[72] Under such circumstances, the standard is elevated to the standard applicable to other constitutional practices, a hybrid rights standard. This has led to the application of the First Amendment speech clause to many religious exercise cases.[73] Speech protection is broader and deeper than free exercise, even under *Sherbert*. Further, the speech clause applies to all styles of expression, not just the verbal or printed word.[74] When interpreting the free exercise clause alone, there is no distinction between religious and nonreligious practices—all practices are similarly construed under the law, ending all preferentialism for religious practices and conflating protection of exercise to the speech clause. Thus, the speech clause is applicable to the wearing of the headscarf and veil in the US.

Congress and state legislators were not happy with the turn to a neutral, generally applicable law standard in *Smith*. By legislative fiat they codified the *Sherbert* standard with the passage of the Religious Freedom Restoration Act (RFRA).[75] The federal act was later struck only for its attempted application to state laws, leaving federal RFRA to regulate federal action and state RFRAs to regulate state laws impacting religious practices.[76] The *Sherbert* compelling interest–narrowly tailored standard applies currently if an act falls within the ambit of an RFRA, federal or state. If the act does not fall within the ambit of an RFRA, the generally applicable neutral law standard of *Smith* applies. The specific impact of recent free exercise RFRA law on the headscarf and veil will be discussed below.

Civil Rights Act of 1964

The final component of American law impacting the veiling debates is American civil rights law. In 1964 the US Congress enacted a civil rights act that greatly expanded the power of the US government to regulate practices throughout the country. The act outlaws discrimination in employment (of employers of fifteen or more nonfamily persons), voting, public accommodation, and public schools on the basis of race, color, religion, or national origin. The act created the Equal Employment Opportunity Commission (EEOC) to prosecute acts of discrimination. Under the law one may file a complaint with the EEOC, and the EEOC may elect to take over prosecution of the case or, as is much more common, grant the individual plaintiff a "right to sue" letter, which enables the individual to file a personal lawsuit for damages against the alleged discriminator. Most states have also enacted anti-discrimination laws and established state EEOC's and/or State Fair Practice in Employment Agencies.[77]

When the immigration law was reformed in 1965 to expand immigration from non-Western, non-Protestant countries, the US had in place a legal and political system designed to aid in the protection of broad individual rights and to restrict the state to an equal treatment standard. Muslim women have benefited from this style of democracy.

THE VEILING DEBATES

Fox News staff member Anne Coulter argued that a woman should be in jail just for wearing a *hijab* because "this immigration policy of us assimilating immigrants into our culture isn't really working. They are assimilating us into their culture." Coulter was immediately chastised by sections of the public for her views and tried to claim it was a joke.[78] The majority of Americans do not seem to accept Ms. Coulter's Islamaphobia. The veiling debates in the US are marked by a lack of national controversy. There is no national legislative or policy movement to restrict wearing the headscarf or veil. Likewise, there are no generalized state movements to restrict either practice, even in states in which other Islamic practices are controversial.[79]

The US approach to personal rights has always entailed a strong level of individualism, a neutral state hands-off approach, and an equal treatment standard for the imposition of restrictions. This level of state neutrality and equal treatment applies across the board to all rights in the US, not just religion. The US motto probably should read "I can do what I want; it is my constitutional right." The Muslim woman in America generally derives a benefit from this view, at least legally, if not socially. Muslim women who wear the scarf and veil may not be subject to less social harassment in the United States, but they are often able to pursue legal recourse and are not the subject of heated political debates. The US federal system means that we must consider the issues on a national and a state level. There is not a sharp distinction between federal and state action due mainly to strong federal control over civil rights and incorporation of the First Amendment.

Religious Garb in the Classroom

The issue of religious garb in the classroom divides along student and teacher lines. The free exercise clause is implicated for both the teacher and student. The establishment clause is also a consideration in the case of a teacher. The only consideration in the US occurs in public schools because of the constitutional restriction on the regulation of private schools. Most regulation of education occurs on the local level.

Students retain a limited right of free speech/expression at school, which includes clothing with a message.[80] Restrictions are limited to those which will "materially or substantially disrupt school discipline."[81] The court has held that religious speech receives the same protection as all other speech.[82] School dress code policies are reviewed for overbreadth. For example, a New York federal district court struck down a school policy which prohibited clothing showing "[a]ny activity, affiliation and/or communication in connection with a non-school sanctioned club/group, including fraternal organizations or gangs."[83] School policies must not stifle student expression; must promote an important interest, such as safety and orderly environment; and must be narrowly tailored.[84] In those states with an RFRA, codifying the *Sherbert* standard, religious garb is expressly protected, and any restriction must emanate from a compelling interest and be narrowly tailored to meet that interest.

Several cases have applied this standard to Muslim schoolgirls. One case from Oklahoma demonstrates the usual course of events. In *Hearn v. Muskogee School District*, No. 6:03-CV-00598 (E.D. Ok. 2003), a Muslim student who had been wearing a headscarf to school for some time was suspended on September 11, 2003, for violating a school policy prohibiting all hats, caps, bandanas, or jacket hoods inside school buildings. The girl and her parents sued the school in federal district court. The US Department of Justice joined the action on behalf of the student, and several *amici* filed briefs in support of the student. Shortly thereafter, the school district settled by reinstating the student and altering the policy to include an exemption for religious dress. Muslim students are subject to harassment and suspension for wearing the headscarf, but they usually are able to find recourse with actual or threatened litigation.[85]

Teachers have greater restrictions on what they can wear at work because of establishment clause considerations and in two states due to state laws. Teachers are protected by Title VII of the Civil Rights Act but, as will be discussed below, the act has been narrowly interpreted and often does not protect religious dress. Further, to pass an establishment clause challenge the garb must not reach the level of proselytizing or be disruptive.[86]

All but two state statutes restricting the wearing of religious garb have been repealed. An Oregon Supreme Court case upheld its statute against a free exercise challenge as "furthering a constitutional obligation beyond an ordinary policy reference of the legislature."[87] In response to this decision, however, the Oregon legislature passed a law repealing the statute and specifically allowing religious dress in the classroom unless it creates an undue hardship on the school.[88] The Oregon Board of Education has issued guidelines to assist schools in implementing the new law, which states that restrictions can be implemented when the clothing is intended to proselytize or create an impression that the school endorses the message. Intent to do either is determined by size and type of clothing, specificity of message, number of employees wearing the clothing, and age and sophistication of the students, parent, and employee.[89]

A Pennsylvania statute has withstood recent challenges under Title VII and the Constitution. In *U.S. v. Board of Education*, 911 F.2d 882 (3rd Cir. 1990), the Pennsylvania law prohibiting teachers from wearing religious garb in the classroom was upheld against a Title VII challenge. The Third Circuit Court of Appeals held that requiring a school district to comply with a Muslim teacher's request to wear the *hijab* amounted to an undue hardship; thus, no accommodation was necessary under Title VII. The court held that to require accommodation amounts to a "significant threat to the maintenance of religious neutrality in the public school system."[90]

In contrast, in 1991 a federal district court in Pennsylvania sustained a Title VII discrimination claim for refusal to hire to a Muslim woman wearing a headscarf because the religious reasons for her dress were not apparent to the observer. The action, consequently, did not fall within the Pennsylvania statute that prohibited the wearing of any dress indicating that the wearer is a member of any religious order, sect, or denomination.[91] In another case from Pennsylvania, a teacher was suspended for wearing a cross necklace.[92] The court held the policy constituted an unconstitutional hostility toward religion when applied to the facts of the case. Proposals to repeal the Pennsylvania statute have been introduced but failed to gain much support.[93]

The only other state with a ban is Nebraska, which apparently is largely unknown to the public, legislators, and school board officials. When brought to their attention, they referred to it as a ridiculous and dead law which no one would be foolish enough to try and impose.[94]

Religious Dress in Other Workplaces

Litigation involving attempts to restrict the wearing of the headscarf in the workplace has arisen across the US. Most cases are brought under Title VII of the Civil Rights Act or its state law equivalent and are either filed by the EEOC or with its approval. Under Title VII employers are not permitted to discharge an employee or refuse to hire an applicant because of religion. An employer is required to make reasonable accommodations for the employee and is only relieved if the accommodation rises to the level of creating an undue hardship on the employer's business or on other employees. A few examples from around the country will demonstrate the issues involved.

In *EEOC v. Alamo-Rent-A-Car*, No. CIV-02–01908-PHX-ROS (D. Ariz. June 2007), a Muslim woman was awarded back pay and punitive damages after her employer refused to allow her to wear a headscarf at work. Alamo employee Bilan Nur had been wearing her headscarf to work during the month of Ramadan for a few years before 9/11. Nur always asked for permission to wear the headscarf, and it had always been granted. Nur worked as a rental agent, so she personally interacted with customers and potential customers. The company had a "Dress Smart Policy" to ensure Alamo employees presented a professional manner of dress to customers. The dress code policy prohibited employees from wearing certain clothing and accessories, including the wearing of more than one earring, open toed shoes, and half-grown beards. The policy did not address head coverings but did contain a catch-all clause which forbade the wearing of any "garment or item of outer clothing not specifically mentioned in this policy."

In November of 2001, Nur requested leave to wear a headscarf during the upcoming Ramadan. She was told that she could wear it while in the back of the office but not when interacting with customers. She twice wore the scarf to work and refused to remove it while at the front counter. On both occasions, she was reprimanded and sent home from work. She was then suspended for three days and warned that she might be terminated. Her employment was terminated shortly thereafter for violating company policy. With the assistance of the EEOC Nur filed suit. In support of her case, Nur showed that she was a devout Muslim and that she was required to cover her head during the religious holiday month of Ramadan. Alamo disputed her religious devotion by claiming Nur had uncovered her head upon the employer's request for a short time at work in November 2000 without objecting.

A US district court judge granted summary judgment in favor of Nur on her religious discrimination claim under Title VII. Summary judgment means the case was proven as a matter of law, that there was no genuine question of material fact on all elements of Alamo's liability. The court decided that Alamo failed to show reasonable attempts to accommodate Nur's religious needs. Moreover, Alamo did not show that a reasonable accommodation would impose an undue hardship as there was little or no cost to comply. The issue of damages was submitted to a jury, and Nur was awarded back wages, compensatory damages, and $250,000 in punitive damages.

Employers are allowed to require a uniform or uniform look of their employees, but they must take reasonable steps to incorporate religious dress upon request. For example, Abercrombie and Fitch has lost claims that wearing the headscarf violates its uniform look of "East Coast preppy," no caps, and no dark colors.[95] Abercrombie defended its action as part of its trade brand, but courts were unconvinced, particularly as to the employees who had little interaction with the public.

In *EEOC v. Abercrombie and Fitch Stores, Inc.*, slip op. 14–86 (June 1, 2015), the Supreme Court further restricted an employer's consideration of religion in hiring decisions in another Abercrombie and Fitch case. Samantha Elauf wore her headscarf to a job interview at Abercrombie and Fitch. Prior to making an employment decision, the interviewer asked two different supervisors what she should do because of the headscarf and told at least one supervisor that she thought that Elauf wore the headscarf for religious reasons. Elauf was not hired and was told by an Abercrombie employee that it was because of her headscarf. She filed a complaint with the EEOC, who on her behalf sued for religious hiring discrimination under Title VII. Abercrombie defended, stating that because Elauf did not specifically tell the interviewer she wore the headscarf for religious purposes, nor did she specifically ask for an accommodation in the uniform policy they could not be guilty of discrimination. The Supreme Court ruled that under Title VII religion must only be a motivating factor in nonhiring. The court held there is no requirement that the employer know of "a conflict between an applicant's religion and a work rule." Abercrombie also defended itself, stating that the policy was a generally applicable neutral one, so there can be no religious discrimination in it. The court disagreed and held that Title VII imposes an affirmative duty on the employer to give religious practices "favored treatment." Thus, a neutral policy must give way when it conflicts with a religious practice unless there is a health or safety concern. If a prospective applicant wears a headscarf to an interview or informs the employer she wants to wear a headscarf at work, the employer may not refuse to hire her due to the wearing of the headscarf and must attempt to accommodate her, even if the employer only suspects that the headscarf is worn for religious reasons.

Employers can require an employee to wear a uniform-approved headscarf or limit size and color but not prohibit its wearing completely except on limited grounds. Employee acceptance of the uniform *hijab* varies.[96] Further, the employee must give the employer a sufficient opportunity to make an accommodation and in any suit must prove a restriction on advancement or discharge due to refusal to accommodate.[97]

State RFRAs and Title VII are usually sufficient to protect the right to wear religious dress in the workplace, but in at least one state, California, a specific law requiring religious dress accommodation in the workplace has been enacted.[98] Keith Blair argues that courts more narrowly interpret the reasonable accommodation standard in religion cases than in other civil rights cases and, thus, Title VII is not sufficient to protect religious rights.[99] This is a matter for legislatures to consider and may be inconsequential given the number of states with RFRA statutes.

The rules for federal government employees are less clear. There is no clear answer about whether they may wear the scarf at work. The White House issued guidelines in 1997 which require agencies to "permit personal religious expression by federal employees to the greatest extent possible," taking into consideration efficiency of operations and establishment clause considerations.[100] As to the US military, the Supreme Court found it to be a special circumstance of unity and order, so no exception for religious clothing need be made.[101] Subsequently, Congress amended military uniform regulations to allow the wearing of religious apparel in uniform with two exceptions: if the secretary of defense deems it would interfere with the performance of duties or if the item is "not neat and conservative."[102] A Sikh TSA officer settled a case and received an accommodation to wear his iron bracelet with his uniform, and an IRS agent was permitted to wear his *kirpan* at work.[103]

In the law enforcement context, *Fraternal Order of Police v. City of Newark*, 170 F.3d 359 (3d Cir. 1999), held that the Newark Police Department had to accommodate Muslim beards in its police force. The regulations required all police officers be clean shaven except for medical necessity. The court held that because there was a secular exception to the policy, a religious one also had to be made.[104] In *Webb v. City of Philadelphia*, 562 F.3d 256, 260 (2009), however, the court held that it was an undue hardship for the

Philadelphia police force to accommodate the wearing of a headscarf. The difference may be that there is no exception to the Philadelphia department's prohibition on wearing religious dress or symbols. The court held that the policy was designed to maintain a strict neutrality and promoted uniformity and cohesiveness of the force without exception. At least one fire department has accommodated a firefighter's request to wear a headscarf with her uniform by designating one of an approved size and color and only requiring its removal for safety reasons when fighting fires.[105]

Public Places Other Than Work

A request to wear the *niqab* for a driver's license photograph was denied in *Freeman v. Department of Highway Safety and Motor Vehicles*, 924 So.2d 48 (Fla Dist Ct App 2006). The court held that obscuring the face amounted to a substantial burden on the state, as the state has a need for a clear photograph to be used by police officers for identification and safety. The court also held that the bureau's offer for the photograph to be taken with only females present was a reasonable accommodation. Several states have required that a driver's license photograph show the full face of the holder since well before the current Muslim dress issue.[106]

There is some controversy over the wearing of the headscarf or other head covering in a driver's license photograph. In at least one state a ban on head covering was allegedly proposed due to an anti-Muslim bias.[107] The proposal was dropped after public outcry. In another state a proposal prohibiting head coverings was amended to include a religious exception and was enacted.[108] Rajdeep Singh has pointed out that laws which do not contain a reference to a state RFRA or provide for a religious exception are subject to a First Amendment challenge.[109] The US State Department requires an open, visible face for all passport photographs and only allows head coverings if always worn for a religious purpose.[110]

Additional cases have arisen for women going about daily life. In Omaha a mother of children wanting to swim was refused entry to a public swimming pool area for wearing Islamic clothing. The city asserted no one was allowed in the pool area in street clothes; however, it was proven that other mothers wearing ordinary clothing were allowed in to supervise their children. After a suit aided by the ACLU, the Omaha Parks Department amended its policies to include a religious accommodation.[111]

A young woman was removed from a water park while on a class trip for wearing a full-body-covering swim suit in accordance with Islamic practice. Again the ACLU aided the student and obtained an accommodation in the policy for religious clothing.[112] Incidents of discrimination abound, but quite often the women find a voice through civil rights or religious rights organizations or the press.[113]

Courts

The issue of religious dress in the courtroom predates issues involving Muslims.[114] The federal Religious Land Use and Institutionalized Persons Act (RLUIPA) protects a Muslim prisoner's right to wear religious garb, subject to security and identity checks.[115] Courts have generally upheld the right of parties to wear religious garb in the courtroom but not practitioners at the bar or court personnel, and the law on witnesses is mixed. Older cases applied the *Sherbert* standard, which is still valid precedent in many places given the number of state RFRAs codifying it. Most courts have held that the wearing of religious dress, no matter the denomination, by a party that is not itself disruptive to the court's interest in decorum should be allowed in deference to free exercise rights.[116]

In a case from Florida a court held that not allowing a jury instruction to prevent prejudice was an error. The defendant belonged to a small sect that required the wearing of unusual clothing; his attorney requested the judge to instruct the jury to disregard the garb in making its decision. The trial court refused and also prohibited the defendant from wearing the clothes in the courtroom. The Florida Court of Appeals held this to be an error. The defendant should have been allowed to wear the clothes and was entitled to the instruction to prevent an improper verdict.[117] Other cases have held that security personnel can require removal of religious garb in performing routine security checks so long as the believer is not subject to greater scrutiny than other persons wearing like nonreligious articles.[118]

Courts are mixed on whether practitioners or witnesses can wear religious garb, as such may prejudice the jury by leaving a bias for or against their action. Vincent LaRocca, a Roman Catholic priest and member of the Bar of New York, repeatedly encountered issues involving his wearing a clerical collar in the courtroom. State courts issued conflicting opinions.[119] More recent cases have left the matter to a case-by-case decision of possible juror bias to be addressed during the jury selection process.[120]

The case of *Muhammad v. Paruk*, 553 F. Supp. 2d 893 (E.D. Mich. 2008), demonstrates a statewide discussion of whether a female may veil in court. Muhammad brought suit in small claims court and wore her face veil to court. The trial judge ordered her to remove it and dismissed her case when she refused. She sued in federal court for violation of her civil rights, but the case was dismissed on technical grounds. She dropped her appeal, but the issue continued. The Michigan Supreme Court amended its rules of evidence to allow a court to "exercise reasonable control over the appearance of parties and witnesses so as to (1) ensure that the demeanor of such persons may be observed and assessed by the fact-finder and (2) ensure the accurate identification of such persons."[121] The controversy is important to other states because Michigan has a sizeable Muslim population. Many asked for a religious exception, which the court denied. One of the reasons for the denial is the confrontation clause of the Constitution, which allows any defendant a right to confront his accusers. Exceptions to face-to-face confrontation are very limited and require extraordinary circumstances.[122] The demeanor of a witness in body language and facial expression is an important part of testimony and is obscured by a face veil; thus, some argue the Constitution prohibits veiling by witnesses. One commentator asserts that the timing of the Michigan amendment and discussion surrounding it show that it was passed to restrict a specific religious practice, and therefore it is invalid under *Lukumi* standards.[123] However, the same commentator argues that laws passed outside these circumstances are valid, generally applicable neutral laws, and the confrontation clause interests outweigh any balancing for a religious exception.

ANTI-MASKING LAWS AND *BURQA* BANS

There are no general laws prohibiting the headscarf. A few existing laws may be used to restrict the general wearing of the face veil in the US. Several states and municipalities have anti-masking laws from the KKK days, which may impact Muslim women who wear the veil in public. Remaining questions in the US are the effect and constitutionality of existing anti-masking laws on a Muslim woman and whether any new law can withstand constitutional scrutiny.

California provides examples of the issues raised. California has both a criminal and a general anti-masking law. The case of *Ghafari v. Municipal Court*, 150 Cal. Rptr. 813 (Cal. Ct. App. 1978), demonstrates the difference between the two and the problem. In *Ghafari*, a group of students was protesting outside the Iranian consulate in San Francisco in 1977 while wearing face masks. They were charged under the general law, as they had not committed any criminal act while masked. The court held the law unconstitutional because it "either inhibits the exercise of free speech or exposes the speaker . . . to retaliation."[124]

In order for the police to charge someone with breach of the criminal law they would have to observe the person committing a crime while wearing the mask. At least one scholar who supports the general laws argues that this is too late and that the prevention of crime before it occurs is the point of general anti-masking laws.[125] However, this raises constitutional issues. The US follows the doctrine of *cogitationis poenam nemo patitur*, no one is punishable solely for his thoughts. The mere intent to commit a crime is not a substitute for criminal conduct. The application of a presumption raises an issue of profiling and, if applied to a Muslim, would be illegal profiling based on religion and possibly race or ethnicity. In a law review article,

Gregory Proseus endorses a US *burqa* ban like the French one by arguing that *burqa*-wearing terrorist acts are inevitable in the US because terrorist acts have been committed elsewhere by *burqa*-clad persons. He also argues that we should ban the *burqa* in the US because countries which require the wearing of the *burqa* do not adhere to American standards of women's rights.[126] This Chicken Little argument would likely fail under US legal standards. As Benjamin Franklin said, "Those who would give up essential liberty to purchase a little temporary safety deserve neither liberty nor safety."[127] If the Muslim woman wearing the face veil is charged with a breach of a general anti-masking law, she can claim violation of her constitutional rights of free exercise and expression (speech).

In the case of an Islamic veil the covering serves the function of direct expression. Direct expression is determined by application of the *O'Brien* test. The *O'Brien* test requires the court to first determine whether the law regulating conduct is unrelated to the content of the expression being made. If so, the conduct can be regulated as the regulation is not intended to stop the expressive nature of the act. Even so, the law banning the conduct must be narrowly tailored to further an important or substantial government interest. Thus, even if the regulation is unrelated to the expressive conduct, the state bears the burden of showing its regulation is the least restrictive means to accomplish an important interest. *U.S. v. O'Brien*, 391 U.S. 367 (1968), involved the burning of a draft card. The Supreme Court held that a federal law against destroying a military draft card was unrelated to O'Brien's act of burning his card as a political protest. Thus, there was no constitutional protection for O'Brien's act. The government's interest was the conduct itself, not the content of the protected communication. Further, the government's interest was important and the regulation was the least restrictive means.[128]

If the face covering is not deemed to be a direct expression, a general ban may still be unconstitutional if it will inhibit the exercise of a First Amendment right. To determine if a lack of anonymity inhibiting the exercise of First Amendment rights is constitutional, the court established a test in the cases of *NAACP v. Alabama*, 357 U.S. 449 (1958), and *Shelton v. Tucker*, 364 U.S. 479 (1960). This test requires that the law serve a compelling government interest and be narrowly tailored. In the case of the Muslim woman the ban inhibits the free exercise of religion. A general ban on all persons covering their face is not narrowly tailored, and it is difficult to imagine a court agreeing that there is a compelling interest in simply being able to see someone's face because social convention prefers it.

One view is that a Muslim woman is directly exercising her religion and communicating that religion to all who see her, so her act is direct expression. The purpose of a general anti-masking law with no exceptions is to stop the wearing of a face covering for any reason. This law directly impairs the woman's rights and would, by these standards, be unconstitutional. A law which has exceptions for certain conduct, such as holiday masks, would have to include an exception for religious reasons because allowing an exception for certain cultural practices and not religion amounts to unequal treatment. A veiling woman may not be able to receive an exemption if a law includes an exception for health or safety only.

Under federal or state RFRA, the Civil Rights Acts, and First Amendment law, any proposed legislation with the motivation to ban the *burqa* would be invalid, so it is not surprising that research reveals no proposals for a *burqa* ban. A *burqa* ban motivated by animus against the Islamic practice would be decided under the *Lukumi* standard as its motivation is anti-religious. Applying the *Lukumi* standard means that a compelling government interest would have to be proven even if the proposal were neutral on its face. The law would also have to be tailored to meet the government interest in the least restrictive manner. A general ban on face covering to stop the Islamic practice would not meet this test. A limited specific ban, such as requiring an uncovered face for a driver's license photograph or when passing through airport security, does survive because it is limited in time and place.

In the US, the robust protection of individual rights offers legal protection for Muslim women, and the judiciary is applying the same standards to Muslim women which they apply to other discrimination claimants. Further, the general attitude of politicians and the public to protect those individual rights inhibits development of any general *burqa* ban. The balance in the US appears to remain close to rule of law standards, with the existing law being neutral in motivation, on its face and in effect.

NOTES

1. 31 U.S.C. § 5112(d) (I). All US laws can be found at http://www.gpo.gov/fdsys/browse/collectionUScode.action?collectionCode=USCODE. The Library of Congress's Thomas system provides legislative information for all US Congressional action at http://www.thomas.loc.gov/home/thomas.php.
2. Tomas Archdeacon, *Becoming American: An Ethnic History* (New York: Free Press, 1984).
3. Richard Middleton and Anne Lombard, *Colonial America: A History to 1763,* 4th ed. (New York: Wiley-Blackwell, 2011).
4. James Hutson, *Religion and the Founding of the American Republic* (Washington, DC: Library of Congress, 1998), 2–48; T. Jeremy Gunn, "Religious Freedom and *Laïcité:* A Comparison of the US and France," *BYU L. Rev*. 2004: 442.
5. Carl Esbeck, "Dissent and Disestablishment: The Church-State Settlement in the Early American Republic," *BYU L. Rev*. 2004: 1385–492, 1415; Gunn, 443–44.
6. Edwin Gaustad, *Faith of the Founders: Religion and the New Nation, 1776–1826.* (Waco, TX: Baylor University Press, 2004), 8–9; Gunn, 443–45.
7. Immigration laws are codified under Title 8 of the U.S.C. Additional laws may be found in Title 50 (defense). These laws bar entry and provide for deportation for any person suspected of criminal activity. For a good synopsis of all these laws, see the University of Massachusetts Amherst's acla.net, http://www.umass.edu/complit/aclanet/USmigrat.html.

8. Armando Navarro, *Mexicano Political Experience in Occupied Aztlan* (Lanham, MD: Rowman and Littlefield, 2005). Aztlan is the name given by some Chicano activists to the portion of the US which used to be part of Mexico.

9. There was no uniform refugee law until 1980. 8 U.S.C. § 1520. Various temporary laws and accords allowed for entry of persons following wars and to escape communism. Post WWII a three-year law allowed up to 250,000 European refugees; there were laws and accords allowing refugees from communist countries to enter, including for Cuban refugees, and a limited-time 1975 law allowing entry for refugees from Vietnam. These laws were enacted as part of the Cold War defense strategy, not general immigration laws.

10. For further details see the Historical Census Statistics on foreign-born population within the United States at census.gov for figures 1850–2000. See also Elizabeth Grieco et al., "The Size, Place of Birth, and Geographic Distribution of the Foreign-Born Population in the United States, 1960–2010," US Census Bureau Working Paper, 2012.

11. Edward E. Curtis, IV, *Muslims in America* (New York: Oxford University Press, 2009); Kambiz Ghanea Bassiri, *A History of Islam in America* (New York: Cambridge University Press, 2010). I will not discuss the roots of the Black Muslim movement as it rests largely on racial issues not a religious freedom argument. Issues faced by Black Muslim women who wear the headscarf or veil are the same as others who wear the scarf or veil.

12. http://www.pewresearch.org/2007/05/22/muslim-americans-middle-class-and-mostly-mainstream/.

13. http://www.pewresearch.org/2007/05/22/muslim-americans-middle-class-and-mostly-mainstream/.

14. Gunn, 412–46.

15. Virginia, South Carolina, North Carolina, Georgia, Maryland. It was also established in parts of New York. Esbeck, *BYU*, 1415; Michael McConnell, "The Origins and Historical Understanding of Free Exercise of Religion," *Harvard L. Rev.* 103, no. 7 (1990): 121–30.

16. New York (1777), North Carolina (1776), Virginia (1776), Georgia (1798), Maryland (1785), and South Carolina (1790). Esbeck, *BYU*, 1458.

17. Congregational churches were established in the New England area, Massachusetts, Connecticut, and New Hampshire. There was no one established religion in Rhode Island, Pennsylvania, Delaware, and New Jersey. Esbeck, *BYU*, 1415, 1457–97; McConnell, 121–30.

18. Carl Esbeck, "Religion during the American Revolution," http://www.papers.ssrn.com/sol3/papers.cfm?abstract_id=2154443. Also available in *Law and Religion*, ed. Silvio Ferrari (Burlington, VT: Ashgate, 2013).

19. Isiah Berlin, "Two Concepts of Liberty," http://www.cas.umt.edu/phil/faculty/walton/Berlin2Concepts.pdf; Noah Feldman, "The Intellectual Origins of the Establishment Clause," *New York University L. Rev.* 77 (2002): 350.

20. John Locke, A Letter Concerning Toleration, http://www.etext.lib.virginia.edu/toc/mod-eng/public/.

21. Declaration of Independence, http://www.archives.gov/exhibits/charters/declaration_transcript.html.

22. Gordon Wood, *The Creation of the American Republic 1776–1787* (Chapel Hill: University of North Carolina Press, 1969).

23. US Const., Article VI.

24. James Madison, *Notes of Our Debates in the Federal Convention of 1787* (New York: W. W. Norton, 1987), 630 et seq.; Catherine Brown, *Miracle at Philadelphia* (New York: Little Brown, 1960), 243–53.

25. Brown, 267 et seq.; Massachusetts, Virginia, New Hampshire, and New York included in their ratification recommendations for the immediate amendment of the Constitution to add a Bill of Rights. North Carolina refused to ratify until progress was made in drafting a Bill of Rights.

26. One of these proposals was ratified as the Twenty-Seventh Amendment in 1992. The other remains pending. See Gunn, 445, 451–52, citations omitted.

27. Gunn, 445–50.

28. Connecticut 1818; Georgia 1789; Maryland 1701 (Catholic), 1776 (COE); Massachusetts 1786, completed 1833; South Carolina 1790; Virginia 1786. Even in disestablished states,

Christian or Protestant preferential laws continued into the twentieth century. Arkansas, Maryland, Massachusetts, North Carolina, Pennsylvania, South Carolina, Tennessee, and Texas all have laws on religious oaths for office. While unenforceable after *Torcaso v. Watkins*, 367 U.S. 488 (1961), the laws have not been repealed.

29. Stephen Monsma, *Positive Neutrality: Letting Religious Freedom Ring* (Grand Rapids, MI: Baker Books, 1995), 113–26; Sydney Ahlstrom identifies the time as between 1815 and 1860, Sydney Ahlstrom, *A Religious History of the American People* (Garden City, NY: Image Books, 1975), 556.

30. Gunn, 446–50.

31. Philip Hamburger, *Separation of Church and State* (Cambridge, MA: Harvard University Press, 2004), 220; Noah Feldman, *Divided by God: America's Church-State Problem and What We Should Do about It* (New York: Farrar, Strauss and Giroux, 2005), 72.

32. Jonathan Sarna and David Dalin, *Religion and State in the American Jewish Experience* (Notre Dame, IN: Notre Dame Press, 1997), 16.

33. Mark Deforrest, "An Overview and Evaluation of State Blaine Amendments: Origin, Scope, and First Amendment Concerns," *Harvard J. of Law and Pub. Policy* 26 (2003): 551–626; Steven Green, "The Blaine Amendment Reconsidered," *American J. Legal History* 36 (1992): 38.

34. "No State shall make any law respecting an establishment of religion, or prohibiting the free exercise thereof; and no money raised by taxation in any State for the support of public schools, or derived from any public fund therefore, nor any public lands devoted thereto, shall ever be under the control of any religious sect; nor shall any money so raised or lands so devoted be divided between religious sects or denominations." 44 Cong. Rec (December 14, 1875); Amendment Congressional Record, 44th Congress, 1st Session, 14 December 1875. www.loc.gov.

35. James Fraser, *Between Church and State: Religion and Public Education in a Multicultural America*, (New York: St. Martin's Press, 1999), 106–13; Michael Sandel, "Religious Liberty: Freedom of Choice or Freedom of Conscience?" in *Secularism and Its Critics*, ed. Rajeev Bhargva (New York: Oxford University Press, 1999), 76. Some of the states included the amendments as part of their constitution as they joined the Union. The state amendments were partially overruled within the US when the Supreme Court ruled in *Zelman v. Simmons-Harris*, 536 U.S. 639 (2002), that state vouchers for education could be used to pay for private, faith-based schools.

36. Roger Williams, *The Bloudy Tenent of Persecution*, http://www.archive.org/stream/thebloudytenento00willuoft/thebloudytenento00willuoft_djvu.txt; for a full discussion of the separation of church-state in history, see John Witte, "Facts and Fictions about the History of Separation of Church-State," *Journal of Church State* 48, no. 1 (Winter 2006): 14–45.

37. Thomas Jefferson, Letter to Messrs. Nehemiah Dodge, et al. January 1, 1802, http://www.etext.lib.virginia.edu.

38. *Reynolds*, 98 U.S. at 167.

39. Kathleen Holscher, "Contesting the Veil in America: Catholic Habits and the Controversy over Religious Clothing in the US," *Journal of Church State* 64 (February 2011): 57–81; Kathleen Holscher, *Religious Lessons: Catholic Sisters and the Captive School Crisis in New Mexico* (New York: Oxford University Press, 2012).

40. Holscher, 64–65.

41. Holscher, 69.

42. Holscher, 70.

43. Holscher, 75.

44. *Zellers v. Huff*, 55 N.M. 501 (1951).

45. Holscher, 74.

46. Wayne Allen, "Klan Cloth and Constitution: Anti-Mask Laws and the First Amendment," *Georgia L. Rev.* 25 (1991): 819, 822.

47. 18 U.S.C. § 241.

48. Stephen Simoni, "Who Goes There—Proposing a Model Anti-Mask Act," *Fordham L. Rev.* 61 (1992–93): 241. According to Simoni, fifteen states and DC have general anti-mask laws. Many more have criminal anti-mask laws, with several having both.

49. Warren Nord, *Religion and American Education: Rethinking a National Dilemma* (Chapel Hill: University of North Carolina Press, 1994), 96.

50. Daniel Okrent, *Last Call: The Rise and Fall of Prohibition* (New York: Scribner, 2010).

51. The Tennessee Supreme Court upheld the statute but reversed the conviction on a legal procedure ground. The law was repealed in 1967 and all such laws were overruled by fiat in the US Supreme Court decision in *Epperson v. Arkansas*, 393 U.S. 97 (1968), which held that such laws violate the establishment clause as their primary purpose is religious.

52. Christian Smith, Preface to *The Secular Revolution: Power Interests, and Conflict in the Secularization of American Public Life*, ed. Christian Smith (Berkeley: University of California Press, 2003), vii. Hereafter, Smith 2003a.

53. Christian Smith, Introduction to *The Secular Revolution: Power Interests, and Conflict in the Secularization of American Public Life*, ed. Christian Smith (Berkeley: University of California Press, 2003), 36–78. Hereafter, Smith 2003b; Robert Wuthnow, *The Struggle for America's Soul: Evangelicals, Liberals, and Secularism* (Grand Rapids, MI: Eerdmans, 1990), 26–27; Philip Hamburger, *Separation of Church and State* (Cambridge, MA: Harvard University Press, 2004), 360 et seq.

54. Jose Casanova, *Public Religions in the Modern World* (Chicago: University of Chicago Press, 1994), 138.

55. Christian Smith, "Secularizing American Higher Education: The Case of Early American Sociology," in *The Secular Revolution: Power Interests, and Conflict in the Secularization of American Public Life*, ed. Christian Smith (Berkeley: University of California Press, 2003), 74–78. Hereafter, Smith 2003c; Eva Marie Garroutte, "The Positive Attack on Baconian Science and Religious Knowledge in the 1870s," in *The Secular Revolution: Power Interests, and Conflict in the Secularization of American Public Life*, ed. Christian Smith (Berkeley: University of California Press, 2003), 197–215; Edward Larson, *Summer for the Gods: The Scopes Trial and Americas Continuing Debate over Science and Religion* (New York: Basic Books, 2006); Feldman, 135–49; Gary Wills, *Under God: Religion and American Politics* (New York: Simon and Schuster, 1990), 7–114; Casanova, 144; Robert Fowler, Allen Hertzke, Laura Olson, and Ken den Dulk, *Religion and Politics in America: Faith Culture, and Strategic Choices* (Boulder, CO: Westview, 2004), 19–21. I acknowledge that there are many arguments that a Protestant preferentialism still exists. I am referring to the strong, open governmental support for Protestantism in opposition to other denominations.

56. Gunn, 446–50.

57. Ahlstrom, 565; William Hutchison, *Religious Pluralism in America: The Contentious History of a Founding Ideal* (New Haven: Yale University Press, 2003), 48–49.

58. Gunn, 449.

59. John Witte, *Religion and the American Constitutional Experiment*, 3rd ed. (Boulder, CO: Westview Press, 2010), 100.

60. This is a very simplified explanation of a complicated and controversial legal interpretation. We need not consider all the ramifications or applications for this discussion. For more information on the controversy see Akhil Amar, *Bill of Rights: Creation and Reconstruction* (New Haven, CT: Yale, 1998); Michael Curtis, *No State Shall Abridge* (Durham, NC: Duke University Press, 1994), or just about any case involving the Bill of Rights since the 1873 *Slaughterhouse Cases*, 83 U.S. 36 (1873). Prior to the religion clause cases the court had already incorporated freedom of speech, *Gitlow v. N.Y.*, 268 U.S. 652 (1925); freedom of the press, *Near v. Minnesota,* 283 U.S. 697 (1931); several criminal defendant rights in the Fifth and Sixth Amendments, *Powell v. Alabama*, 287 U.S. 45 (1931); and a generic incorporation of the "fundamental rights" enumerated in the Bill of Rights, *Palko v. Connecticut*, 302 U.S. 319 (1937).

61. *Abingdon Sch. Dist. v. Schempp*, 374 U.S. 203, 222 (1963).

62. McCollum involved a release-time program in the Champaign, Illinois, public schools. During release time, students were permitted to attend religious devotional instruction rather than regular school classes during the school day. Religious instructors paid for by local religious groups conducted the instruction without input from the school.

63. Wuthnow, 17.

64. 4 U.S.C. § 4; 36 U.S.C. §§ 119, 302.

65. Jon Meacham, *American Gospel: God, the Founding Fathers, and the Making of a Nation* (New York: Random House, 2007), 176–79.

66. *Zorach* involved a school release-time program. The court held the release-time program constitutional as it was off school grounds and with parental permission.

67. *Zorach v. Clausen,* 343 U.S. 306 (1952).

68. *Lemon*, 403 U.S. at 612–13.

69. *Sherbert*, 374 U.S. at 304–10.

70. *Thomas*, 450 U.S. at 713–14.

71. *Frazee v. Illinois Department of Employment Security,* 489 U.S. 829, 933 (1989); *U.S. v. Seeger*, 30 U.S. 163, 185 (1965).

72. *Smith* at 879.

73. See cases cited in Ronald Flowers, Melissa Rogers, and Stephen Green, *Religious Freedom and the Supreme Court* (Waco, TX: Baylor University Press, 2008), 765–851.

74. *Tinker v. Des Moines Indep. Sch. Dist.*, 393 U.S. 503 (199), wearing of an armband is protected speech; *Texas v. Johnson*, 491 U.S. 397 (1989), burning the flag is protected speech.

75. 42 U.S.C. § 2000bb-4. The number of state RFRAs is extensive and all are substantially similar. For example, see Alabama, Arizona, California, Connecticut, Florida, Idaho, Illinois, Missouri, New Mexico, Oklahoma, Pennsylvania, Rhode Island, South Carolina, Texas, and Virginia. According to Douglas Laycock, some state constitutions include the *Sherbert* standard, so an RFRA is unnecessary. Douglas Laycock, "Theology Scholarship, the Pledge of Allegiance and Religious Liberty: Avoiding the Extremes but Missing the Liberty," *Harvard L. Rev*. 118 (2004): 211–12.

76. *City of Boerne v. Flores*, 521 U.S. 507 (1997); Jerold Waltman, *Congress, the Supreme Court and Religious Liberty: The Case of City of* Boerne v. Flores (New York: Palgrave, 2013).

77. To my knowledge, only Arkansas and Mississippi have neither.

78. "Ann Coulter: Bombing Suspect's Wife Should Be Jailed for Wearing Hijab," http://www.huffingtonpost.com/2013/04/23/ann-coulter-hijab_n_3139513.html. In the same tirade, Coulter asserted the police arresting the Boston bombing suspect should have given "him an automatic death penalty right there." Coulter later claimed she was making a joke about the *hijab* but made no retraction as to her call for summary execution, a clear violation of US law.

79. A number of states have attempted to implement other restrictions on Muslim practices. Several attempted to or did implement statutes prohibiting consideration of shari'a law in family decisions. Oklahoma did so with a constitutional amendment. All have been ruled invalid as violations of the US Constitution.

80. *Tinker v. Des Moines ISD*, 393 U.S. 503 (1969).

81. *Tinker*, 393 U.S. at 509.

82. *Westside Community Schools v. Mergens*, 496 U.S. 226, 250 (1990). Numerous cases, from around the country have upheld the wearing of message T-shirts and buttons. For a list see http://www.aclj.org/education/religious-clothing-at-school.

83. *Lopez v. Bay Shore Free Sch. Dist.*, 668 F. Supp. 2d 406 (E.D. N.Y. 2009).

84. See, generally, *Palmer v. Waxahachie ISD,* 579 F.3d 502 (5th Cir. 2009), *cert. denied,* 130 S.Ct. 1055 (2010).

85. CAIR publishes a widely distributed newsletter requesting Muslims report incidents of discrimination and aid in finding assistance for litigation. It also publishes a yearly report of incidents of discrimination against Muslim students. The ACLU also encourages reporting of religious discrimination and assists in litigation.

86. *Nichol v. ARIN Intermediate Unit 28,* 268 F. Supp. 536 (W.D. Pa. 2003); *James v. Bd. of Edu. of Central Dist. No. 1 of Town of Addison, et al,* 461 F.2d 566 (1972).

87. *Cooper v. Eugene Sch. Dist. No. 41*, 301 Ore. 350, 375 (1986), app. dism'd, 480 U.S. 942 (1987).

88. Michael Peabody, "The Right Thing," *Liberty*, March/April 2011, 8–11.

89. "Oregon Education Board Model Policy regarding Religious Clothing of Public School Employees," 8 December 2010.

90. *U.S. v. Board of Education*, 911 F.2d at 894.

91. *EEOC v. READS*, 759 F. Supp. 1150 (E.D. Penn. 1991).

92. *Nichol v. ARIN Intermediate Unit 28*, 268 F. Supp. 536 (W.D. Pa. 2003).

93. http://www.triblive.com/x/pittsburghtrib/news/s_747107.html (accessed September 8, 2012).

94. Neb. Stat. §79–1274. Alexander Panetta, "Nebraska Shocked to Learn It Has PQ-Style Religion Law," http://www.ctvnews.ca, 9 March 2014.

95. *EEOC v. Abercrombie and Fitch Stores, Inc.*, No. 09-CV-602-GKF-FHM (N.D. Ca. April 9, 2013).

96. For example, Disney, a strict-uniform-policy company, has created a uniform *hijab* which at least one employee accepts and one does not. The one who did not accept it sued, but the suit was later dismissed on undisclosed grounds. See http://www.huffingtonpost.com/2010/09/30/disneyland-hijab-dispute-_n_745610.html (accessed September 9, 2012) and *Boulal v. Disney*, No. 8:12-CV-01306 (C. D. Cal., dismissed March 3, 2014).

97. *EEOC v. Regency Health Associates*, No. 1:05-CV-2519-CAP-CCH (N.D. Ga. 2007).

98. http://www.articles.latimes.com/2012/sep/09/local/la-me-workplace-discrimination-20120909 (accessed September 9, 2012).

99. Keith Blair, "Better Disabled Than Devout? Why Title VII Has Failed to Provide Adequate Accommodations against Workplace Religious Discrimination," *U. Ark L. Rev.* 63 (2010): 515–57.

100. http://www.clinton2.nara.gov/WH/New/html/19970819–3275.html.

101. *Goldman v. Weinberger*, 457 U.S. 503 (1986).

102. 10 U.S.C. § 774(b) (2006).

103. http://www.articles.washingtonpost.com/2012–06–06/national/35460413_1_turbans-sikh-and-muslim-workers-kara (accessed September 10, 2012).

104. It is interesting to note that Justice Alito wrote the opinion while on the circuit court and is now a member of the US Supreme Court.

105. "Muslim Firefighter May Wear Scarf," *Washington Post*, July 13, 2001, http://www.pqasb.pqarchiver.com/washingtonpost/access/75379231.html?dids=753.startpage=B.05anddesc=Muslim+Firefighter+ May+Wear+Scarf (accessed September 8, 2012).

106. For example, see Texas Transportation Code § 521.21(a)(2) (2012): "a color photograph of the entire face of the holder" is required on all driver's licenses or government issued IDs. The rule also applies to all licenses issued by the state which require a photo be attached, such as beautician and barber licenses.

107. http://www.tulsaworld.com/article.aspx/Anti_scarf_bill_draws_concern/20090305_298_0_oklaho793247 (accessed September 8, 2012).

108. Minn. Stat. § 171.071 (2010).

109. Rajdeep Singh Jolly, "How State Photo Identification Standards Can Be Used to Undermine Religious Freedom," *Asian American Law Journal* 19 (2012). http://www.ssrn.com/abstract=2204832 (accessed January 23, 2013). There are twenty-one statutory state RFRAs and a further eleven by judicial fiat.

110. http://www.travel.state.gov/passport/pptphotoreq/pptphotoreq_5333.html.

111. *Hussein v. City of Omaha*, No. 8:04-cv-00268 (D. Neb. 2004).

112. Wahentaw County Parks and Recreation, January 2006, http://www.aclu.org/womens-rights/gen/35367res200601.html. The style of swimsuit the student wore is called a burkini and looks a lot like a jumpsuit made of swimsuit fabric.

113. See reports of ACLU, Anti-Defamation League, and CAIR.

114. For a synopsis of this issue across time and place, see Samuel Levine, "Religious Symbols and Religious Garb in the Courtroom: Personal Values and Public Judgments," *Fordham L. Rev.* 66 (1998): 1510.

115. 42 U.S.C. § 2000cc.

116. For example, see *McMillan v. State*, 265 A.2d 453 (Md. 1970), and *In re Palmer*, 386 A.2d 1112 (R.I. 1978).

117. *Joseph v. State*, 642 So.2d 613 (Fla. Dist. Ct. App. 1994).

118. *Spanks-E v. Finley*, 845 F.2d 1023 (7th Cir. 1988) (plaintiff could be required to remove his fez when passing through security because removal was temporary and all person were required to remove all head coverings); *Kaukab v. Harris*, No. 2-cv-0371 (N.D. Ill. 2003) (plaintiff alleging TSA excessive screening of Muslim woman is a violation of civil rights).

119. For a synopsis of the long saga of LaRocca, see Levine 1515–21.
120. *Ryslik v. Krass*, 6532 A.2d 767 (N.J. Super. Ct. App. Div. 1995).
121. Mich. R. Evid. 611(b).
122. *Coy v. Iowa*, 487 U.S. 1012 (1988); *Maryland v. Craig*, 497 U.S. 836 (1990) (even with children testifying against defendants accused of abusing them there is no absolute right for the child to not have to testify face-to-face with the defendant).
123. Sean Clerger, "Timing Is of the Essence: Reviving the Neutral Law of General Applicability Standard and Applying It to Restrictions against Religious Face Coverings while Testifying in Court," *Geo. Mason L. Rev.* 18 (2010–2011): 1013, 1038. *Lukumi Babalu Aye v. City of Hialeah,* 508 U.S. 520 (1993) (an ordinance neutral on its face but targeted in passage and effect to prohibit a specific religious practice is subject to strict scrutiny, the compelling interest–narrowly tailored standard, and not the *Smith* test, the lenient rational basis–generally applicable neutral law standard).
124. *Ghafari* at 816.
125. Allen, 840.
126. Gregory Proseus, "Reconciling Religious Free Exercise and National Security: Triumph of the Ultimate Compelling Government Interest," *Wm. and Mary J. Women and Law* 18 (2011–2012): 363–94.
127. Ben Franklin, Reply to the Governor no. 11 (1755), in *Papers of Ben Franklin*, ed. Leonard W. Labaree (New Haven, CT: Yale University Press, 1963), 242.
128. *O'Brien* at 381–82.

Chapter Eight

Conclusion

We have spent a great deal of time reviewing each country's history, institutional structure, and responses to controversy about Islamic women's dress. This background was necessary for the reader to be able to compare the reactions. The introduction queried whether there are any common factors driving state actions or if the actions are merely a reflection of local variations. In each country proponents of restrictions give similar reasons for their actions: protection of women from male dominance, domestic condemnation of an intolerant foreign ideology, promotion of an essential aspect of national identity. Additional reasons given for restrictions on women's dress are that the state is protecting and promoting women's equality and ensuring state neutrality. Now we can examine these presumptions cross-nationally to show that they are based on false assumptions and are unlikely to achieve the desired result. Cross-nationally the restrictions are not mere variations in local institutional structure. They demonstrate movement away from the center balance point of state neutrality and legal equality. Thus, they cannot be reconciled with liberal democratic theory.

Forces constantly pull the pendulum of democracy away from the center point of ideal. Liberal democracy has proved elastic when incorporating new cultures in the past, and there is no reason why it should not be able to do so now. What is different is that in response to those forces some countries are moving away from the center point of ideal democracy. No nation can ever achieve lasting ideal democracy because new situations are encountered every moment of every day. However, liberal democracies should strive for proximity to that center point.

In a liberal democracy citizens should share a desire to achieve that ideal, a balance between the individual right and community need. There have always been differences in ideas, regional cultures, and even religions. The introduction of Islamic women's dress into the West is another addition to the mix. The addition is not a reason to abandon liberal democratic principles.

Each of the countries studied is coping with new religious adherents. Some of the differences in how each country is responding to the new religious adherents emanate from the local historical-institutional structure. However, the reasons underlying local action or inaction are common and grounded in a reaction to forces tending to pull the country away from the ideal balance point for liberal democracy. Religious dress may run counter to a social norm, but the enactment of laws prohibiting conduct in a liberal democracy is supposed to be limited to those issues which are fundamental to sustaining and furthering the democracy, not for social comfort.

As early as Plato and Aristotle, the essential values of democracy were seen as liberty and equality. Democratic states enshrine liberty and equality through constitutional rules. A democracy cannot be a full one if citizens lack freedom to associate or express themselves as they wish, including religious expression. There is an interest in stopping assembly or expression that genuinely threatens democratic principles, which is the only point at which free expression in the liberal democracy should be curtailed.

Just as important is equality of persons. If citizens lack equal opportunity to express themselves, to seek legal redress, to participate in governance and the benefits of community, then democracy falters. The evolution of religion into a human right places diversity, rather than theological or elitist assertions of supremacy at the center of thought. In a liberal democracy tolerance holds primacy of place, and equal treatment is the goal. A continual balancing of community and individual occurs, requiring respect for the other in her humanness as opposed to a particular belief or practice other than democracy itself. Globalization results in exposure to more diverse ideas and practices and allows us to better isolate the essence of liberal democracy. It moves national identity from a regional culture to adherence to an abstract ideal balancing individual and community, with regional culture serving only as the flavor on top.

All three countries are signatories to the International Covenant on Civil and Political Rights (ICCPR), which provides for implementation of its norms through national structures. The ICCPR, incorporating the UN Declaration on Human Rights, declares that freedom of religion is to be guaranteed by the signatory states and that freedom to manifest religious beliefs includes religious dress. The only limitations allowed are as necessary for public safety, order, health, morals, and fundamental rights of others.

France signals that its practical interpretation of these ideals may differ from other Western liberal democracies by its refusal to accept article 27, which requires adherents to allow minority religious groups the freedom to enjoy their own culture and practice their religion. Article 27 does not require the state to give official recognition to the minority group separate from other citizens. It requires that the state leave the groups alone, an implied recognition of difference. The French reaction to article 27 is our first clue that, when putting agreed-to international liberal democratic norms into practice, states may interpret those norms differently and impose community biases.

The UN Declaration of Human Rights of 1948 begins by proclaiming that "recognition of the inherent human dignity and of the equal and inalienable rights of all members of the human family is the foundation of freedom, justice, and peace in the world." The UN stance is the liberal democratic one: *in dubio pro liberate*—any doubt should benefit liberty. The recognition of dignity of each person undergirds both liberty and equality. It is only when we acknowledge the dignity of each person that we acknowledge her right of self-governance.

Ober asserts two relevant features of democracy's dignity are nonhumiliation (having respect as a moral equal) and noninfantilization (having recognition as a choice-making adult).[1] Formal rhetoric on equality and formal self-participation are inadequate to demonstrate recognition of the dignity necessary for liberal democracy. This dignity calls for a recognition of those differences in the public sphere.

> Lowly (humiliating or infantilizing) circumstances preclude the activities of speech choice, and execution demanded of self-governing citizens. . . . [Dignity] stabilizes democracy by mediating between demands of liberty and equality, forbidding libertarian neglect of basic needs and egalitarian paternalism alike. Democracy without secure dignity is at best a fragile construct. At worst, it is a façade masking the despotism of entrenched and unaccountable elites. Like equality and liberty, dignity stands in a reciprocal relationship to democracy sustaining and sustained by it. Dignity makes democracy robust: Democratic institutions defend dignity, whereas the habits of dignified citizens provide behavioral foundations for defending democracy and for improving constitution over time.[2]

In a liberal democracy human dignity is an *a priori* position of individual self-worth, which is reinforced in the community as the social recognition of that worth.

The rule of law incorporates human dignity by requiring that all be given the same consideration in the government structure and implementing rules to impose this equality on wider society. Substantive rule of law is the implementation of the principles of liberal democracy. Substantive rule of law requires that all law be neutral in motivation, neutral on its face, and neutral in effect. All law is a value determination, a choice between what is considered valuable and allowed and what is so unacceptable that the state must prohibit it. In a liberal democracy the margin of individual choice is to be as wide as possible and, in one view, restrictive laws are only to prevent damage to the continuation of democracy. For example, a law against murder is clearly necessary to sustain democracy because violence directly impedes the coexistence of diverse individuals. Also, laws for property distribution after death assist in maintaining democracy because they create a method for orderly transition. Where do laws restricting the religious dress of Islamic women fall?

The laws restricting religious dress may be neutral on their face, but they are not neutral in motivation or effect. The laws arose specifically in response to issues with Islamic women. All hearings on the proposed laws focused on Islamic women. Moreover, the popular names given to the laws refer to Islamic women. The inception of these laws is thus not neutral in motivation. Additionally, the laws are not neutral in effect because there are no other identifiable groups of persons affected by the laws. The laws act as a type of poll tax on Islamic women appearing in public.[3] The enforcement of the laws at schools falls almost exclusively on Muslim students. In the school context, administrators are given arbitrary authority to determine what constitutes religious dress. They are making suppositions about the meaning of dress worn by a Muslim student that are not applied to other students, resulting in arbitrary enforcement of the law and targeting based on religion, both violations of liberal democratic rule of law standards.

The bans unfairly target Islamic women because they are the only group in Western society which regularly engages in the practice of veiling. They are unfairly targeted for a religious practice and prevented from being active members of society due to discrimination against their religion. Proponents of the laws argue that they are properly balancing individual and community interests and are furthering democracy by protecting order and promoting women's rights. The evidence casts doubt on these justifications.

THE MALE DOMINANCE ARGUMENT

Humor sometimes exposes a truth we are too embarrassed to admit. The cartoon by Malcolm Evans, shown in figure 8.1, points out the fallacy of the assumption that a woman who wears the *burqa* only does so due to male dominance and that she is the only one subjected to male dominance. The same argument can be made that women who undress or wear scanty or sexually suggestive clothing, are just as much objects of male dominance as *burqa*-clad women. In Western cultures women's identity and power are determined by male standards of sexuality. Thus, it is imperative for women to make their own reasoned decision about appearance and thoughtfully determine the image they want to project.

The *burqa* ban does not assist women in attaining power over their own lives. In countries which require women to wear the *burqa* and in those

Figure 8.1. Cruel Culture, Malcolm Evans, 06 Jan 11. *Source:* Malcolm Evans, "Cruel Culture," January 6, 2011. http://www.evanscartoons.com/image.php?id=1294733061 (accessed January 30, 2013).

which prohibit its wearing, the state chooses the women's dress. In a liberal democracy personal appearance is a part of dignity. The state humiliates and infantilizes women by denying them the power to determine their own identity. In countries which require women to wear the *burqa* and in those which prohibit veiling, the state is implementing an egalitarian paternalism, an illiberal action. In a liberal democracy a woman should choose how to dress unless neutral factors, health or safety, require the imposition of restrictions.

The liberal democratic state claims that it works to ensure that each person is accorded equality in voice and association. In the *burqa* laws the state is saying that the women have submitted themselves to an unhealthy degree to the dominance of another. The state supposes that the women, by making a choice others would not make, must be mentally inferior, thereby infantilizing them. In the West there used to be laws and social norms that required women to cover their bodies, but those laws have been almost universally repealed because they unfairly targeted women. This has led to a social norm that anyone who does not uncover is ashamed and unable to take control over her own body. Of course, it can be argued just as forcefully that this actually promotes the increased objectification of women by emphasizing beauty and sexual desirability.

There is no evidence that all women who veil are doing so due to male dominance. The women surveyed indicated they did so as an act of piety.[4] The girls interviewed about wearing the scarf stated that they did so as an exploration of their faith.[5] It is true that all are influenced by their community, which may be a conservative one. But that influence is true of every person. Our thoughts and identity are constantly shaped by our experiences and perceptions. The evidence does not support an assumption that every girl who wears the scarf or every woman who veils is unduly influenced by a male.

Laws restricting dress also elevate physical appearance over human dignity. The state prohibits that which it finds different and which makes the majority uncomfortable. The state sends a message to women that their appearance must comport with its norms, and those who do not comply are unworthy and unequal. On the basis of appearance the state is declaring who is a worthy member of society. The effect on Muslim women is potentially humiliating when one considers the impact of choosing between religious practices and social acceptance. In a liberal democracy equality of citizens is supposed to emanate from their humanity, not their appearance. The criminalization of religious dress causes a lasting stigma in the minds of the women that they are somehow different or even deviant, thwarting the development of the strong ego needed to be in control of their own identity. If the women had a physical deformity, the same state would be outraged at the injustice of forcing them to be ashamed and to hide.

Another argument against veiling is that Islam is a patriarchal religion, so it is per se misogynist and thus incompatible with Western liberal democratic values. Christianity and Judaism are also patriarchal religions and also have some elements of female subjugation in their theology. There are a variety of Judaic and Christian, as well as Muslim, interpretations which accord women different roles in society, with some being very restrictive and others as equal partners. Bans singling out Islam due to some fundamentalist branches which are anti-democratic are illiberal, as they do not apply the same restrictions to other patriarchal religions. Further, some of the objectors to patristic religion object to all religion as backward and seek to restrict all religion to such a point that practice becomes too onerous for the average believer. In implementing this strategy these proponents of strict secularism act illiberally by restricting individual freedom and the guaranteed liberal right to freedom of religion.

It is clear that education and exposure to a multiplicity of philosophies is the best means of personal empowerment. The *burqa* ban serves to isolate women whom the state has already identified as marginalized. The restriction on school dress serves to prevent girls from attaining education or forces them to attend a private school where the state has even less control over their exposure to ideas which the state may find objectionable. If the state wants to ensure that all women are masters of their own destinies, the state will focus on increasing educational and economic opportunities, decreasing the women's dependence on others. The issue is no different from that faced by all other socioeconomically deprived persons; in that sense, there is no justification for a law targeting Muslim women. The repeal of these laws will move the state closer to balanced democracy. The state can then adequately address real problems by encouraging women's access to education and employment and advising them of their domestic rights.

INTOLERANT IDEOLOGY PROTEST

The bans are also justified by claims that they promote equality by offsetting the oppressive effects of forced veiling in other countries. Either way women are made pawns in a state tit-for-tat debate. Domestic laws are to deal with domestic situations. It is for international laws and actions to attempt to influence other states. There is no evidence that the enactment of a national veiling ban has ever influenced another sovereign state to alter its treatment of women. In fact, the evidence shows that it causes an entrenchment of ideology as a prideful reaction to what is viewed as outsider meddling.

Further, the bans create the same gender inequality as the mandates. They both affect and are specifically targeted toward Muslim women. They create a gender inequality, which is what they are supposedly protesting. The mere fact that any state has decided women are too infantile to decide for themselves how to dress is proof of gender inequality. The bans are part of the problem, not the solution. The solution is to allow women to make their own choice about their own bodies and appearance and for states to stop telling women what to or not to wear. The way to combat intolerance is to be tolerant. None of the women surveyed agreed with the political policies of countries which commanded wearing of the veil, and all expressed gratitude for the tolerance and opportunities for individual development in their home country.

PRESERVATION OF NATIONAL IDENTITY

One of the arguments given for veil bans is the continuation and fostering of national identity. Many asked about veiling practices in all three countries respond that "we just don't do that here"—it is un-French, un-Dutch, or un-American. However, is it? Is the majority sartorial culture so important to the continuation of the democracy that minority religious practice must be formally/institutionally curtailed for the good of the state, or can new minority religious sartorial practice be added to the mosaic national culture?

In France the standard for toleration is lack of harm to a third party, including the state. With the *burqa* ban that third party has become an amorphous national identity which did not exist previously. There is no imposed, even acceptable, French national dress; each individual and region decides the acceptability of appearance. No other religious dress has been generally banned, and others can wear any religious identifier on the public street without interference from the state. Thus, the argument that the French public space is religious-symbol free so that the veil bans are necessary for national identity or are acts of equal treatment is incorrect.

THREAT OF JURISTOCRACY

One of the questions asked at the beginning was whether the judiciary is expanding rights, possibly creating a juristocracy, so that political reaction is an assertion of their authority and maintenance of existing religion-state relations. In no instance has the judicial been expanding rights, so any argument that the political is merely acting to prevent implementation of a juristocracy is false. In the Netherlands the judicial has continued to apply the same principles to Islamic women that they apply to other minority groups. In France, the judicial at first held steady to recent rulings, but when the political retreated from liberal democratic principles, the judicial acquiesced.

The Council of Europe has also held steady against attempts by France to alter liberal democratic policies. However, the Court of Human Rights has not done so. Prior to the French *burqa* ban, the standard set by the Court of Human Rights was that when restricting individual religious rights, the state must prove a pressing need for the restriction and must use the least restrictive means to meet that need. The court had struck a Turkish blanket ban on the wearing of religious dress on the street and wearing of the headscarf in public school. It had also struck a prohibition on public school teachers wearing headscarves in Switzerland. The court applied the same reasoning to restrictions on the wearing of Christian symbols in two cases from the UK.

Only in the UK cases did the court even hint that some restriction is possible, and those restrictions were on neutral grounds. One of the cases involved a nurse, and the court ruled that for safety and hygiene she could be required to keep a necklace with a cross inside her uniform while on duty. The court emphasized that any restriction, even if allowed on neutral grounds, must be proportional to the need. In all cases, the court emphasized that pluralism and broadmindedness are hallmarks of democracy and that majority and minority views must be balanced to prevent dominance by either. The court relied on specific portions of the Charter of Human Rights in ruling in each of these cases. However, it retreated from its accepted precedent to uphold the French *burqa* ban and itself retreated to an illiberal position.

In upholding the *burqa* ban the court explicitly stated that the ban *did not* violate express provisions of the charter but then went on to engraft a penumbral right of "living together" to justify upholding the ban. The court retreated to a position that living together means majority social norm dominance, and minority rights are not even entitled to recognition. As Anna Galeotti points out, this minimal tolerance by recognition, a public acceptance of a minority group's visible difference, is the beginning of public legitimacy for the minority group and their inclusion as members of the community.[6] Without even this minimal tolerance, the minority will be marginalized and treated as suspect.

In the US a recent decision by the Supreme Court demonstrates that religion is again being placed in a preferentialist position. In the past the US position was one of Protestant preferentialism with minority religions subjugated. The institutional structure moved away from this preferentialism as it began to recognize plurality was a hallmark of liberal democracy. The Supreme Court moved the standard to one of strict neutrality; if a law is one of general applicability, its effect on religious practice is not considered. A political backlash statutorily reinstituted a religious preferentialism. Courts have since instituted this religious preferentialism, particularly in two cases in 2013–2014. It can be argued that movement in the US is away from state neutrality toward individuality, so it too could be admonished for moving from the center point of balance, albeit in the opposite direction of France. The preservation of national identity in France is definitely moving illiberally to a homogenous dominant majority while the US is moving to a more individualist diversity position.

STATE NEUTRALITY AND LEGAL EQUALITY

A neutral state is nondiscriminatory. It regulates its own conduct and that of private actors to maximize openness and tolerance. Restrictions on conduct are only to counter prejudice and discriminatory practice by private actors. The neutral state does not grant special status to religion or nonreligion. In a liberal democracy the state neither promotes nor disadvantages one human right over another except when balancing *directly conflicting rights* and one *must* be accorded priority due to neutral factors. For example, a white supremacist preacher can discuss biblical tenets which he believes support his views, but he cannot instruct his flock to kill designated people in order to please God. The fundamental right of the targeted people to safety trumps the preacher's right of speech or religion.

The French laws are both overbroad and underinclusive. They unduly restrict women's right to expression and religion while failing to sufficiently address the underlying justification of other rights, such as safety or a purged public square. The uncovered head or face as a social norm does not rise to the level of a fundamental right. If the justification is security, the law amounts to profiling without supporting evidence because it assumes all covered women, and only covered women, are engaged in criminal activity. Laws on probable cause address the issue more directly and less restrictively affect religion or expression. The balancing of rights weighs in favor of allowing the women to cover. A person does have a right of privacy entitling her to limit her engagement with others on the street, including remaining anonymous, except when done with the intent to commit a distinct crime, a neutral restriction. If identification is the issue, then it should be limited in time and place.

The proposed Netherlands law is closer to meeting liberal democratic norms. The law limits when women must unveil; however, its provision that she must unveil while on public transportation is troubling. If a transportation official needs to verify identity with a rider's pass, limiting veiling at that moment is neutral. However, to require the woman to remain unveiled while using public transport restricts her fundamental right of travel and serves no neutral purpose other than social comfort to other riders. It subjugates the individual's fundamental rights of autonomy, religion, and travel to a community social norm.

The federalism of the US creates its own obstacle to full engagement of Muslim women and assurances of state neutrality. The hodge-podge of local laws inhibits travel, which is a fundamental right in liberal democracy and in the US a constitutionally protected fundamental right. A national law would remedy these variations but probably violates constitutional federal-state separation. The institutional structure may therefore inhibit liberal democratic implementation. On the other hand, the French *burqa* ban is not the result of an inherent structure; it is the product of an institutionalized social norm that violates the liberal democratic balancing of community and individual.

The French bans also do not achieve the social norm of strictly privatized religion, creating a completely neutral public square, because the restrictions on religious clothing apply only to Muslim women. All other religious dress and symbols are allowed in the public square. The argument that it is the face which must be uncovered is a straw man argument because no one else regularly covers his or her face in public, and the Islamic women are the only religious group affected. Exceptions to the ban on face covering exist for safety and cultural and religious processions. An exception for religion at all times could easily have been added to the law and would make the law compliant with the liberal democratic principle France espouses.

There is some argument for the restriction on public employees wearing religious dress since they represent the state, and the state may choose to present a strictly secular face. However, the ban must apply to all religious symbols and dress and not single out Islamic women. This type of ban would be neutral among religions but illiberal due to its oppressive effect on religious freedom. There is no all-time-all-places neutral reason for banning all religious symbols and dresses other than imposing a state secularism, which also violates liberal democratic freedom norms. The neutral liberal democratic norm requires limitation of the wearing of religious symbols to those instances when it directly impacts peoples' ability to perform their job, such as the UK nurse. An individual wearing a religious symbol does not equate to an institutional display or an endorsement of the wearer's religion because the wearing differs with each employee. It does serve as a symbol of liberal democracy by embracing a diversity of individuals and religious faiths.

Another neutrality argument made by the French state focuses on public schools. The French state asserts it must ensure its schools are free of all religion so students develop a solely French identity and all feel equal. Because the French state allows religious instruction at the public school, it has not completely eliminated all religious content. The ban in schools is only to ostentatious religious symbols, and the principal of the school decides what is ostentatious and religious. The school principal dictates which signs of religion must be removed from the school; practices by one minority can be singled out for unique treatment. The principal is thus arbiter of what is acceptable, a capricious standard given the number of principals in France. A principal may find small cross necklaces acceptable but a multicolored head covering unacceptable just because the principal knows the student is Muslim or thinks the head covering *could be* worn for religious reasons. The problem in France is that the state is not creating a strictly secular or neutral place in the public school; the problem is its loss of state control over the individual, which causes the state to declare the conduct illegal. The state is inhibiting individual development to infantilize and humiliate the girls into believing there is something degenerate in their culture, religion, and parental teaching, psychologically forcing them to conform to the community standard, an illiberal action.

The liberal state is to ensure the widest margin of freedom to the individual and to the parent. In a liberal democracy the broad individual freedom from state interference applies to parental rights to make choices in the raising of a child. Intervention by the state, just as in individual action, is justified only when there is demonstrable physical or psychological harm. There are due process safeguards to protect the parent from abuse of their right to raise their child. The French school ban removes the right of the parents to direct and guide their child's development and forces an illiberal uniform sameness of thought on the children.

Freedom is not uniformity and equality is not sameness. Freedom is granting to each individual the widest possible range of choice to develop and pursue her own beliefs. Equality is diversity. The courts in the Netherlands and the US appear to be adhering to these principles and generally applying the same interpretation to Muslim women that they apply to all other persons. While the general anti-masking laws present some constitutional issues in the US, they predate the Muslim issue, and no other laws are proposed which target the women. In fact, the opposite appears to be occurring by the repeal of school bans and employers' efforts to accommodate religious dress. In the Netherlands the law is a bit of a muddle. A strong illiberal force appeared to be taking control but at present is being held in check. Only time will tell with the Netherlands' political picture, but the courts' strong adherence to liberal principles bodes well for a correction if the politicians move to an illiberal position.

OTHER LIBERAL DEMOCRACIES

I asked at the beginning if the reaction to Islamic women's religious dress is merely a reflection of an individual country's historical institutional structure or if it demonstrates movement away from agreed-to international democratic norms. I also noted that religion and state as competitors for authority are always in some kind of tension, and increasing pluralism in the West is causing a reassessment of the place of visible minority religions in public. Does this tension only exist in pluralist Western democracies? Clearly not, as many states which identify themselves as liberal democracies face the same pluralist issues, with some doing so for centuries. When religion forms national identity or permeates everyday life, it creates a continuing challenge to liberal democracy. The constitutional design of each country nudges the pendulum to a particular position while nation-state involvement on the international stage checks local majority forces. Thus, the analysis applied here to the US, France, and the Netherlands, can be applied to any state claiming it is a liberal democracy.

For example, India and Turkey both identify themselves as secular democracies. India adopted a British constitutional style and Turkey a French *laïcité* style.[7] In both, reaction to Islamic women's dress is but one symptom of the deeper challenge of religion to democracy. Both India and Turkey face the same forces as Western democracies, and the evidence shows they are reacting in a similar manner. Even in states which are declared democracies with a specific religious identity, such as Israel, the analysis can be applied. The internal and external forces pulling on the pendulum cause continual reflection on state neutrality and legal equality for Islamic women's dress. One can move the question "What is fundamental to continuation of democracy?" to any religious practice and to any country claiming to be a liberal democracy. What formal and informal actions lead the minority to feel they are equal citizens? What formal and informal actions do not cause the majority to feel the minority is being granted a preference over other minorities or are endangering a base cultural identity? Is the majority sartorial culture so important to the continuation of democracy that minority religious sartorial practices must be formally curtailed for the good of the continuation of the democracy, or can minority religious sartorial practices be allowed in the mosaic of national culture?

COMMON FACTORS

In the beginning we asked whether there are any common factors driving state action or if the actions are traceable to each state's structure. A common factor to each state's actions is that in each, individuals or groups, who seek to maintain a status quo social norm react restrictively toward the women. The difference is how the state structure reacts. In France the state structure institutionalized the status quo social norm. Two justifications for the different reactions are that they are a reaction to extremist elements or a result of underlying cultural feelings toward religion.

Individuals or groups who impute extreme elements of the religion to all followers of the religion create stereotypes. Stereotypes have been used against many groups, racial, ethnic, gender, and sexual orientation, to justify discriminatory practices. With other groups, liberal democracy has dismantled institutional discrimination and moved social discrimination to a suspect position. The states frame neutrality as the center point, accepting moderate elements of the different groups as equal members of community, thus strengthening liberal democratic values. The French reaction seeks to maintain the status quo neutrality and structure, making all change suspect. The women seeking change are per se a threat to the status quo structure, which is perceived as the ideal structure.

Local reaction begins from long-term cultural view of religion's value in the world. The US prizes religion; France is skeptical of it; the Netherlands views it as a thing to be domesticated and made useful. Entering the conversation of liberal democracy from these different starting points colors the trajectory of each to becoming a vibrant liberal democracy. But, as each now claims liberal democratic values as their pole star, each has agreed to limit following local cultural tendencies. France is falling short while the Netherlands and the US appear to be following the stars of state neutrality and legal equality to the center of liberal democracy. In the US and the Netherlands, while some calls for maintenance of status quo neutrality have been made, the majority continues to balance the democratic ideal, enabling the state to look beyond appearance to check motivations against liberal democratic values. In balancing the individual and neutral community needs, restrictions on the individual have been limited in time and place.

John Stuart Mill once noted that in liberal society the law should never act upon mere social disgust or dislike vis-à-vis a minority practice. States adhering to liberal democratic norms can take steps to ensure that proposed laws address real issues faced by Muslim women and are not motivated by illiberal forces claiming otherwise. The states claiming to be liberal democracies must adhere to their principles. The addition of Muslim women to the West should not disrupt the pendulum of liberal democracy's rhythmic sway in the center, maintaining that critical balance between individual and community.

NOTES

1. Josiah Ober, "Democracy's Dignity," *American Political Science Review* 106, no. 4 (November 2012): 828.
2. Ober, 827–28.
3. In the United States, poll taxes were used to prevent nonwhites, recent immigrants, and lower-socioeconomic persons from voting. Poll taxes were implemented after the Constitution was amended to prohibit denial of the right to vote to African Americans. A poll tax is a fee charged by the state to register to vote. In the United States, someone cannot vote unless they have previously registered to do so. The poll tax laws contained many exceptions which applied to white voters. Additionally, the amount charged prevented many lower-socioeconomic persons from voting, regardless of race. The poll taxes prevented individuals from exercising their right to be fully engaged citizens in the democracy and thwarted the exercise of their constitutional rights.
4. Open Society Foundation, *Unveiling the Truth: Why 32 Muslim Women Wear the Full Veil in France* (2011), http://www.scros.org/initiatives/home/articles_publications/publications/unveiling the truth.
5. Pierre Trevanie, Ismahane Chouder, and Malika Latreche, *Les filles voilles parlent* (Paris: La fabrique, 2008).
6. Anna Galeotti, *Toleration as Recognition* (New York: Cambridge University Press, 2002).
7. Gary Jacobsohn, *The Wheel of Law* (Princeton: Princeton University Press, 2003) (India). Ahmet Kuru, *Secularism and State Policies toward Religion in the United States, France, and Turkey* (New York: Cambridge University Studies, 2009).

Bibliography

Ahdar, Rex, and Ian Leigh. *Religious Freedom in the Liberal State*. New York: Oxford University Press, 2005.

Ahlstrom, Sydney. *A Religious History of the American People*. Garden City, NY: Image Books, 1975.

Allen, Wayne. "Klan Cloth and Constitution: Anti-Mask Laws and the First Amendment" *Georgia Law Review* 25 (1991): 819–60.

Amar, Akhil. *Bill of Rights: Creation and Reconstruction*. New Haven, CT: Yale University Press, 1998.

Ames, Glenn. *The Globe Encompassed: The Age of European Discovery, 1500–1700*. New York: Prentice Hall, 2005.

Andeweg, Rudy, and Galen Irwin. *Governance and Politics of the Netherlands*. 3rd ed. New York: Palgrave, 2009.

Arblaster, Paul. *A History of the Low Countries*. 2nd ed. New York: Palgrave, 2011.

Archdeacon, Tomas. *Becoming American: An Ethnic History*. New York: Free Press, 1984.

Arai-Takahashi, Y. *The Margin of Appreciation and the Principles of Proportionality in the Jurisprudence of the ECHR*. Antwerp: Intersentia, 2002.

Arjomand, Said Amir. "Religion and Constitutionalism in Western History and in Modern Iran and Pakistan." In *The Political Dimension of Religion*, edited by Said Amir Arjomand, 69–100. Albany: State University of New York Press, 1993.

Asad, Talal. "Trying to Understand French Secularism." In *Political Theologies: Public Religions in a Post-Secular World*, edited by Hent de Vries and Lawrence Sullivan, 494–526. New York: Fordham University Press, 2006.

Assemblée Nationale. *Rapport d'information au nom de la mission d'information sur la pratique du port du voile intégral sur le territoire national*. January 26, 2010. http://www.assemblee-nationale.fr/13/pdf/rap-info/i2262.pdf.

Bache, Ian, Stephen George, and Simon Bulmer. *Politics in the European Union*. New York: Oxford University Press, 2011.

Barry, Brian. *Culture and Equality: An Egalitarian Critique of Multiculturalism*. Cambridge, MA: Harvard University Press, 2001.

Bassiri, Kambiz Ghamaea. *A Short History of Islam in America: From the New World to the New World Order*. New York: Cambridge University Press, 2010.

Baubérot, Jean. "Existe-t-il une religion civile republicaine?" *French Politics, Culture, & Society* 25, no. 2 (Summer 2007): 3–18. http://www.EBSCOhost.com.

———. *Histoire de la Laïcité Francaise*. Paris: Pressses de Universitaires de France, 2000.

———. "Secularism and French Religious Liberty: A Sociological and Historical View." *Brigham Young University Law Review* 2003 no. 2: 451–64.

———. "Two Thresholds of Laicization." In *Secularism and Its Critics*, edited by Rajee Bhargava, 94–136. New York: Oxford University Press, 1999.

Bell, John. "What Is the Function of the Conseil D'État in the Preparation of Legislation." *The International and Comparative Law Quarterly* 49, no. 3 (July 2000): 661–72.

Berlin, Isaiah. "Two Concepts of Liberty." http://www.cas.umt.edu/phil/faculty/walton/Berlin2Concepts.pdf.

Berman, Harold. *Law and Revolution: The Formation of the Western Legal Tradition*. New York: Cambridge University Press, 1983.

———. *Law and Revolution, II: The Impact of the Protestant Reformation on the Western Legal Tradition*. Cambridge, MA: Harvard University Press, 2003.

Berque, J. *Les enfants de l'immigration a l'ecole Rapport au Ministre de l'Education Nationale*. Paris: La Documentation Francaise, 1985.

Bielefeldt, Heiner. "Freedom of Religion or Belief—A Human Right Under Pressure." *Oxford Journal of Law and Religion* l, no. 1 (2012): 15–35.

Birnbaum, Pierre. *The Idea of France*. New York: Hill and Wang, 2001.

Blair, Keith. "Better Disabled Than Devout? Why Title VII Has Failed to Provide Adequate Accommodations against Workplace Religious Discrimination." U. Ark. L. Rev. 63 (2010): 515–57.

Blom, J. C. H. "The Second World War and Dutch Society: Continuity and Change." In *Britain and the Netherlands VI: War & Society*, edited by A. C. Duke and C. A. Tamse, 228–48. The Hague: Nijhoff, 1977.

Blom, J. C. H., and E. Lambert, eds. *History of the Low Countries*, Amsterdam: Berghahn, 2006.

Blumenthal, Uta-Renate. *The Investiture Controversy: Church and Monarchy from the 9th to the 12th Century*. Philadelphia: University of Pennsylvania Press, 1988.

Bocker, Anita. "Paving the Way to a Better Future: Turks in the Netherlands." In *Immigrant Integration: The Dutch Case*, edited by Hans Vermeulen and Rinus Penninx, 153–65. Amsterdam: Spinhuis, 2000.

Bognetti, Giovanni. "The Concept of Human Dignity in European and US Constitutionalism," In *European and US Constitutionalism*. edited by George Nolte, 85–107. New York: Cambridge University Press, 2005.

Bollinger, Lee. *The Tolerant Society: Freedom of Speech and Extreme Speech in America*. New York: Oxford University Press, 1988.

Bond, Martyn. *The Council of Europe: Structure, History and Issues in European Politics*. New York: Routledge, 2011.

Bossi, Elle. "The Burqa Ban: An Insight into Its Compatibility with Human Rights." http://www.academia.edu/338326/The_burqa_ban_law_an_insight_into_its_compatibility_with_human_rights.

Bowen, John. *Why the French Don't Like Headscarves*. Princeton, NJ: Princeton University Press, 2007.

Brown, Catherine. *Miracle at Philadelphia*. New York: Little Brown, 1960.

Burdy, Jean-Paul, and Jean Marcou. "Laicite/Laklik: Introduction." *CEMOTI (Cahiers d'etudes sur la mediteranee orientale et de le monde turco-iranien)* 19 (1995): 5–34. http://www.cemoti.revues.org/1677.

Burns, Tony. "Aquinas's Two Doctrines of Natural Law." *Political Studies* 48 (2000): 929–46.

Buruma, Ian. *Murder in Amsterdam: The Death of Theo Van Gogh and the Limits of Tolerance*. New York: Penguin Books, 2006.

Casanova, Jose. *Public Religions in the Modern World*. Chicago: University of Chicago Press, 1994.

Cesari, Jocelyne. "Demande d'islam en banileue: Un défi a la citoyen-néte?" *CEMOTI Cahiers d'études sur la Mediterranée orientale est le mond turco iranien)* 19 (1995): 167–81. http://www.cemoti.revues.org/1677.

———. "L'unité républicaine menace par les ideologies multiculturelles." In *La laicite une valeur d'aujourd'hui? Contestations et renégociations de modéle francais*, edited by Jean Baudouin and Philippe Portier. Rennes, France: Presser Universitatat de Rennes, 2001.

Chazan, Robert, ed. *Church, State and Jew in the Middle Ages*. New York: Behrman House, 1980.

Chua, Amy. *Day of Empire: How Hyperpowers Rise to Global Dominance and Why They Fall*. New York: Doubleday, 2007.

Clerger, Sean. "Timing Is of the Essence: Reviving the Neutral Law of General Applicability Standard and Applying It to Restrictions against Religious Face Coverings while Testifying in Court." *Geo. Mason L. Rev* 18 (2010–2011): 1013–43.

Comite Preside par Simone Veil. *Nationale Redcouvrir le Preambule de la Constitution—Rapport du Comite Preside par Simone Veil*. December 17, 2008. http://www.openlibrary.org/books/OL23659501M/Red%C3%A9couvrir_le_Pr%C3%A9ambule_de_la_Constitution.

Commission de Reflexion sur L'Application du Principe de Laicite dans La Republique. *Rapport au President de la Republique*. December 11, 2003. http://www.lesrapports.ladocumentationfrancaise.fr/BRP/034 000725/0000.pdf.

Curtis, Edward E., IV. *Muslims in America*. New York: Oxford University Press, 2009.

Curtis, Michael. *No State Shall Abridge*. Durham, NC: Duke University Press, 1994.

Daalder, Hans. "On the Origins of the Consociational Democracy Model." *Acta Politica* 19, no. 1 (1984): 97–116.

Davis, Michael. "The Law/Politics Distinction, the French Conseil Constitutionnel, and the U.S. Supreme Court." *The American Journal of Comparative Law* 34, no. 1 (Winter 1986): 45–92.

Deforrest Mark. "An Overview and Evaluation of State Blaine Amendments: Origin, Scope, and First Amendment Concerns." *Harvard J. of Law and Public Policy* 26 (Spring 2003): 551–626.

Dekker, Paul, and Peter Ester. "Depillarization, Deconfessionalization, and De-ideologization: Empirical Trends in Dutch Society, 1958–1992." *Review of Religious Research* 317, no. 4 (June 1996): 325–341. http://www.jstor.org. stable /3512012.

Devrell, William. "Church-State Issues in the Period of the Civil War." In *Church and State in America: A Bibliographical Guide, The Civil War to the Present Day*, vol. 2, edited by John Wilson, 1–32. New York: Greenwood Press, 1987.

Duby, Georges. *France in the Middle Ages, 987–1460: From Hugh Capet to Joan of Arc*. New York: Wiley,1993.

Duby, Georges, and Robert Mondrau. *Histoire de la Civilisation Francaise*. Paris: A. Colin, 1984.

Dworkin, Ronald. *Taking Rights Seriously*. Cambridge, MA: Harvard University Press, 1977.

Ellemers, J. E. "The Netherlands in the Sixties." *The Netherlands Journal for Sociology* 17 (1981): 113–35. http://www.webdoc.ubn.kun.nl/tijd/n/nethjoofs/.

Ericksen, T. H. *Ethnicity & Nationalism: Anthropological Perspective*. London: Pluto Press, 1993.

Esbeck, Carl. "Dissent and Disestablishment: The Church-State Settlement in the Early American Republic." *BYU L. Rev*. 2004, no. 4: 1385–492.

———. "Religion During the American Revolution." http://www.papers.ssrn.com/sol3/papers.cfm?abstract_id=2154443. Also available in *Law and Religion*, edited by Silvio Ferrari. Burlington, VT: Ashgate, 2013.

European Foundation for the Improvement of Living and Working Conditions. "Work and Health Statistics in the Netherlands." http://www.eurofound.europa.eu/ewcol/surveys/NL0403SR01/NL0403SR01.pdf.

Favell, Adrian. *Philosophies of Integration: Migrants, Minorities, and Citizenship*. New York: Palgrave, 1998.

Feldman, Noah. *Divided by God: America's Church-State Problem and What We Should Do about It*. New York: Farrar, Strauss & Giroux, 2005.

———. "The Intellectual Origins of the Establishment Clause." *New York University L. Rev*. 77 (2002): 346–428.

Fetzer, Joel, and Christopher Soper. *Muslims and the State in Britain, France, and Germany*. New York: Cambridge University Press, 2005.

Flowers, Ronald, Melissa Rogers, and Stephen Green. *Religious Freedom and the Supreme Court.* Waco, TX: Baylor University Press, 2008.

Fowler, Robert, Allen Hertzke, Laura Olson, and Ken den Dulk. *Religion and Politics in America: Faith Culture, and Strategic Choices*. Boulder, CO: Westview, 2004.

Fraser, James. *Between Church and State: Religion and Public Education in a Multicultural America.* New York: St. Martin's Press, 1999.

Friedrich, Carl. *Transcendent Justice*. Durham, NC: Duke University Press,1964.

Galeotti, Anna Elisabetta. *Toleration as Recognition.* New York: Cambridge University Press, 2002.

Garroutte, Eva Marie. "The Positive Attack on Baconian Science and Religious Knowledge in the 1870s." In *The Secular Revolution: Power Interests, and Conflict in the Secularization of American Public Life*, edited by Christian Smith, 197–215. Berkeley: University of California Press, 2003.

Gaustad, Edwin. *Faith of the Founders: Religion and the New Nation, 1776–1826*. Waco, TX: Baylor University Press, 2004.

Giordian, H. *Democratic culturelle et droit a la difference*. Paris: Ministere de la Culture, 1982.

Green, Steven. "The Blaine Amendment Reconsidered." *American Journal of Legal History* 36 (1992): 38–70.

Gregory, Brad. *The Unintended Reformation: How a Religious Revolution Secularized Society.* Cambridge, MA: Harvard University Press, 2012.

Grillo, R. D. *Pluralism and the Politics of Difference: State, Culture, and Ethnicity in Comparative Perspective*. New York: Clarendon Press, 1998.

Gunn, T. Jeremy. "Deconstructing Proportionality in Limitation Analysis." *Emory International Law Review* 19 (2005): 465–98.

———. "Religious Freedom and Laïcité: A Comparison of the United States and France." *BYU L. Rev.* 2004, no. 2: 419–506.

———. "Under God but Not the Scarf: The Founding Myths of Religious Freedom in the United States and Laicite in France." *Journal of Church and State* 46, no. 1 (2004): 7–24.

Guterman, Simeon. *Religious Toleration and Persecution in Ancient Rome.* Westport, CT: Greenwood Press, 1971.

Hall, S. "The Question of Cultural Identity." In *Modernity and Its Future*, edited by S. Hall, D. Held, and T. McGrew, 274–316. Cambridge: Polity Press, 1992.

Hamburger, Philip. *Separation of Church and State*. Cambridge, MA: Harvard University Press, 2004.

Hart, H. L. A. *The Concept of Law*. New York: Oxford University Press, 1961.

Haut conseil a l'integration. *L'Islam dans la Republique*. 2001. http://www.ladocumentationfrancaise/fr/rapports-publics/014000017.

Hirschl, Ran. *Towards Juristocracy*. Cambridge, MA: Harvard University Press, 2004.

Holscher, Kathleen. "Contesting the Veil in America: Catholic Habits and the Controversy over Religious Clothing in the US." *Journal of Church and State* 64, no. 1 (2011): 57–81.

———. *Religious Lessons: Catholic Sisters and the Captive School Crisis in New Mexico.* New York: Oxford University Press, 2012.

Hoving, Isabel. "Circumventing Openness: Creating a new Sense of Dutchness." *TRANSIT: Migration, Culture and the Nation-State* 1, no. 1 (2005): 1–9. http://www.escholarship.org/uc/item/1g62t/wx.

Hutchison, William. *Religious Pluralism in America: The Contentious History of a Founding Ideal.* New Haven, CT: Yale University Press, 2003.

Hutson, James. *Religion and the Founding of the American Republic*. Washington, DC: Library of Congress, 1998.

Israel, Jonathan. *The Dutch Republic: Its Rise Greatness and Fall, 1477–1806*. Oxford: Clarendon Press, 1995.

Jacobsohn, Gary. *The Wheel of Law.* Princeton, NJ: Princeton University Press, 2003.

James, Edward. *The Origins of France: From Clovis to the Capetians, 500–1000.* New York: St. Martin's Press, 1982.

Jenkins, Philip. *The New Anti-Catholicism: The Last Acceptable Prejudice*. New York: Oxford University Press, 2003.

Jolly, Rajdeep Singh. "How State Photo Identification Standards Can Be Used to Undermine Religious Freedom." *Asian American Law Journal* 19 (2012). http://www.ssrn.com/abstract=2204832.

Jones, Peter. "The Ideal of the Neutral State." In *Liberal Neutrality*, edited by Robert Goodin and Andrew Reeve. New York: Routledge, 1989.

Joppke, Chistian. "State Neutrality and Islamic Headscarf Laws in France and Germany." *Theory and Society* 36 (2007): 313–42. http://www.springer.com/social+sciences/journal/11/86.

Joppke, Christian, and John Torpey. *Legal Integration of Islam.* Cambridge, MA: Harvard University Press, 2013.

Kant, Immanuel. "Metaphysics of Morals (1797)." In *Practical Philosophy: The Cambridge edition of the Works of Immanuel Kant*, edited and translated by Mary Gregor, 353–604. New York: Cambridge University Press, 1999.

Kaplan, Benjamin. *Divided by Faith: Religious Conflict and the Practice of Toleration in Early Modern Europe.* Cambridge, MA: Harvard University Press, 2007.

Kastoryano, Riva, and Angeline Escafre-Dublet. "Tolernace and Cultural Diversity Discourses in Franbce." *Accept Pluralism Project of the Council of Europe.* Sandomenico di Fresole, Italy: European University Institute, 2010. http://www.acceptpluralism.eu/Home.aspx.

Kennedy, James. *Building the New Babylon: The Netherlands in the Sixties.* 3rd ed. Amsterdam: Boom, 1999.

Kuru, Ahmet. *Secularism and State Policies toward Religion.* New York: Cambridge Press, 2009.

Kymlicka, Will. *Multicultural Citizenship.* New York: Clarendon Press, 1995.

Laborde, Cecile. *Critical Republicanism.* New York: Oxford University Press, 2008.

Larson, Edward. *Summer for the Gods: The Scopes Trial and America's Continuing Debate over Science and Religion.* New York: Basic Books, 2006.

Laycock, Douglas "Theology Scholarship, the Pledge of Allegiance and Religious Liberty: Avoiding the Extremes but Missing the Liberty." *Harvard L. Rev.* 118 (2004): 211–12.

Levine, Samuel. "Religious Symbols and Religious Garb in the Courtroom: Personal Values and Public Judgments." *Fordham L. Rev.* 66 (1998): 1505–40.

Lincoln, C. Eric. *The Black Muslims in America.* Boston: Beacon Press, 1961.

Lindo, Flip. "The Silent Success: The Social Advancement of Southern European Labor Migrants in the Netherlands." In *Immigrant Integration: The Dutch Case*, edited by Hans Vermeulen and Rinus Penninx, 123–52. Amsterdam: Spinhuis, 2000.

Lucassen, Jan, and Rinus Penninx. *Newcomers: Immigrants and Their Descendants in the Netherlands, 1550–1995.* Translated by Michael Wintle. Amsterdam: Het Spinhus, 1997.

Maas, Willem. "Citizenship and Immigration in the Netherlands." In *Migrant and Minorities: The European Response*, edited by Adam Luedtke, 226–243. New York: Cambridge Scholars Publishing, 2010.

MacCulloch, Diarmaid. *The Reformation: A History.* New York: Penguin, 2003.

Madison, James. *Notes of our Debates in the Federal Convention of 1787.* New York: W. W. Norton, 1987.

Margry, Peter Jan. "The Murder of Pim Fortuyn and Collective Emotions: Hype, Hysteria and Holiness in the Netherlands." *Etnofoor: Antropologiseh tijdschrift* 16 (2003): 106–131. http://www.jstor.org/stable/25758060.

Marineau, Erin. "'Too Much Tolerance': Hang-Around Youth, Public Space and the Problem of Freedom in the Netherlands." PhD diss., City University of New York, 2006.

McConnell, Michael. "The Origins and Historical Understanding of Free Exercise of Religion." *Harvard L. Rev.* 103, no. 7 (1990): 121–30.

McCrudden, Christopher. "Human Dignity and Judicial Interpretation of Human Rights." *The European Journal of International Law* 19, no. 4 (2008): 655–724. http://dx.doi.org/10.1093/ejil/chn043.

McGoldrick, Dominic. *Human Rights and Religion: The Islamic Headscarf Debates in Europe.* Portland, OR: Hart, 2006.

Meacham, Jon. *American Gospel: God, the Founding Fathers, and the Making of a Nation.* New York: Random House, 2007.

Merrick, Jeffrey. *The Desacralization of the French Monarchy in the Eighteenth Century*. Baton Rouge: Louisiana State University, 1990.

Middleton, Richard, and Anne Lombard. *Colonial America: A History to 1763*. 4th ed. New York: Wiley-Blackwell, 2011.

Monsma, Stephen. *Positive Neutrality: Letting Religious Freedom Ring*. Grand Rapids, MI: Baker Books, 1995.

Morris, Colin. *The Discovery of the Individual, 1050–1200*. Toronto: University of Toronto Press, 1987.

Morton, F. L. "Judicial Review in France: A Comparative Analysis." *The American Journal of Comparative Law* 36, no 1. (Winter 1988): 89–110.

Motley, John Lothrop. *The Rise of the Dutch Republic*. 1856. Project Gutenberg, 2004. http://www.gutenberg.org/ebooks/4836.

Navarro, Armando. *Mexicano Political Experience in Occupied Aztlan*. Lanham, MD: Rowman & Littlefield, 2005.

Nielsen, Jörgen. *Muslims in Western Europe*, 2nd ed. Edinburg: Edinburg University Press, 975.

Nord, Warren. *Religion & American Education: Rethinking a National Dilemma*. Chapel Hill: University of North Carolina Press, 1994.

Noiriel, Gérard. *The French Melting Pot: Immigration, Citizenship, and National Identity*. Minneapolis: University of Minnesota Press, 1996.

———. "Immigration and National Memory in the Current French Historiography." *IMIS Beitrage* 10 (1999): 39–56. http://www.imis.uni-osnabrueck.de/pdffiles/ imis10.pdf.

———. *Le Creuset francais: histoire de l'immigration XIXe–XXe siècle*. Paris: Seuil, 2006.

Ober, Josiah. "Democracy's Dignity." *American Political Science Review* 106, no. 4 (November 2012): 827–46.

Okrent, Daniel. *Last Call: The Rise and Fall of Prohibition*. New York: Scribner, 2010.

Open Society Foundation. "Unveiling the Truth: Why 32 Muslim Women Wear the Full Veil in France." 2011. http://www.scros.org/initiatives/home/articles_publications/publications/unveilingthetruth.

Ozment, Steven. *The Age of Reform, 1250–1530: An Intellectual and Religious History of Late Medieval and Reformation Europe*. New Haven, CT: Yale University Press, 1986.

Parekh, Bhikhu. *Rethinking Multiculturalism: Cultural Diversity and Political Theory*. 2nd ed. New York: Palgrave, 2006.

Pena-Ruiz, Henri. *Qu'est-ce que la laicite?* Paris: Gallimard, 2003.

Portegijs, Wil, Annemarie Boelens, and Linda Olsthorn. "Emancipatiemonitor 2004." Sociaal en Cultureel Plaanbureau. http://www.scp.nl/dsresource?objectid=20863&typ e=org .

Poulat, Emile. *Notre Laicite Publique*. Paris: Editeurs Berg International, 2003.

Proseus, Gregory. "Reconciling Religious Free Exercise and National Security: Triumph of the Ultimate Compelling Government Interest." *Wm. & Mary J. Women and Law* 18 (2011–2012): 363–94.

Rawls, John. *A Theory of Justice*. Cambridge, MA: Harvard University Press, 1998.

———. *Political Liberalism*. New York: Columbia University Press, 1996.

Renouard, Yves. *The Avignon Papacy, 1305–1403*. Translated by Denis Bethell. Hamden, CT: Archon Books, 1970.

Roald, Anne. *Women in Islam*. New York: Routledge, 2001.

Roy, Olivier. *Vers un Islam européen*. Paris: Espirit, 1999.

Saharso, Sawatri. "Headscarves: A Comparison of Public Thought in Germany and the Netherlands." *Critical Review of International Social And Political Philosophy* 10, no. 4 (December 2007): 513–30. http://dx.doi.org/10.1080/13698230701660204.

Sandel, Michael. "Religious Liberty: Freedom of Choice or Freedom of Conscience?" In *Secularism and Its Critics*, edited by Rajeev Bhargva, 73–93. New York: Oxford University Press, 1999.

Sarna, Jonathan, and David Dalin. *Religion and State in the American Jewish Experience*. Notre Dame, IN: Notre Dame Press, 1997.

Sauer, Brigit. "Headscarf Regimes in Europe: Diversity Policies at the Intersection of Gender Culture and Religion." *Comparative European Politics* 7, no. 1 (2009): 75–94. http://dx.doi.org/10.1057/cep.2008.41.

Schyff, Gehard van der, and Adriaan Overbeeke. "Exercising Religious Freedom in the Public Space: A Comparative and European Convention Analysis of General Burqa Bans." *European Constitutional Law Review* 7 (2011): 424–52. http://dx.doi.org/10.1017/S1574019611300041.

Scott, Joan. *Politics of the Veil*. Princeton, NJ: Princeton University Press, 2007.

Seksig, Alain, Patrick Kessel, and Jean-Marc Roirant. "Ni Plurielle ni de combat la Laicite." *Hommes and Migrations* 1218 (1999): 64–75. http://www.hommes-et-migrations.fr/index:php?12=2340.

Selby, Jennifer. *Questioning French Secularism*. New York: Palgrave, 2012.

Shadid, W., and P. S. van Koningeveld. "Muslim Dress in Europe: Debates on the Headscarf." *Journal of Islamic* Studies 16, no. 1 (2005): 35–61. http://dx.doi.org/10.1091/jis/eti002.

Shetter, William. *The Netherlands in Perspective: The Dutch Way of Organizing a Society and its Setting*. Utrecht: Nederlands Centrum Buitenlanders, 1997.

Shultziner, Doron, and Itai Rabinovici. "Human Dignity, Self-Worth, and Humiliation: A Comparative Legal-Psychological Approach." *Psychology, Public Policy, and Law* 18, no. 1 (2012) : 105–43. http://dx.doi.org/10.1037/a0024585.

Simoni, Stephen. "Who Goes There—Proposing a Model Anti-Mask Act." *Fordham L. Rev.* 61 (1992–93): 241–74.

Smeets, Henk, and Justus Veenman. "More and More at Home: Three Generations of Moluccans in the Netherlands." In *Immigrant Integration: The Dutch Case*, edited by Hans Vermeulen and Rinus Penninx, 36–63. Amsterdam: Spinhuis, 2000.

Smith, Christian. Introduction to *The Secular Revolution: Power Interests, and Conflict in the Secularization of American Public Life*, edited by Christian Smith, 1–96. Berkeley: University of California Press, 2003.

———. Preface to *The Secular Revolution: Power Interests, and Conflict in the Secularization of American Public Life*, edited by Christian Smith, vii–xii. Berkeley: University of California Press, 2003.

———. "Secularizing American Higher Education: The Case of Early American Sociology." In *The Secular Revolution: Power Interests, and Conflict in the Secularization of American Public Life*, edited by Christian Smith, 97–159. Berkeley: University of California Press, 2003.

Smith, Stephen. *Getting Over Equality*. New York: New York University Press, 2001.

Steinberg, Theodore. *Jews and Judaism in the Middle Ages*. Westport, CT: Praeger Publishers, 2008.

Sunier, Thijl. "The National 'Domestication' of Religion in Europe." In *Religious Newcomers and the Nation State*, edited by Erik Sengers and Thijl Sunier, 1–22. Delft, Netherlands: Eburon Academic Publishers, 2010.

Sweeney, J. A. "Margins of Appreciation: Cultural Relativity and the ECHR." *International and Comparative Law Quarterly* 54 (2005): 459–74.

Sweet, Alex. *Governing with Judges*. New York: Oxford University Press, 2000.

Sweet, Alex, and Thomas Brunell. "Trustee Courts and the Judicialization of International Regimes." *Journal of Law and Courts* 1, no. 1 (Spring 2013): 61–88.

Tamahara, Brian. *On the Rule of Law*. New York: Cambridge University Press, 2004.

Taylor, Charles. "The Politics of Recognition." In *Multiculturalism: Examining the Politics of Recognition*, edited by Amy Gutman, 25–74. Princeton, NJ: Princeton University Press, 1994.

Tevanian, Pierre, Ismahane Chouder, and Malika Latreche. *Les filles voilles parlent.* Paris: Lafabrique 2008.

Tierney, Brian. *The Crisis of Church-State, 1050–1300.* Toronto: University of Toronto Press, 1988.

———. *The Idea of Natural Rights: Studies in Natural Rights, Natural Law, and Church Law, 1150–1625*. Atlanta: Scholars Press, 1997.

———. *The Middle Ages*. New York: Knopf, 1970.

———. *Religion, Law, and the Growth of Constitutional Thought, 1150–1650*. New York: Cambridge University Press, 1982.
Troper, Michel. "Religion and Constitutional Rights: French Secularism, or Laïcité." *Cardozo L. Rev.* 21 (February 2000): 1267–84.
Uitermark, Justus. *Dynamics of Power in Dutch Integration Politics: From Accommodation to Confrontation*. Amsterdam: Amsterdam University Press, 2012.
Van Hulst, Hans. "A Continuing Construction of Crisis: Antilleans, Especially Curacaoans, in the Netherlands." In *Immigrant Integration: The Dutch Case*, edited by Hans Vermeulen and Rinus Penninx, 93–122. Amsterdam: Spinhuis, 2000.
Van Niekerk, Mies. "Paradoxes in Paradise: Integration and Social Mobility of the Surinamese in the Netherlands." In *Immigrant Integration: The Dutch Case*, edited by Hans Vermeulen and Rinus Penninx, 64–92. Amsterdam: Spinhuis, 2000.
Van Rooden, Peter. "History, the Nation and Religion: The Transformation of the Dutch Religious Past." In *Nation and Religion: Perspectives on Europe and Asia*, edited by Hartmut Lehmann and Peter van de Veer, 96–111. Princeton, NJ: Princeton University Press, 1999.
Verhaar, Odile, and Sawitri Sharso. "The Weight of Context: Headscarves in Holland." *Ethical Theory and Moral Practice* 7, no. 2 (2004): 179–95. http://www.jstor. org/stable/27504308.
Vermeulen, Hans, and Rinus Penninx. Introduction to *Immigrant Integration: The Dutch Case*, edited by Hans Vermeulen and Rinus Penninx, 6–7. Amsterdam: Het Spinhus, 2000.
Visser, J., and A. Hemerijck. *"A Dutch Miracle": Job Growth, Welfare Reform and Corporatism in the Netherlands*. Amsterdam: Amsterdam University Press, 1997.
Voorhoes, Joris. *Peace, Profits and Principles: A Study of Dutch Foreign Policy*. The Hague: Nijihoff, 1979.
Waltman, Jerold. *Congress, the Supreme Court and Religious Liberty: The Case of* City of Boerne v. Flores. New York: Palgrave, 2013.
Walzer, Michael. *Spheres of Justice: A Defense of Pluralism and Equality*. New York: Basic Books, 1983.
Warren, Nord. *Religion and American Education: Rethinking a National Dilemma*. Chapel Hill: University of North Carolina Press, 1994.
Weber, E. *Peasants in Frenchmen.* Stanford, CA: Stanford University Press, 1976.
Weil, Patrick. *La France et des étrangers.* Paris: Gallimard, 2004.
———. "A Nation in Diversity: France, Muslims and the Headscarf." *Open Democracy* (March 25, 2004). http://www.opendemocracy.net/faith-europe-islam/article_1811.jsp.
Weiner, Michael. "The Mandate of the Special Rapporteur on Freedom of Religion or Belief—Institutional Procedural and Substantive Legal Issues." *Religion and Human Rights,* 2 (2007): 3–17. http://dx.doi.org/10.163/1187103107X218911.2.
White, Ronald. *Lincoln's Greatest Speech.* New York: Simon and Schuster, 2002.
Williame, Jean Paul. "The Cultural Turn in the Sociology of Religion in France." *Sociology of Religion* 65, no. 4 (2004): 373–89.
———. *Europe et religion: Les enjeux du XXIe siècle.* Paris: Fayard, 2004.
———. "L'Union europennee est-ell laique." In *Les entriens d'auxerre: De la separation des eglises et de l'etat a l'avenir et la laicite*, edited by Jean Baubérot and Michael Wieviorka. Paris: L'Aube, 2005.
———. "The Paradoxes of Laïcité in France." Translated by Allyn Hardyck in *The Centrality of Religion in Social Life: Essays in Honour of James A. Beckford*, edited by Eileen Barker, 41–54. Burlington, VT: Ashgate, 2010.
Wills, Gary. *Under God: Religion and American Politics*. New York: Simon & Schuster, 1990.
Wing, Adrien, and Monica Smith. "Critical Race Feminism Lifts the Veil: Muslim Women, France and the Headscarf Ban." *U. C. Davis L. Rev.* 39 (2006): 743–86.
Witte, John. "Facts and Fictions about the History of Separation of Church-State." *Journal of Church State* 48, no. 1 (Winter 2006): 14–45.
———. *Religion and the American Constitutional Experiment*. 3rd ed. Boulder, CO: Westview Press, 2010.
Wood, Gordon. *The Creation of the American Republic, 1776–1787.* Chapel Hill: University of North Carolina Press, 1969.

Wuthnow, Robert. *The Struggle for America's Soul: Evangelicals, Liberals, and Secularism.* Grand Rapids, MI: Eerdmans, 1990.

Young, Iris. *Justice and the Politics of Difference*. Princeton, NJ: Princeton University Press, 1990.

Index

About the Author

Brenda J. Norton is a practicing attorney of thirty years and adjunct professor of political science at Baylor University. She has a JD from Texas Tech University, master of theology from Southern Methodist University, and PhD from Baylor University.

www.ingramcontent.com/pod-product-compliance
Ingram Content Group UK Ltd.
Pitfield, Milton Keynes, MK11 3LW, UK
UKHW012041150926
475560UK00001B/121

9 781498 523967